The Life of Friedrich Nietzsche

by

Daniel Halevy

The Echo Library 2017

Published by

The Echo Library

Echo Library
Unit 22
Horcott Industrial Estate
Horcott Road
Fairford
Glos. GL7 4BX

www.echo-library.com

Please report serious faults in the text to complaints@echo-library.com

ISBN 978-1-40688-379-4

THE LIFE OF FRIEDRICH NIETZSCHE

BY

DANIEL HALÉVY

TRANSLATED BY J. M. MONE

WITH AN INTRODUCTION BY
T. M. KETTLE, M.P.

T. FISCHER UNWIN
LONDON: ADELPHI TERRACE
LEIPSIC: INSELSTRASSE 20

1911

CONTENTS

INTRODUCTION

The duel between Nietzsche and civilisation is long since over; and that high poet and calamitous philosopher is now to be judged as he appears in the serene atmosphere of history, which—need it be said?—he infinitely despised. The crowd, the common herd, the multitude—which he also despised—has recorded its verdict with its usual generosity to the dead, and that verdict happens to be an ample revenge. It has dismissed Nietzsche's ideas in order to praise his images. It has conceded him in literature a brilliant success, and has treated his philosophy as fundamental nonsense of the sort that calls for no response except a shrug of the shoulders. The immoralist who sought to shatter all the Tables of all the Laws, and to achieve a Transvaluation of all Values, ends by filling a page in *Die Ernte* and other Anthologies for the Young. And in certifying his style to be that of a rare and real master the "crowd" has followed a true instinct. More than Schopenhauer, more even than Goethe, Nietzsche is accounted by the critics of his country to have taught German prose to speak, as Falstaff says, like a man o' this world. The ungainly sentences, many-jointed as a dragon's tail, became short, definite, arrowy. "We must 'Mediterraneanise' German music," he wrote to Peter Gast, and in fact he did indisputably "Mediterraneanise" the style of German literature. That edged and glittering speech of his owed much to his acknowledged masters, La Rochefoucauld, Voltaire, and Stendhal, the lapidaries of French. But it was something very intimately his own; he was abundantly dowered with the insight of malice, and malice always writes briefly and well. It has not the time to be obscure. Nietzsche had this perfection of utterance, but a far richer range and volume. He was a poet by grace divine, and a true Romantic for all the acid he dropped on Romanticism; the life of his soul was an incessant creative surge of images, metaphors, symbolisms, mythologies. These two tendencies produced as their natural issue that gnomic and aphoristic tongue which sneers, preaches, prophesies, chants, intoxicates and dances through the pages of *Also Sprach Zarathustra.* German critics have applied to Nietzsche, and with even greater fitness, Heine's characterisation of Schiller: "With him thought celebrates its orgies. Abstract ideas, crowned with vine-leaves, brandish the thyrsus and dance like bacchantes; they are drunken reflections." Of many aspects of his own personality Nietzsche may have thought not wisely but too well; but in this regard it appears that he did not exaggerate himself. "After Luther and Goethe," he wrote to Rohde, "a third step remained to be taken.... I have the idea that with *Zarathustra* I have brought the German language to its point of perfection." The German world of letters has not said No! to a claim so proud as to seem mere vanity. Friedrich Nietzsche holds a safe, and even a supreme position in the history of literature.

What is to be said of his place in the history of philosophy? Höffding allows him a high "symptomatic value," but only that. His work has the merit of a drama, in which the contradictions of modern thought, vibrant with passion, clash and crash together in a tumultuous conflict which, unhappily, has no issue. M. Alfred Fouillée, who has contrasted him with Guyau—that noblest of "modern" thinkers—in his book *Nietzsche et l'immoralisme,* draws out a table of antitheses, and cancelling denials against affirmations, arrives at a result that looks remarkably like zero. Nietzsche in truth was a man of ecstasies and intuitions, rather than of consequent thought. He troubled little to purge himself of self-contradictions, as became a writer whose first word had been a vehement assault on that Socratic rationalism which, as he believed, had withered up the vital abundance of Greece. His instincts were those of an oracle, a mystagogue; and mystagogues do not argue. Heinrich von Stein, in styling his first book an *Essay in Lyrical Philosophy,* spoke in terms of his master's mind.

With Nietzsche reason deliberately abdicates, bearing with it into exile its categories of good and evil, cause and end. Schopenhauer had suggested to him that the true key to the riddle of existence was not intellect but will; behind the mask of phenomena the illuminated spirit discerned not a Contriving but a Striving, a monstrous Will, blind as old Œdipus, yearning like him through blood and anguish to a possible redemption. But in time he cast off Schopenhauer and pessimism. The Will to Live he "construed in an optimistic sense," and it darkened into that other mystery, at once vaguer and more malign, the Will to Power. The problem remained to find a ground for optimism, and a clue to the harmony, to the recurring rhythms and patterns of reality as we know it. So was born what is perhaps the characteristic idea of Nietzsche. The universe is not a phenomenon of Will, it is a phenomenon of Art. "In my preface to the book on Wagner I had already," wrote Nietzsche in 1886, "presented art, and not morality, as the essentially metaphysical activity of man: in the course of the present book I reproduce in many forms the singular proposition that the world is only to be justified as an artistic phenomenon." For the optimist *quand-même* this interpretation has many advantages. Cruelty, sorrow and disaster need no longer dismay him; since a world may at the same time be a very bad world and a very good tragedy. "It may be," the lyricist, turned philosopher, wrote later, "that my *Zarathustra* ought to be classified under the rubric Music." These two passages, with a hundred others, determine the atmosphere into which we are introduced. We have to deal not with a thinker who expounds a system, but with a prophet who dispenses a Revelation: Nietzsche is not the apologist but the mystic of Neo-Paganism.

Coming to closer range, we may dismiss at once a great part of his polemical writings. They were a sort of perpetual bonfire in which from time to time Nietzsche burned what he had once adored, and much more beside. They bear witness to that proud independence, one may almost say that savage isolation, which was the native climate of his soul. *Niemandem war er Untertan,* "he was no man's man," he wrote of Schopenhauer, and that iron phrase expressed his own ideal and practice. His brochures of abuse he regarded as a mode, though an unhappy mode, of liberation. He had little love of them himself in his creative moments: he desired with a fierce desire to rid his soul of hatreds and negatives and rise to a golden affirmation. "I have been a fighter," declares Zarathustra, "only that I might one day have my hands free to bless." "In dying I would offer men the richest of my gifts. It was from the sun I learned that, from the sun who when he sets is so rich; out of his inexhaustible riches he flings gold into the sea, so that the poorest fishermen row with golden oars." It is not the Will to Power that speaks here, but that older and more sacred fountain of civilisation, the Will to Love. But if Nietzsche had that inspiration one is tempted to say of him what he said of Renan: He is never so dangerous as when he loves. The truth is that he had the genius of belittlement. It was the other side of his vanity, a vanity so monstrous that it seems from the first to have eaten of the insane root. There is no humour, no integral view of things, behind his critical work. It is sick with subjectivity. And yet Zarathustra in a temper is, by times, far more amusing than sinister. What could be better than some of the characterisations in *A Psychologist's Hedge-School*, "Seneca, the Toreador of virtue ... Rousseau, or the return to nature *in impuris naturalibus*. ... John Stuart Mill; or wounding lucidity"? But when, in this mood, he gnaws and nibbles about the sanctuaries of life; when he tells us that the true Fall of Man was the Redemption, that the two most noxious corruptions known to history are Christianity and alcohol; when he presses his anti-Feminism to a point that goes beyond even the gross German tradition of which Luther's *Table Talk* is a monument, the best that one can do for him is to remember that he often took too much chloral. It may be that to the circles in these countries to whom the cult of Nietzscheanism appeals, this strain of his thought also appeals. This particular music is not played on many trumpets, but every Superman ought to know it. And he ought to know further that Zarathustra, being brave, gibes not only at St. Paul, but even at Herbert Spencer, and has no more toleration for the gospel according to Marx than for that according to Matthew.

What is the gospel of this ambiguous prophet? It is, he himself declares, a long "Memento vivere." His own experience taught him that the characteristic of life, in its highest moments, is to be unimaginably alive. From a mere process it becomes a sudden intoxication, and on the psychology of that intoxication, which is the psychology of the artist and also that of the lover and the saint, he has written pages which are a wonder of pure light. From this standpoint he criticises justly the mechanical theory of adjustments in which there is nothing to adjust, of adaptations in which there is nothing to adapt, the whole *ab extra* interpretation of life popularised by Darwin, Spencer, and the English school in general. The living unit is more than a mere node or knot in a tangle of natural selection; it is a fountain of force, of spontaneity, constantly overflowing. "The general aspect of life is not indigence and famine, but on the contrary richness, opulence, even an absurd prodigality." To live is for Nietzsche, as for the Scholastics, to be a centre of self-movement. With the Pragmatists he asserts the primacy of life over thought. But this tension of consciousness, this Dionysiac drunkenness, is only a foundation, it is not yet a philosophy. Philosophy, or at all events moral philosophy, begins with the discovery that there are other people in the world. Your ego, thus drunken and expansive, collides sharply with another ego, equally drunken and expansive, and it becomes at once necessary to frame a code of relations, a rule of the road. Is this force and spontaneity of the individual to flow out towards others through the channel of domination or through that of love?

Zarathustra had marched with the Germans over prostrate France, he had said in his Gargantuan egoism: "If there were Gods, how could I bear not to be a God? *Consequently* there are no Gods." If the Goths and the Vandals had read Hegelian metaphysics, observes Fouillée, they would have answered this question as Nietzsche answered it. The living unit accumulates a superabundance of force in order to impose its power on others ... *an andern Macht auslassen.* The Will to Power is the sole source of human activity. The strong must live as warriors and conquerors, adopting as their three cardinal virtues pride, pleasure, and the love of domination. Pity is the deepest of corruptions; it but doubles pain, adding to the pain of him who suffers the pain of him who pities. If you have helped any one, you must wash the hands that helped him, for they are unclean. The Crusaders brought home but one treasure, the formula, namely, of the Assassins, "Nothing is true, everything is permitted." Science is mere illusionism; but the warrior, knowing how to be hard—for that is the new law—will impose his own arbitrary values on all things, and will make life so good that he will desire it to be indefinitely repeated. The earth, thus disciplined, will bring forth the Superman, who, having danced out his day, will disappear to be recreated by the Eternal Return. Thus spake Zarathustra.

The greatest difficulty that one experiences before such a doctrine as this is the difficulty of taking it seriously. Nietzsche, who had a tendency to believe that every reminiscence was an inspiration, is by no means as original as he thought. After all, there were sceptics, optimists, tyrants and poets before Zarathustra. The "common herd" may not be given to discussing ethical dualism, but it knows that since society began there have been two laws, one for the rich and another for the poor. Scepticism as to the objectivity of human values, moral and intellectual, is no new heresy, but a tradition as old as science, and almost as old as faith. The notion of an Eternal Return, crystallised by Plato from a mist of earlier speculation, had exercised many modern thinkers; one has only to name Heine, Blanqui, von Naegeli, Guyau, Dostoievsky. The Romantics had, at the beginning of Nietzsche's century, as Schlegel wrote, "transcended all the ends of life," and, fascinated with the idea of mere power, had filled the imagination of Europe with seas and storms that raged for the sole sake of raging. There was no Scholastic compiler of a text-book on Ethics but had "posed morality as a problem," and asked in his first *quæstio* whether there was a science of good and evil. The Superman so passionately announced by Nietzsche had already been created by the enigmatic and dilettante fancy of Renan. The name itself was as old as Goethe, though it is to be recalled that not Goethe but Mephistopheles applies it to Faust as a sneer and a temptation. Zarathustra is not a prophet nor even a pioneer; he brings but a new mode of speech, his triumphant and dancing phrase sweeps into its whirl a thousand ghosts and phantoms. And what is to be said of the doctrine itself? Perhaps the most adequate answer to Nietzsche, on the plane of his own ideas, is that of Guyau. Both were poets, strayed into philosophy, both seize upon life as the key to all reality. But Guyau finds in the spontaneous outflow of individual life, itself the spring of sociability, fraternity, love. An organism is more perfect as it is more sociable, there can be no full intensity without wide expansion. "There is a certain generosity inseparable from existence, without which one withers up interiorly and dies. The mind must flower; morality, altruism are the flower of human life." The reduction of all consciousness to one mode—in Nietzsche the Will to Power—is neither new nor difficult. La Rochefoucauld tracked down behind all motives the motive of self-interest, and modern simplifiers have amused themselves by analysing passion into unconscious thought. The soul, as St. Augustine tells us, is all in every part; and since the same self is always present, it is obviously possible in some fashion or another to translate any one mood of its life into any other. But such suppression of the finer details, while interesting as a tour de force, is not scientific psychology. The Will to Power is not sufficiently definite to serve the turn of a moralist or even an immoralist. Power is of many kinds. Love hath its victories not less renowned than hate. Had Cleopatra's nose been shorter, history would, says Pascal, have been different, and in the phrase of the French *chanson* there are often more conquests ambushed in the hair of Delilah than in that of Samson. Nietzsche himself perceived that it was necessary to establish a hierarchy of values as between different manifestations of "power," but this *Umwerthung aller Werthe* was never either achieved or achievable. The evangel of Zarathustra dissolves into mere sound and fury for lack of what the Court of Equity calls reasonable particularity. Most notable is this in regard to the two laws. Am I a Superman—or rather a potential ancestor of the Superman, for in this case hereditary privilege runs backwards—with the right to found my life on pride, pleasure, and the love of power, or am I a slave with no right except to remain a slave? The test is astral, and even nebulous. If you can compel the stars to circle about you as their centre, if you have a chaos in you and are about to beget a dancing star, then you are of the seed of the Superman. Unhappily, the only people who could seriously entertain such an estimate of themselves are the very wealthy and the very mad. Zarathustra derides the mob in order to flatter the snob; he is *malgré lui* the casuist of the idle rich, the courtier of international finance.

Friedrich Nietzsche was an optimist. It was a paradox of courage. There is nothing nobler or more valiant in the history of thought than his refusal to let the sun be dimmed by the mist of his own suffering. "No invalid has the right to be a pessimist." "Let them beware: the years in which my vitality sank to its minimum were those in which I ceased to be a pessimist." That is magnificent, but it is not philosophy. If Nietzsche by his insomnia and his wounded eyes is pledged on the point of honour to optimism, is not Schopenhauer by his fixed income and excellent digestion similarly pledged to pessimism? But Zarathustra's optimism is not merely positive, it is ecstatic: to express its fulness he creates the formula of the Eternal Return. He claps his hands and cries "Encore!" to life. He is drunken with joy as men are in the taverns with corn and the grape, and he shouts "The same again!"

This Eternal Return is presented to us as a conclusion of mathematical physics and spectrum analysis. St. Thomas Aquinas taught, following Aristotle, that the stars were composed of a substance nobler than that of earth, not subject to birth or death, and so immune from corruption. But Fraunhofer and his successors have, with their prisms and telescopes, discovered in the stars the same eighty-one or eighty-two elements which constitute the earth. Since then we have but a finite number of indestructible elements and forces, and an infinite space and time—or at least a space and time to which we can conceive no limits—it must follow that the same combinations will repeat themselves incessantly both in space and time. There is not only an Eternal Return, but an Infinite Reduplication. And if thought, as Nietzsche assumed, is only the phosphorescence accompanying certain arrangements of matter, the same conscious life must also repeat itself. One does not stay to discuss this phantasy of mathematics except to say that whoever was entitled to entertain it Zarathustra was not. If science is, as he held, a mere linked illusionism, how can it give so absolute a prophecy? To Nietzsche it was no conclusion, but a reminiscence from Greek speculation which came to him, disguised in the flame of an inspiration, under that pyramidal rock near Sorlei, "six thousand feet above men and time." He accepted it because it seemed to him the supreme formula of optimism. His mind was incited to it perhaps by that sombre passage in which his rejected master, Schopenhauer, declares that if you were to knock on the graves, with power to summon forth the dead to rise up and live their lives again, none would answer to your call. Christianity agrees with Schopenhauer; for though Christianity is an optimism, it is founded on pessimism. It is an optimism poised on a centre that does not lie within the walls of space and time. Christianity called a new world into existence to redress the balance of the old; and were this old world all—a closed circuit, a rounded whole—Zarathustra might dance and chant through all its Campo Santos without finding more than a very few to rise up and follow him.

The practical consequences to which Nietzsche was led were in his own phrase inactual, out of time and out of season. Zarathustra is, by a natural kinship, a prophet of the Anarchists, but he hated Anarchism; by a strange transformation, the genius of a certain school of Socialists, but he despised Socialism. German officials in Poland may find in him a veritable Oppressors' Handbook; he danced through the streets at the victory over France, but he derided the German State and Empire as a new idol. He contemned women, but praised indissoluble marriage. He preached pleasure, but celebrated chastity in a noble hymn. He was all for authority and inequality, "a Joseph de Maistre," says Fouillée, "who believes in the hangman without believing in the Pope"; but when he looked at a criminal on trial he acquitted everybody except only the judge. He denounced Bismarck and the Kaiser for being too democratic; he regarded Science, too, as disastrously democratic, because it subjected all phenomena, great and small, to the same uniform laws. Will was his god, but he saw the world under the aspect of a Mahometan determinism, and submitted himself to a resignation, an adoption of the hostile ways of existence, an *amor fati* which a Stoic might think extravagant. A German proletarian, full of German prejudices, he thought himself Polish and noble, and boasted of being a *sans-patrie* and a "good European." Pity, generosity, self-immolation, the whole ritual of civilisation, were condemned by Zarathustra and practised by him. In brief, Nietzsche never rose above a sort of philosophical cinematograph; he had the glitter but never the hard definiteness of the diamond which he chose as his symbol.

But it would be very superficial to suppose that a thought so passionate could be altogether unreal. Zarathustra is a counter-poison to sentimentalism, that worst ailment of our day. He brings a sort of ethical strychnine which taken in large doses is fatal, but in small doses is an incomparable tonic. He disturbed many who were woefully at ease in Zion, and was a poet of the heroic life. Germany, so apt to lose herself in the jungle of scholarship, needed to be reminded that erudition exists for the sake of life and not life for the sake of erudition. To literature, when he wrote in conformity with its settled and common tradition, he gave great chants of courage, loneliness and friendship. In M. Halévy's book, founded on that of Madame Förster-Nietzsche, we have in English for the first time a portrait of him in the intimacies of his life and thought. It exhibits him as better than his gospel, a hundred times better than most of those disturbers of civilisation who call themselves his disciples.

T. M. KETTLE

The Life of Friedrich Nietzsche

CHAPTER I

CHILDHOOD

Karl-Ludwig Nietzsche, a young clergyman of the Lutheran Church, came of an ecclesiastical family. His father and his grandfather had taught theology. His wife was the daughter and the granddaughter of clergy-men. Ignoring modern thought and all the agitations and desires of his time, he followed the safe path of the double tradition, which had at once been revealed by God to the faithful and indicated by Princes to their subjects. His superiors thought highly of him. Frederick William IV., King of Prussia, condescended to take him under his wing, and he might have hoped for a fine career had he not suffered from headaches and nerves. As it was, rest became essential.

He asked for a country parish, and that of Röcken was confided to him. The situation of this poor village, whose little houses uprear themselves in a vast plain on the confines of Prussia and Saxony, was melancholy; but Karl-Ludwig Nietzsche liked the place, for solitude was acceptable to him. He was a great musician, and often, at the fall of day, would shut himself up in his church and improvise upon the rustic organ whilst the good folk of his parish stood without and listened in admiration.

The pastor and his young wife waited four years for their first child, who was born on October 15,1844, the King's birthday. The coincidence increased the father's joy. "O month of October, blessed month," he wrote in his church register, "ever have you overwhelmed me with joy. But of all the joys that you have brought me, this is the deepest, the most magnificent: I baptize my first child.... My son, Friedrich Wilhelm, such shall be your name on earth in remembrance of the royal benefactor whose birthday is yours."

The child soon had a brother, then a sister. There are women who remember Friedrich's infancy, and those quickly passing days of joy round the Nietzsches' hearth. Friedrich was slow in learning to speak. He looked at everything with grave eyes, and kept silent. At the age of two and a half he spoke his first word. The pastor liked his silent boy, and was glad to have him as a companion of his walks. Never did Friedrich Nietzsche forget the sound of distant bells ringing over the immense pool-strewn plain as he wandered with his father, his hand nestled in that strong hand.

Misfortune came very quickly. In August, 1848, Nietzsche's father fell from the top of the stone steps leading up to his door, and struck his head violently against the edge of one of them. The shock brought on a terrible attack, or, perhaps, for one cannot be certain, only hastened its approach: Karl-Ludwig Nietzsche lost his reason, and, after a year of aberration and decline, died. Friedrich Nietzsche was then four years old. The incidents of this tragic time made a deep impression upon his mind:

night-alarms, the weeping in the house, the terrors of the closed chamber, the silence, the utter abandonment to woe; the tolling bells, the hymns, the funeral sermons; the coffin engulfed beneath the flagstones of the church. His understanding of such things had come too early, and he was shaken by it. His nights were troubled with visions, and he had a presentiment of some early disaster. He had dreams—here is the naïve recital that he makes in his fourteenth year:

"When one despoils a tree of its crown it withers and the birds desert its branches. Our family had been despoiled of its crown; joy departed from our hearts, and a profound sadness entered into possession of us. And our wounds were but closing when they were painfully reopened. About this time I had a dream in which I heard mournful organ music, as if at a burial. And as I was trying to discover the cause of this playing, a tomb opened sharply and my father appeared, clad in his shroud. He crossed the church, and returned with a little child in his arms. The tomb opened again, my father disappeared into it, and the stone swung back to its place. At once the wail of the organ ceased, and I awoke. The next morning I told the dream to my dear mother. A short while after, my little brother Joseph fell ill, and after a nervous crisis of a few hours, he died. Our grief was terrible. My dream was exactly fulfilled, for the little body was placed in the arms of its father. After this double calamity the Lord in heaven was our sole consolation. It was towards the end of January, 1850."

In the spring of this year the pastor's widow left the parochial house and went to reside in the neighbouring town of Naumburg-zur-Saale, where she was near her own people. Relations of hers lived in the neighbouring countryside. Her husband's mother and his sister came to stay with her in the small house, to which the children, who at first had been disconsolate, gradually grew accustomed.

Naumburg was a royal city, favoured by the Hohenzollerns and devoted to their dynasty. A bourgeois society of officials and pastors, with some officers' families and a few country squires, lived within the grass-grown ramparts, pierced with five gates, which were closed every evening. Their existence was grave and measured. The bell of the metropolitan church, flinging its chimes across the little town, awoke it, sent it to sleep, assembled it to State and religious festivals. As a small boy Nietzsche was himself grave and measured. His instincts were in accord with the customs of Naumburg, and his active soul was quick to discover the beauties of his new life. He admired the military parades, the religious services with organ and choir, the majestic anniversary celebrations. He found himself deeply moved every year by the return of Christmas. His birthday stirred him less deeply, but was a source of great joy.

"My birthday being also that of our beloved King," he wrote, "I am awakened that day by military music. I receive my presents: the ceremony is quickly over, and we go together to the church. Although the sermon is not directed to my special benefit, I choose the best of it and apply it to myself. Afterwards we all assemble at the school to celebrate the great festival.... Before the break-up a fine patriotic chorus is sung, and the director *concilium dimisit*. Then comes for me the best moment of all; my friends arrive and we spend a happy day together."

Friedrich did not forget his father, and wished to follow his example and to become, like all the men of his race, a pastor, one of the elect who live near God and speak in His name. He could conceive no higher vocation, nor any more congenial to himself. Young as he was, he had an exacting and meticulous conscience. The slightest scolding pained him, and he liked to take his own line, unaided. Whenever he felt a scruple he would retire to some obscure hiding-place and examine his conscience, nor would he resume his play with his sister until he had deliberately arrived at a condemnation or a justification of his conduct. One day, when it was raining in torrents, his mother saw him coming back from school with slow, regular steps, although he was without umbrella or cloak. She called him, and he came sedately up to her. "We have always been told not to run in the streets," he explained. His companions nicknamed him "the little pastor," and listened, in respectful silence, when he read them aloud a chapter from the Bible.

He was careful of his prestige. "When one is master of oneself," he gravely taught his sister, "then one is master of the whole world." He was proud, and believed in the nobility of the Nietzsches. This was a family legend which his grandmother loved to relate, and of which he and his sister Lisbeth used to dream. Remote ancestors of theirs, Counts, Nietzski by name, had lived in Poland. During the Reformation they defied persecution, and broke with the Catholic Church. Thereafter they wandered wretchedly for three years, outcasts, pursued from village to village. With them was their son, who had been born on the eve of their flight. The mother nursed this child with devoted constancy, and he thus acquired, in spite of all ordeals, wonderful health, lived to a great age, and transmitted to his line the double virtue of strength and longevity.

Friedrich was never tired of listening to so fine an adventure. Often also he asked to be told the history of the Poles. The election of the King by the Nobles, gathered together on horseback in the midst of a great plain, and the right which the meanest of them had to oppose his veto to the will of all the rest, struck him with admiration: he had no doubt that this race was the greatest in the world. "A Count Nietzski must not lie," he declared to his sister. Indeed, the passions and the powerful desires which, thirty or forty years later, were to inspire his work, already animated this child with the bulging forehead and the big eyes, whom unhappy women loved to fold in their tender caresses. When he was nine years old his tastes widened, and music was revealed to him by a chorus from Handel, heard at church. He studied the piano. He improvised, he accompanied himself in chanting the Bible, and his mother, remembering her husband's fate, was troubled, for he, too, like the child, used to play and improvise on the organ at Röcken.

The instinct of creation—an instinct that was already tyrannical—seized hold of him; he composed melodies, fantasies, a succession of mazurkas, dedicated to his Polish ancestors. He wrote verses, and mother, grandmother, aunts, sister, received, every anniversary, a poem with his music. Games themselves became the pretext for work. He drew up didactic treatises, containing rules and advice, which he handed over to his comrades. First he taught them architecture; then, in 1854, during the siege of Sebastopol, the capture of which made him weep—for he loved all Slavs and hated the revolutionary French—he studied ballistics and the defence of fortified places. At the same time, he and two friends founded a theatre of arts, in which they played dramas of antiquity and of primitive civilisations, of which he was the author: *The Gods of Olympus* and an *Orkadal.*

He left school to enter college at Naumburg. There he showed from the first such conspicuous ability that his professors advised his mother to send him to study in a superior institute. The poor woman hesitated. She would have liked to keep her child near her.

This was in 1858. Nietzsche's vacation was of rather a serious character. He spent it as usual in the village of Pobles, under the shadow of wooded hills, on the banks of the fresh and lazy Saale, in which each morning he bathed. His maternal grandparents had him and his sister Lisbeth to stay with them. He was happy, with a heaped abundance of life; but his mind was preoccupied with the uncertainty of his future.

Adolescence was coming; and perhaps he was about to leave his own people and change his friends and his home. With some anxiety he foresaw the new course which his life was going to follow. He called to mind his boyish past, all the long years of childhood, at which one should not smile—thirteen years filled with the earliest affections and the earliest sorrows, with the first proud hopes of an ambitious soul, with the splendid discovery of music and poetry. Memories came, numerous, vivid, and touching: Nietzsche, who had a lyric soul, suddenly became, as it were, intoxicated with himself.

He took up his pen, and in twelve days the history of his childhood was written. He was happy when he had finished.

"Now I have brought my first notebook to a proper end," he writes, "and I am content with my work. I have written with the greatest pleasure and without a moment's fatigue. It is a grand thing to pass in review before one the course of one's first years, and to follow there the development of one's soul. I have sincerely recounted all the truth without poetry, without literary ornamentation. That I may write many more like it!"

Four little verses followed:

"Ein Spiegel ist das Leben
In ihm sich zu erkennen,
Möcht' ich das erste nennen
Wonach wir nur auch streben."[1]

---

[1] "Life is a mirror. I might say that the recognition of ourselves in it is the first object to which we all strive."

The school of Pforta is situated five miles from Naumburg, on the bank of the Saale. Ever since a Germany has existed there have been teachers and scholars in Pforta. Some Cistercian monks, come in the twelfth century from the Latin West to convert the Slavs, obtained possession of this property, which lies along both banks of the river. They built the high walls which surround it, the houses, the church, and founded a tradition which is not extinct. In the sixteenth century they were expelled by the Saxon princes, but their school was continued, and their methods conserved by the Lutherans who were installed in their place.

"The children shall be brought up to the religious life," says an instruction of 1540. "For six years they shall exercise themselves in the knowledge of letters, and in the disciplines of virtue." The pupils were kept separated from their families, cloistered with their teachers. The school had its fixed rules and customs: anything in the shape of easy manners was forbidden. There was a certain, established hierarchy: the oldest scholars had charge of the youngest and each master was the tutor of twenty pupils. Religion, Hebrew, Greek, and Latin were taught. In this old monastery German rigour, the spirit of humanism, and the ethic of Protestantism formed a singular and deep-rooted alliance, a fruitful type of life and sentiment. Many distinguished men owed their education to Pforta: Novalis, the Schlegels, Fichte—Fichte, philosopher, educator, patriot, and chief glory of the school. Nietzsche had long desired to study at Pforta, and in October, 1858, a scholarship being awarded him, he left his family to enter the school.

He now disappears for a time from our ken. An heroic and boyish anecdote is the sole memory of his first year. The story of Mucius Scævola seemed an improbable one to some of his comrades; they denied it: "No man would have the courage to put his hand in fire," opined these young critics. Nietzsche did not deign to answer, but seized from the stove a flaming coal and placed it in the palm of his hand. He always carried the mark of this burn, the more visible because he had taken care to keep in repair and enlarge so glorious a wound by letting melted wax run over it.

Assuredly, he did not easily endure this new life of his. He played little, not caring to attach himself to unfamiliar people; moreover, the tender customs of the maternal hearth had ill prepared him for the disciplines of Pforta. He only went out once a week, on Sunday afternoon. Then his mother, his sister, and two Naumburg friends of his came to meet him at the school door, and spent the day with him in a neighbouring inn.

In July, 1859, Nietzsche had a month's liberty. The holidays of pupils at Pforta were never longer. He revisited the people and places that he liked, and made a rapid voyage to Jena and Weimar. For a year he had written only what he had to write as a task, but now the inspiration and delight of the pen returned to him, and he composed out of his impressions of summer a sentimental fantasy which is not barren of pathos.

"The sun has already set," he writes, "when we leave the dark enclosure. Behind us, the sky is bathed in gold; above us, there is a glow of rosy clouds: before us, we see the town, lying at rest under the gentle breeze of evening. Ah, Wilhelm, I say to my friend, is there any joy greater than that of wandering together across the world? Oh, pleasure of friendship, faithful friendship: oh, breath of this magnificent summer night, perfume of flowers, and redness of evening! Do you not feel your thoughts soar upward, to perch like the jubilant lark on a throne of golden clouds? The wonder of these evening landscapes! It is my own life that unveils itself to me. So are my own days arranged: some shut within the dark penumbra, others lifted up in the air of liberty! At this moment our ears are pierced by a shrill cry: it comes from the madhouse which stands near our path. Our hands join in a tighter clasp, as if some evil genius had touched us with a sweep of menacing wings. Go from us, ye powers of Evil! Even in this beautiful world there are unhappy souls! But what, then, is unhappiness?"

At the beginning of August he returned to Pforta, as sadly as he had gone there in the first instance. He could not accept the brusque constraint of the place, and, being unable to cease thinking of himself, he kept for some weeks an intimate diary which shows us how he employed his time and what his humours were from one day to another. We find, to begin with, certain courageous maxims against ennui, given him by his professor and transcribed; then a recital of his studies, his distractions, his readings, and the crises which depress him. The poetic soul of the child now resists, now resigns itself to its impressions and bows painfully beneath a discipline. When emotion urges him he abandons prose, which is not musical enough to express his melancholy. Rhythm and rhyme appear; under an inspiration he makes a few verses, a quatrain, a sextain; but he does not seek after the lyrical impulse, nor hold to it; he merely follows it when it rises within him; and, as soon as it weakens, prose takes its place, as in a Shakesperean dialogue.

Life at Pforta was, however, brightened by hours of simple and youthful joy. The pupils went out for walks, sang in chorus, bathed. Nietzsche took part in these delights, and related them. When the heat was too heavy, the life of the water replaced the life of study. The two hundred scholars would go down to the river, timing their steps to the tunes they had struck up. They would throw themselves into the water, following the current without upsetting the order of their ranks, accomplish a swim long enough to try, and yet elate, the youngest members of the party, then clamber up the bank at their master's whistle, put on their uniforms, which a ferry boat had convoyed in their wake; then, still singing, still in good order, would march back to their work and to the old school. "It is absolutely stunning," says Nietzsche in effect.

So time went by, and the end of August came. The Journal is silent for eight days, then for six, then for a whole month. When he reopens his notebook, it is to bring it to an end.

"Since the day on which I began this Journal my state of mind has completely changed. Then we were in the green abundance of the late summer; now, alas! we are in the late autumn. Then I was an *unter-tertianer* (a lower form boy); now I am in a higher form.... My birthday has come and gone, and I am older—time passes like the rose of spring, and pleasure like the foam of the brook.

"At this moment I feel myself seized by an extraordinary desire for knowledge, for universal culture. That impulse comes to me from Humboldt, whom I have just read. May it prove as lasting as my love for poetry!"

He now mapped out a vast programme of study in which geology, botany, and astronomy were combined with readings in the Latin stylists, Hebrew, military science, and all the techniques. "And above all things," said he, "Religion, the foundation of all knowledge. Great is the domain of knowledge, *infinite* the search after truth."

A winter and spring-time sped away while the boy worked on. But now came his second holidays, then the third return to school; it was when autumn had denuded the great oaks on the estate of Pforta. Friedrich Nietzsche is seventeen years of age, and he is sad. Too long had he imposed upon himself a painful obedience; he had read Schiller, Hölderlin, Byron; he dreams of the Gods of Greece, and of the sombre Manfred, that all-powerful magician who, weary of his omnipotence, vainly sought repose in the death which his art had conquered. What cares Nietzsche for the lessons of his professors? He meditates on the lines of the romantic poet:

> "Sorrow is knowledge; they who know the most
> Must mourn the deepest o'er the fatal truth,
> The tree of knowledge is not that of life."

He grows weary at last. He longs to escape from the routine of classes, from tasks which absorb his whole life. He would listen to his soul alone, and thus come to understand the dreams with which his mind overflows. He confides in his mother and his sister, and declares that his projects for the future have changed. The thought of the University bores him; he now wants to be not a professor, but a musician. His mother reasons with him, and succeeds in appeasing him a little. But her success is not for long. The death of a master to whom he had been attached completes his confusion of mind. He neglects his work, isolates himself, and meditates.

He writes. From his earliest childhood he had had the instinct of the phrase and the word, the instinct of visible thought. He writes incessantly, and not one shade of his unrest has remained hidden from us. He surveys the vast universe of romanticism and of science, sombre, restless, and loveless. This monstrous vision fascinates and frightens him. The pious ways of his boyhood still hold him under their influence; he reproaches himself for his inclinations towards audacity and negation, as if for sins. He strives to retain his religious faith, which is dwindling day by day. He does not break with it sharply in the French and Catholic manner, but slowly and fearfully detaches himself; slowly, because he venerates those dogmas or symbols which stand for all his past, for his memories of his home and his father; fearfully, because he knows that in renouncing the old security he will find not a new security to take its place, but a surging throng of problems. Weighing the supreme gravity of the choice imposed on him, he meditates:

"Such an enterprise," he writes, "is the work not of a few weeks but of a life-time: can it be that, armed solely with the results of a boy's reflections, any one will venture to destroy the authority of two thousand years, guaranteed as it is by the deepest thinkers of all the centuries? Can it be that with his own mere fancies and rudiments of thought any one will venture to thrust aside from him all that anguish and benediction of religion with which history is profoundly penetrated?

"To decide at a stroke those philosophical problems about which human thought has maintained an unending war for many thousands of years; to revolutionise beliefs which, accepted by men of the weightiest authority, first lifted man up to the level of true humanity; to link up Philosophy with the natural sciences, without as much as knowing the general results of the one or the others; and finally to derive from those natural sciences a system of reality, when the mind has not yet grasped either the unity of universal history, or the most essential principles—it is a masterpiece of rashness....

"What then is humanity? We hardly know: one stage in a whole, one period in a process of Becoming, an arbitrary production of God? Is man aught else than a stone evolved through the intermediary worlds of flora and fauna? Is he from this time forward a completed being, or what has history in reserve for him? Is this eternal Becoming to have no end? What are the springs of this great clock? They are hidden; but however long be the duration of that vast hour which we call history, they are at every moment the same. The crises are inscribed on the dial-face: the hand moves on, and when it has reached the twelfth hour, it begins another series: it inaugurates a period in the history of humanity.

"To risk oneself, without guide or compass, on the ocean of doubt is for a young brain loss and madness; most adventurers on it are broken by the storms, few indeed are the discoverers of new lands.... All our philosophy has very often appeared to me a very Tower of Babel.... It has as its desolating result an infinite disturbance of popular thought; we must expect a vast upheaval when the multitude discovers that all Christianity is founded on gratuitous affirmations. The existence of God, immortality, the authority of the Bible, Revelation, will for ever be problems. I have attempted to deny everything: ah, to destroy is easy, but to construct!"

What a marvellous instinct appears in this page! Friedrich Nietzsche poses the precise questions which are later to occupy his thought and gives a foretaste of the energetic answers with which he is to trouble men's souls: humanity is a nothing, an arbitrary production of God; an absurd Becoming impels it towards recommencements without a term, towards eternal returns; all sovereignty is referable in the last instance to force, and force is blind, following only chance....

Friedrich Nietzsche affirms nothing: he disapproves of rapid conclusions on grave subjects, and, so long as he is hesitant, likes to abstain from them. But when he commits himself, it will be with a whole heart. Meanwhile he stays his thought. But, despite himself, it overflows at times in its effort towards expression. "Very often," he writes, "submission to the will of God and humility are but a mantle thrown over the cowardice and pusillanimity which we experience at the moment when we ought to face our destiny with courage." All the Nietzschean ethics, all the Nietzschean heroism are included in these few words.

We have named the authors who were Nietzsche's favourites at this time: Schiller, Byron, Hölderlin—of these he preferred Hölderlin, then so little known. He had discovered him, as one discovers, at a glance, a friend in a crowd. It was a singular encounter. The life of this child, now scarcely begun, was to resemble the life of the poet who had just died. Hölderlin, the son of a clergyman, had wished to follow his father's vocation. In 1780 he is studying theology at the University of Tübingen with comrades whose names are Hegel, Sendling. He ceases to believe. He comes to know Rousseau, Goethe, Schiller, and the intoxication of romanticism. He loves the mystery of nature, and the lucid mind of Greece; he loves them together, and dreams of uniting their beauties in a German work. He is poor, and has to live the hard life of a needy poet. As a teacher, he endures the ennui of wealthy houses in which he is despised generally, and once is loved too much—a brief rapture that ends in distress. He returns to his native village, for its air and its people are pleasant to him. He works, writes at his leisure, but as it pains him to live at the expense of his own family, he goes away again. He has some of his verses published; but the public shows no taste for those fine poems in which the genius of an unknown German calls up the Gods of Olympus to people the deep forests of Suabia and the Rhineland. The unhappy Hölderlin dreams of vaster creations, but goes no farther than a dream: Germany is a world in itself, and Greece is another; the inspiration of a Goethe is needed to unite them, and to fix in eternal words the triumph of Faust, the ravisher of Helen. Hölderlin writes fragments of a poem in prose: his hero is a young Greek, who laments over the ruin of his race and, frail forerunner of Zarathustra, calls for the rebirth of a valorous humanity. He composes three scenes of a tragedy, taking for his hero Empedocles, tyrant of Agrigentum, poet, philosopher, haughty inspirer of the multitude, a Greek isolated among the Greeks by reason of his very greatness, a magician, who, possessing all nature, wearies of the satisfactions which one life can offer, retires to the summit of Etna, sends away his family, his friends, his appealing people, and flings himself, one evening, at sunset, into the crater.

The work is full of power; but Hölderlin abandons it. His melancholy enfeebles and exalts him. He wishes to leave Germany where he has suffered so much, and to free his relatives from the inconvenience of his presence. Employment is offered to him in France, at Bordeaux, and he disappears. Six months later he returns home sunburnt and in rags. He is questioned, but he does not reply. Enquiries are made and it is, with great difficulty, discovered that he had crossed France on foot under the August sun. His mind is gone, swallowed up in a torpor which is to last for forty years. He dies in 1843, a few months before the birth of Nietzsche. It might please a Platonist to think that the same genius passed from one body to the other. Surely the same German soul, romantic by nature, and classic in aspiration, broken at length by its desires, animated these two men, and predestined them to the same end. One seems to surprise across the tenor of their lives the blind labour of the race, which, pursuing its monotonous bent, sends into the world, from century to century, like children for like ordeals.

That year, at the approach of summer, Nietzsche suffered severely from his head and eyes. The malady was uncertain in its nature, but possibly had its origin in the nerves. His holidays were spoilt. But he arranged to be able to stay at Naumburg until the end of August, and the joys of a prolonged leisure compensated him for previous vexations.

He returned to Pforta in a wholesome frame of mind. He had not resolved his doubts but he had explored them, and could without wronging himself become once more a laborious student. He was careful not to interrupt his reading, which was immense. From month to month he sent punctually to his two friends at Naumburg, poems, pieces of dance and song music, essays in criticism and philosophy. But these occupations were not allowed to interrupt his work as a student. Under the direction of excellent masters, he studied the languages and the literatures of antiquity.

He would have been happy, had not the pressing questions of the future and of a profession begun to torment him.

"I am much preoccupied with the problem of my future," he wrote to his mother in May, 1862. "Many reasons, external and internal, make it appear to me troubled and uncertain. Doubtless I believe myself to be capable of success in whatever province I select. But strength fails me to put aside so many of the diverse objects which interest me. What shall I study? No idea of a decision presents itself to my mind, and yet with myself alone it lies to reflect and to make my choice. What is certain is that whatever I study I shall be eager to probe to its depths. But this fact only renders the choice more difficult, since the question is to discover the pursuit to which one can give one's whole self. And how often they deceive us, these hopes of ours! How quickly one is put on the wrong track by a momentary predilection, a family tradition, a desire! To choose one's profession is to make one in a game of *lotto,* in which there are many blanks, but only very few prizes! At this moment my position is uncomfortable. I have dispersed my interest over so many provinces that if I were to satisfy my tastes I would certainly become a very learned man, but only with great difficulty a professional animal. My task is to destroy many of my present tastes, that is clear, and, by the same process, to acquire new ones. But which are the unfortunates that I am to throw overboard? Precisely my dearest children, maybe! ..."

His last holidays slipped by into the beginning of his last year. Nietzsche returned without vexation to the old school which he was soon to leave. The rules had grown lighter, and he had a room to himself, and certain liberties. He went out to dine on the invitation of this or that professor, and thus, even in the monastery, he had his first taste of the pleasures of the world. At the house of one of his tutors he met a charming girl; he saw her again, and, for the first time in his life, fell in love. For some days his dreams were all of the books which he wished to lend her, of the music which he wished to play with her. His emotion was delicious. But the girl left Pforta, and Nietzsche returned to his work. The *Banquet* of Plato, the tragedies of Æschylus, were his last diversions before he gave himself up to the ordinary round of tasks. Sometimes he sat down to the piano just before the supper hour; two comrades who were to remain his friends, Gersdorff and Paul Deussen, listening while he played them Beethoven or Schumann, or improvised.

Poetry is always by him. If he has the slightest leisure, if there is a delay of some hours in his work, the lyricist reappears. On Easter morning he leaves school, returns home, goes straight to his room, where he is alone, dreams for a moment; then finds himself assailed by a multitude of impressions. He writes with intense pleasure after his long privation. And is not the page, which we transcribe here, worthy of Zarathustra?

"Here I am on the evening of Easter Day, seated at my fire, enveloped in a dressing-gown. Outside a fine rain is falling. All about me is solitude. A sheet of white paper lies on my table; I look at it in a muse, rolling my pen between my fingers, embarrassed by the inextricable multitude of subjects, feelings, thoughts which press forward and ask to be written. Some of them clamour and make a great tumult: they are young and eager for life. Others gesture and struggle there also: they are old thoughts, well matured, well clarified; like elderly gentlemen they regard with displeasure the mêlée of young bloods. This struggle between an old world and a new it is that determines our mood; and the state of combat, the victory of these, the weakness of those, we call at any moment our state of mind, our *Stimmung*.... Often when I play the spy on my thoughts and feelings, and study them in religious silence, I am impressed as with the hum and ferment of savage factions, the air shudders and is torn across as if a thought or an eagle had shot up towards the sun.

"Combat is the food which gives strength to the soul. The soul has skill to pluck out of battle sweet and glorious fruits. Impelled by the desire for fresh nutriment, it destroys; it struggles fiercely—but how gentle it can be when it allures the adversary, gathers it close against itself, and wholly assimilates it.

"That impression, which at this moment makes all your pleasure or all your pain, will, it may be, slip off in an instant, being the mere drapery of an impression still more profound, will disappear before something older and higher. Thus our impressions grave themselves deeper and deeper on our souls, being ever unique, incomparable, unspeakably young, swift as the instant that brought them.

"At this moment I am thinking of certain people whom I have loved; their names, their faces pass before my mind. I do not mean that in fact their natures become continually more profound and more beautiful; but it is at least true that each of these reminiscences, when I recover it, leads me on to some acuter impression, for the mind cannot endure to return to a level which it has already passed; it has a need of constant expansion. I salute you, dear impressions, marvellous undulations of an agitated soul. You are as numerous as Nature, but more grandiose, for you increase and strive perpetually—the plant, on the contrary, gives out to-day the same perfume that it gave out on the day of creation. I no longer love now as I loved a few weeks ago, and I find myself in a different disposition at this moment from that in which I was when I took up this pen."

Nietzsche returned to Pforta to undergo his last examinations. He all but failed to pass; and, indeed, in mathematics he did not obtain the required number of marks. But the professors, overlooking this inadequacy, granted him his diploma. He left his old school, and left it with pain. His mind easily adjusted itself to the places where it lived, and clung with equal force to happy memories and to melancholy impressions.

The break-up of the school was a prescribed ceremony. The assembled students prayed together for the last time; then those who were about to leave presented their masters with a written testimony of gratitude. Friedrich Nietzsche's letter moves one by its pathetic and solemn accent. First he addresses himself to God: "To Him who has given me all, my first thanks. What offering should I bring Him, if not the warm gratitude of my heart, confident of His love? It is He who has permitted me to live this glorious hour of my life. May He, the All-Bountiful, continue to watch over me." Then he thanks the King, "through whose goodness I entered this school...; him and my country I hope one day to honour. Such is my resolve." Then he speaks to his venerated masters, to his dear comrades, "and particularly to you, my dear friends: what shall I say to you at the instant of parting? I understand how it is that the plant when torn from the soil which has nourished it can only take root slowly and with difficulty in a foreign soil. Shall I be able to disaccustom myself to you? Shall I be able to accustom myself to another environment? Adieu!"

These long effusions were not enough, and he wrote, for himself alone, certain lines in which they are repeated:

"So be it—it is the way of the world:
Let life deal with me as with so many others:
They set forth, their frail skiff is shattered,
And no man can tell us the spot where it sank.

Adieu, adieu! the ship's bell calls me,
And as I linger the shipmaster urges me on.
And now to confront bravely waves, storms, reefs.
Adieu, adieu!..."

CHAPTER II

YEARS OF YOUTH

In the middle of October, 1862, Nietzsche left Naumburg for the University of Bonn, accompanied by Paul Deussen, his comrade, and a cousin of the latter. The young people did not hurry. They made a halt on the banks of the Rhine. They were gay, a little irresponsible even, in their sudden enjoyment of complete liberty. Paul Deussen, to-day a professor at the University of Kiel, tells us of those days of exuberant laughter with all the satisfaction of a very good bourgeois who brightens up at the memory of his far-off pranks.

The three friends rode on horseback about the country-side. Nietzsche—perhaps he had appreciated too highly the beer supplied at the neighbouring inn—was less interested in the beauty of the landscape than in the long ears of his mount. He measured them carefully. "It's a donkey," he affirmed. "No," replied Deussen and the other friend, "it's a horse." Nietzsche measured again and maintained, with praiseworthy firmness: "It's a donkey." They came back at the fall of day. They shouted, perorated, and generally scandalised the little town. Nietzsche warbled love songs, and girls, drawn by the noise to their windows and half-hidden behind curtains, peeped out at the cavalcade. Finally an honest citizen, who had left his house for the express purpose, cried shame on the roisterers, and, not without threats, put them back on the road to their inn.

The three friends installed themselves at Bonn. The Universities enjoyed at that time an uncommon prestige. They alone had remained free, and maintained in a divided Germany a powerful life in a weakly body. They had their history, which was glorious, and their legends, which were more glorious still. Every one knew how the young scholars of Leipsic, of Berlin, of Jena, of Heidelberg, and of Bonn, kindled by the exhortations of their teachers, had armed themselves against Napoleon for the salvation of the German race; every one also knew that these valiant fellows had fought, and were still fighting, against despots and priests to lay the foundations of German liberty; and the nation loved these grave professors, these tumultuous youths who represented the Fatherland in its most noble aspect, the laborious Fatherland, armed for labour. There was not a small boy but dreamt of his student years as the finest time of his life; there was not a tender girl but dreamt of some pure and noble student; and among all the dreams of dreamy Germany there was none more alluring than that of the Universities. She was infinitely proud of those illustrious schools of knowledge, bravery, virtue, and joy. Their arrival at Bonn moved Nietzsche and his comrades very deeply. "I arrived at Bonn," says one of the numerous essays in which Nietzsche recounts his own life to himself, "with the proud sense of an inexhaustibly rich future before me." He was conscious of his power, and impatient to make the acquaintance of his contemporaries, with whom, and on whom, his thoughts were to work.

Most of the students at Bonn lived grouped together in associations. Nietzsche hesitated a little before following this custom. But from fear of too unsociable a withdrawal should he not impose upon himself some obligation of comradeship, he joined one of these Vereine. "It was only after ripe reflection that I took this step, which, given my character, seemed to me an almost necessary one," he wrote to his friend Gersdorff.

During the next few weeks he allowed himself to be absorbed by the course of his new life. No doubt he never touched either beer or tobacco. But learned discussions; boatings upon the river; hours of light-headedness in the riverside inns, and, at evening on the way home, improvised choruses—Nietzsche made the best of these simple pleasures. He even wished to fight a duel so that he might become a "finished" student, and, lacking an enemy, chose for his adversary an agreeable comrade. "I am new this year," said he to him, "and I want to fight a duel. I rather like you. Let us fight." "Willingly," said the other. Nietzsche received a rapier thrust.

It was impossible that such a life should content him for long. The mood of infantile gaiety soon passed away. At the beginning of December he withdrew a little from this life. Disquiet was again gaining on him. The festival of Christmas and that of the New Year, passed far from his own people, were causes of sadness. A letter to his mother lets us divine his emotion:

"I like anniversaries, the feast of St. Sylvester or birthdays. To them we owe those hours in which the soul, brought to a pause, discovers a fragment of its own existence. No doubt it is in our own power to experience such moments more frequently; but we allow ourselves too few. They favour the birth of decisive resolutions. At such moments it is my custom to take up again the manuscripts, the letters, of the year that has just gone by, and to write for myself alone the reflections which come to me. During an hour or two, one is, as it were, raised above time, drawn out of one's own existence. One acquires a view of the past that is brief and certain, one resolves with a more valiant and a firmer heart to strike forward on the road once more. And when good wishes and family benedictions fall like soft rain on the soul's intents—Ah! that is fine!"

Of the reflections written by the young student "for himself alone" we possess some traces. He reproaches himself for wasted hours, and decides upon a more austere and concentrated life. Nevertheless, when the time came for him to break with his companions, he hesitated. They were somewhat coarse, it is true, but yet young and brave, like himself. Should he keep in with them? A delicate fear troubled him; he might, as the result of long indulgence, accustom himself to their low way of living, and so come to feel it less acutely. "Habit is a powerful force," he wrote to his friend Gersdorff. "One has already lost much when one has lost one's instinctive distrust of the evil things which present themselves in daily life." He took a third course, a very difficult course, and decided that he would talk frankly to his friends, that he would try to exercise an influence on them, to ennoble their lives. Thus he would commence the apostolate which he dreamed of extending one day over the whole of Germany. He proposed therefore a reform of the rules of the association; he called for the suppression, or at least for a reduction, of those smoking and drinking parties which provoked his disgust.

The proposal met with no success. The preacher was silenced, and set aside. Nietzsche, prompt with sarcasm, avenged himself with words which did not win him any love. Then he knew the worst of solitudes, the solitude of the vanquished. He had not retired from the world; he had been asked to leave it. He was proud, and his stay at Bonn became a misery. He worked energetically and joylessly. He studied philology, which did not interest him. It was an exercise which he had taken up to discipline his mind, to correct his tendencies towards a vague mysticism and dispersion of thought. But it pleased him in no way, this minute analysis of Greek texts the sudden beauty of which he felt by instinct. Ritschl, his master in philology, dissuaded him from any other study. "If you wish to become a strong man," he said, "acquire a speciality." Nietzsche obeyed. He renounced the idea, which he had entertained, of making a deep study of theology. In December he had composed some melodies: now he decided that he would not, for a whole year, allow himself the enjoyment of so vain a pleasure; he wished to submit, and to break himself in to ennui. He was recompensed for his pains, and was able to write a work which Ritschl commended for its rigour and sagacity.

A poor pleasure! It was thought that Nietzsche needed. He listened to the talk of the students. Some repeated without any ardour of conviction the formulas of Hegel, of Fichte, of Schelling: those great systems had lost all their power to stimulate. Others, preferring the positive sciences, read the materialistic treatises of Vogt and Büchner. Nietzsche read these treatises, but did not re-read them. He was a poet and had need of lyricism, intuition, and mystery; he could not be contented with the clear and cold world of science. Those same young people, who called themselves materialists, also called themselves democrats; they vaunted the humanitarian philosophy of Feuerbach; but Nietzsche was again too much of a poet and, by education or by temperament, too much of an aristocrat to interest himself in the politics of the masses. He conceived beauty, virtue, force, heroism, as desirable ends, and he desired them for himself. But he had never desired a happy life, a smooth and comfortable life: therefore he could not interest himself in men's happiness, in the poor ideal of moderate joy and moderate suffering.

Little satisfied as he was by all the tendencies of his contemporaries, what joy could he experience? Repelled by a base politics, a nerveless metaphysics, a narrow science, whither could he direct his mind? Certainly he had his clear and well-marked preferences. He was certain of his tastes. He loved the Greek poets, he loved Bach, Beethoven, Byron. But what was the drift of his own thought?

He had no answer to the problems of life, and now in his twenty-first, as formerly in his seventeenth year, preferring silence to uncertain speech, he kept himself under a discipline of silence. In his writings, his letters, his conversation, he was always on his guard. His friend Deussen suggested that prayer has no real virtue, and only gives to the mind an illusory confidence. "That is one of the asininities of Feuerbach," Nietzsche replied tartly. The same Deussen was speaking on another occasion of the *Life of Jesus* which Strauss had just published in a new edition, and expressing approval of the sense of the book. Nietzsche refused to pronounce upon the subject. "The question is important," said he. "If you sacrifice Jesus, you must also sacrifice God." These words would seem to show that Nietzsche was still attached to Christianity. A letter addressed to his sister removes this impression. The young girl, who had remained a believer, wrote to him: "One must always seek truth at the most painful side of things. Now one does not believe in the Christian mysteries without difficulty. Therefore the Christian mysteries are true." She at once received from her brother a reply which betrays, by the harshness of its language, the unhappy condition of his soul.

"Do you think that it is really so difficult to receive and accept all the beliefs in which we have been brought up, which little by little have struck deep roots into our lives, which are held as true by all our own kith and kin, and a vast multitude of other excellent people, and which, whether they be true or not, do assuredly console and elevate humanity? Do you think that such acceptance is more difficult than a struggle against the whole mass of one's habits, waged in doubt and loneliness, and darkened by every kind of spiritual depression, nay more, by remorse; a struggle which leaves a man often in despair, but always loyal to his eternal quest, the discovery of the new paths that lead to the True, the Beautiful, and the Good?

"What will be the end of it all? Shall we recover those ideas of God, the world, and redemption which are familiar to us? To the genuine seeker must not the result of his labours appear as something wholly indifferent? What is it we are seeking? Rest and happiness? No, nothing but Truth, however evil and terrible it may be.

"... So are the ways of men marked out; if you desire peace of soul and happiness, believe; if you would be a disciple of Truth, enquire ..."

Nietzsche tried to endure this painful life. He walked in the country. Alone in his room he studied the history of art and the life of Beethoven. They were vain efforts; he could not forget the people of Bonn. Twice he went to listen to the musical festivals at Cologne. But each return added to his malaise. In the end he left the town.

"I left Bonn like a fugitive. At midnight I was on the quay of the Rhine accompanied by my friend M. I was waiting for the steamship which comes from Cologne, and I did not experience the slightest impression of pain at the moment of leaving a country-side so flourishing, a place so beautiful, and a band of young comrades. On the contrary, I was actually flying from them. I do not wish to begin again to judge them unjustly, as I have often done. But my nature could find no satisfaction among them. I was still too timidly wrapt up in myself, and I had not the strength to stick to my rôle amid so many influences which were exercising themselves on me. Everything obtruded on me, and I could not succeed in dominating my surroundings.... I felt in an oppressive manner that I had done nothing for science, and little for life, and that I had only clogged myself with faults. The steamer came, and took me off. I stayed on the bridge in the damp wet night, and as I watched the little lights which marked the river bank at Bonn slowly disappear, everything conspired to give me the impression of flight."

He went to spend a fortnight at Berlin with a comrade whose father was a rich bourgeois, ready with his censure and his regrets. "Prussia is lost," this old man affirmed; "the Liberals and the Jews have destroyed everything with their babblings ... they have destroyed tradition, confidence, thought itself." Young Nietzsche welcomed these bitter words. He judged Germany from the students of Bonn and saw his own sick discomfort everywhere. At the concert he suffered from being in community of impressions with a low public. In the cafés whither his hosts took him he would neither drink nor smoke, nor did he address a word to the people who were introduced to him.

He was determined not to see Bonn again, and decided to go to Leipsic to complete his studies. He arrived in the unknown town and at once inscribed himself on the roll of the University. The day was a festival. A Rector harangued the students and told them that on that same date a hundred years before Goethe had come to inscribe himself among their elders. "Genius has its own ways," the prudent official was quick to add, "and it is dangerous to follow them. Goethe was not a good student; do not take him for model during your years of study." "Hou, hou!" roared the laughing young men; and Friedrich Nietzsche, lost in the crowd, was glad at the chance that had brought him thither at the moment of such an anniversary.

He resumed work, burnt some verses which had remained among his papers, and disciplined himself by studying philology according to the most rigorous methods. Alas, weariness at once laid hold of him again. He feared a year similar to that at Bonn, and one long complaint filled his letters and notebooks. Soon there was an end, and this is the event which delivered his soul. On a bookstall he picked up and turned over the pages of a work by an author then unknown to him: it was Arthur Schopenhauer's *The World as Will and Idea.* The vigour of a phrase, the precision and flair of a word struck him. "I do not know," he wrote, "what demon whispered to me, 'Go home and take that book with you.' Hardly had I entered my room when I opened the treasure which I had thus acquired, and began to submit myself to the influence of that energetic and sombre genius."

The introduction to the book is grandiose: it consists of the three prefaces which the neglected author wrote at long intervals, for each of the three editions of 1818, 1844, and 1859. They are haughty and bitter, but in no way unquiet; rich in profound thoughts, and in the sharpest sarcasm; the lyricism of a Goethe shows itself in union with the cutting realism of a Bismarck. They are beautiful with that classic and measured beauty which is rare in German literature. Friedrich Nietzsche was conquered by their loftiness, their artistic feeling, their entire liberty. "I think," wrote

Schopenhauer, "that the truth which a man has discovered, or the light which he has projected on some obscure point, may, one day, strike another thinking being, may move, rejoice, and console him; and it is to this man one speaks, as other spirits like to ours have spoken to us and consoled us in this desert of life." Nietzsche was moved: it seemed to him that a strayed genius was addressing him alone.

The world which Schopenhauer describes is formidable. No Providence guides it, no God inhabits it, inflexible laws draw it in chains through time and space; but its eternal essence is indifferent to laws, a stranger to reason: it is that blind Will which urges us into life. All the phenomena of the universe are rays from that Will, just as all the days of the year are rays from a single sun. That Will is invariable, it is infinite; divided, compressed in space. "It nourishes itself upon itself, since outside of it there is nothing, and since it is a famishing Will." Therefore, it tortures itself and suffers. Life is a desire, desire is an unending torment. The good souls of the nineteenth century believe in the dignity of man, in Progress. They are the dupes of a superstition. The Will ignores men, the "last comers on the earth who live on an average thirty years." Progress is a stupid invention of the philosophers, under the inspiration of the crowd: Will, an offence to reason, has neither origin nor end; it is absurd, and the universe which it animates is without sense....

Friedrich Nietzsche read greedily the two thousand pages of this metaphysical pamphlet, which had struck at all the naïve beliefs of the nineteenth century with terrible force, and had struck from the head of puerile humanity all its crown of dreams. He experienced a strange and almost startling emotion. Schopenhauer condemns life, but so vehement an energy is in him that in his accusing work it is yet life that one finds and admires. For fourteen days Nietzsche scarcely slept; he went to bed at two o'clock, rose at six, spent his days between his book and the piano, meditated, and, in the intervals of his meditations, composed a *Kyrie.* His soul was full to the brim: it had found its truth. That truth was hard, but what matter? For a long time his instinct had warned and prepared him for this. "What do we seek?" he had written to his sister. "Is it repose or happiness? No, truth alone, however terrible and evil it may be." He recognised the sombre universe of Schopenhauer. He had had a presentiment of it in the reveries of his boyhood, in his readings of Æschylus, of Byron, and of Goethe; he had caught a glimpse of it across the symbolism of Christianity. What was this evil Will, the slave of its desires, but under another name, that fallen nature pictured by the Apostle, yet more tragic, now that it was deprived of the divine ray which a Redeemer had left to it? The young man, in alarm at his inexperience and his temerity, had recoiled before so formidable a vision. Now he dared to look it in the face. He no longer feared, for he was no longer alone. By trusting in Schopenhauer's wisdom he satisfied at last one of the profoundest of his desires—he had a master. He struck even a graver note in giving to Schopenhauer the supreme name in which his orphaned childhood had enshrined a mystery of strength and tenderness—he called him his father. He was exalted; then, suddenly swept by a desolating regret. Six years earlier Schopenhauer still lived; he might have approached him, listened to him, told him of his veneration. Destiny had separated them! Intense joy mixed with intense sorrow overwhelmed him; and he was shattered by a nervous excitement. He grew alarmed, and it needed an energetic effort on his part to bring him back to human life, to the work of the day, to the sleep of the night.

Young people experience a need to admire, it is a form of love. When they admire, when they love, all the servitudes of life become easy to bear. It was as Schopenhauer's disciple that Friedrich Nietzsche knew his first happiness. Philology caused him less weariness. Some pupils of Ritschl, his comrades, founded a society of studies. He joined with them, and, on the 18th of January, 1866, some weeks after his great reading of Schopenhauer, he expounded to them the result of his researches on the manuscripts and the *variæ lectiones* of Theognis. He spoke with vigour and freedom, and was applauded. Nietzsche liked success and tasted it with the simple vanity which he always avowed. He was happy. When he brought his memoir to Ritschl and was congratulated very warmly upon it, he was happier yet. He wished to become, and in fact did become, his master's favourite pupil.

No doubt he had not ceased to consider philology as an inferior duty, as a mere intellectual exercise and means of livelihood, and his soul was hardly satisfied; but what vast soul is ever satisfied? Often, after a day of parching labour, he was melancholy, but what young and ardent soul is ignorant of melancholy? At least his sadness had ceased to be mournful, and a fragment of a letter like the following, which opens with a complaint and ends in enthusiastic emotion, suggests an excessive plenitude rather than pain.

"Three things are my consolations," he wrote in April, 1866. "Rare consolations! My Schopenhauer, the music of Schumann, and lastly solitary walks. Yesterday a heavy storm gathered in the sky; I hastened towards a neighbouring hill (it is called Leusch, can you explain the word to me?), I climbed it; at the summit I found a hut and a man, who, watched by his children, was cutting the throats of two lambs. The storm broke in all its power, discharging thunder and hail, and I felt inexpressibly well, full of strength and *élan,* and I realised with a wonderful clearness that to understand Nature one must, as I had just done, go to her to be saved, far from all worries and all our heavy constraints. What mattered to me, then, man and his troubled Will! What mattered to me then the Eternal *Thou Shalt* and *Thou Shalt Not!* How different are lightning, storm, and hail, free powers without ethics! How happy they are, how strong they are, those pure wills which the mind has not troubled!"

At the beginning of the summer of 1866 Nietzsche was spending all his days in the library of Leipsic, engaged in deciphering difficult Byzantine manuscripts. Suddenly he allowed his attention to be distracted by a spectacle of a grandiose kind; Prussia, discreetly active for fifty years, reappeared in a warlike rôle. Frederick the Great's kingdom once more found a chief: Bismarck, the passionate, irascible, and crafty aristocrat who wished to realise at last the dream of all Germans and to found an empire above all the little States. He quarrelled with Austria, whom Moltke humiliated after twenty days of fighting. "I am finishing my *Theognidea* for the *Rheinisches Museum* during the week of Sadowa," we read in a memorandum made by Nietzsche. He did not stop his work, but political preoccupations entered into his thoughts. He felt the pride of national victory; he recognised himself as a Prussian patriot, and a little astonishment was mixed with his pleasure: "For me this is a wholly new and rare enjoyment," he writes. Then he reflected on this victory, and discerned its consequences, which he enunciated with lucidity.

"We hold the cards; but as long as Paris remains the centre of Europe, things will remain in the old condition. It is inevitable that we should make an effort to upset this equilibrium, or at least to try to upset it. If we fail, then let us hope to fall, each of us, on a field of battle, struck by some French shell."

He is not troubled by this view of the future, which satisfies his taste for the sombre and the pathetic. On the contrary, he grows animated and is ready to admire.

"At certain moments," he writes, "I make an effort to free my opinions from the turn which my momentary passion and my natural sympathies for Prussia give them, and then what I see is this: an action conducted with grandeur by a State, by a chief; an action carved out of the true substance of which history is really made; assuredly by no means moral; but, for him who contemplates it, sufficiently edifying and beautiful."

Was it not a similar sentiment which he had experienced on that hill with the queer name, Leusch, on a stormy day, by the side of that peasant who was cutting the throats of two lambs with such calm simplicity? *"Free powers, without ethics! How happy they are, how strong, those pure Wills which the mind has not troubled!"*

The second year which he passed at Leipsic was perhaps the happiest of his life. He enjoyed to the full that intellectual security which his adhesion to his master Schopenhauer assured him. "You ask me for a vindication of Schopenhauer," he wrote to his friend Deussen; "I will simply say this to you: I look life in the face, with courage and liberty, since my feet have found firm soil. The waters of trouble, to express myself in images, do not sweep me out of my road, because they come no higher than my head; I am at home in those obscure regions."

It was a year of composure and of comradeship. He did not worry himself about public affairs. Prussia, on the morrow of her victory, fell back to the low level of everyday life. The babblings of the tribune and the press succeeded the action of great men, and Nietzsche turned away from it all. "What a multitude of mediocre brains are occupied with things of real importance and real effect!" he writes. "It is an alarming thought." Perhaps he regretted having allowed himself to be seduced by a dramatic incident. Nevertheless he knew—Schopenhauer had taught him—that history and politics are illusory games. He had not forgotten; he wrote in order to affirm his thought, and to define the mediocre meaning and value of human agitations.

"What is history but the endless struggle for existence of innumerable and diverse interests? The great 'ideas' in which many people believe that they find the directing forces of this combat are but reflections which pass across the surface of the swelling sea. They have no action on the sea; but it often happens that they embellish the waves and thus deceive him who contemplates them. It matters little whether this light emanates from a moon, a sun, or a lighthouse; the waves will be a little more or a little less lit up—that is all."

His enthusiasm had no other object but art and thought, the study of the genius of antiquity. He conceived a passion for his master Ritschl: "That man is my scientific conscience," said he. He took part in the friendly soirées of the Verein, spoke, and discussed. He planned more undertakings than he had time for, and then proposed them to his friends. He elected to study the sources of Diogenes Laertius—that compiler who has preserved for us such precious information with regard to the philosophers of Greece. He dreamed of composing a memoir which should be sagacious and rigorous, but also beautiful: "All important work," he wrote to Deussen, "you must have felt it yourself, exercises a moral influence. The effort to concentrate a given material, and to find a harmonious form for it, I compare to a stone thrown into our inner life: the first circle is narrow, but it multiplies itself, and other more ample circles disengage themselves from it."

In April Nietzsche collected and systematised his notes, wholly preoccupied with this concern for beauty. He did not wish to write in the manner of scholars who misunderstand the savour of words, the equilibrium of phrases. He wished to *write,* in the difficult and classical sense of the word.

"The scales fall from my eyes," he wrote; "I have lived too long in a state of innocence as regards style. The categorical imperative, 'Thou shalt write, it is necessary that thou writest,' has awakened me. I have tried to write well It is a thing which I had forgotten since leaving Pforta, and all at once my pen lost its shape between my fingers. I was impotent, out of temper. The principles of style enunciated by Lessing, Lichtenberger, Schopenhauer were scolding in my ears. At least I remembered, and it was my consolation, that these three authorities agreed in saying that it is difficult to write well, that no man naturally writes well, and that one must, in order to acquire a style, work strenuously, hew blocks of hard wood.... Above all, I wish to imprison in my style some joyous spirits; I shall apply myself to it as I apply myself upon the keyboard, and I hope to play at length, not only the pieces that I have learnt, but free fantasies, free as far as possible, though always logical and beautiful."

A sentimental joy completed his happiness: he found a friend. Nietzsche had long been faithful to the comrades of his early childhood: one was dead, and the other, their lives and occupations having been separate for ten years, was becoming a stranger to him. At Pforta he had been fond of the studious Deussen, the faithful Gersdorff: the one was studying at Tübingen, the other at Berlin. He wrote to them with much zeal, but an exchange of letters could not satisfy that need for friendship which was an instinct of his soul. Finally, he made the acquaintance of Erwin Rohde, a vigorous and perspicacious spirit; he liked him at once; he admired him, for he was incapable of loving without admiring; he adorned him with the sublime qualities with which his soul overflowed. Every evening, after laborious hours, the young men came together. They walked or rode, talking incessantly. "I experience for the first time," wrote

Nietzsche, "the pleasure of a friendship founded on a moral and philosophic groundwork. Ordinarily, we dispute strongly, for we are in disagreement on a multitude of points. But it suffices for our conversation to take a more profound turn; and then at once our dissonant thoughts are silenced, and nothing resounds between us but a peaceable and total accord."

They had promised each other that they would spend their first holiday weeks together. At the beginning of August, being both free, they left Leipsic and sought isolation in walks in a tramp on the frontiers of Bohemia. It is a region of wooded heights, which recalls, with less grandeur, the Vosges. Nietzsche and Rohde led the life of wandering philosophers. Their luggage was light, they had no books, they walked from inn to inn, and, throughout the days unspoilt by a care, they talked about Schopenhauer, about Beethoven, about Germany, about Greece. They judged and condemned, with youthful promptitude; they were never weary of defaming their science. "Oh childishness of erudition!" they said. "It was a poet, it was Goethe, who discovered the genius of Greece. He it was who held it up to the Germans, absorbed always on the confines of a dream, as an example of rich and clear beauty, a model of perfect form. The professors followed him. They have explained the ancient world, and, under their myopic eyes, that wonderful work of art has become the object of a science. What is there that they have not studied? In Tacitus, the ablative case, the evolution of the gerund in the Latin authors of Africa; they have analysed to the last detail the language of the *Iliad,* determined in what respect it is connected with this other and that other Aryan language. What does it all signify? The beauty of the *Iliad* is unique; it was felt by Goethe, and they ignore it. We shall stop this game; that will be our task. We shall go back to the tradition of Goethe; we shall not dissect the Greek genius, we shall revitalise it, and teach men to feel it. For long enough the scholars have carried out their minute enquiries. It is time to make an end. The work of our generation shall be definitive; our generation shall enter into possession of the grand legacy transmitted by the past. And science, too, must serve progress."

After a month of conversation, the young men left the forest and went to Meiningen, a little town in which the musicians of the Pessimist school were giving a series of concerts. A letter of Friedrich Nietzsche's has preserved a chronicle of the performance. "The Abbé Liszt presided," he wrote. "They played a symphonic poem by Hans von Bülow, *Nirvana,* an explanation of which was given on the programme in maxims from Schopenhauer. But the music was awful. Liszt, on the contrary, succeeded remarkably in finding the character of the Indian *Nirvana* in some of his religious compositions; for example, in his *Beatitudes.* "Nietzsche and Rohde separated on the morrow of these festivals, and returned to their families.

Alone at Naumburg, Nietzsche took up work of various kinds and read widely. He studied the works of the young German philosophers, Hartmann, Dühring, Lange, Bahnsen; he admired them all, with the indulgence of a brother-in-arms, and dreamt of making their acquaintance and collaborating with them in a review which they should found together. He projected an essay, perhaps a sort of manifesto upon the man whom he wished to give to his contemporaries as a master, Schopenhauer. "Of all the philosophers," he writes, "he is the truest." No false sensibility shackles his mind. He is brave, it is the first quality of a chief. Friedrich Nietzsche notes rapidly: "Ours is the age of Schopenhauer: a sane pessimism founded upon the ideal; the seriousness of manly strength, the taste for what is simple and sane. Schopenhauer is the philosopher of a revived classicism, of a Germanic Hellenism...."

He was working ardently, and then, suddenly, his life was turned upside down. He had been exempted from military service on account of his very short sight. But the Prussian army in 1867 had great need of men; and he was enrolled in a regiment of artillery, in barracks at Naumburg.

Nietzsche made the best of this vexation. It was always a maxim of his that a man should know how to utilise the chances of his life, extracting from them, as an artist does, the elements of a richer destiny. Therefore, since he had to be a soldier, he resolved that he would learn his new trade. The military obligation had, in this time of war, a solemnity which it lacks to-day. Nietzsche thought it a good and healthy thing that he should shut his dictionaries and get on horseback; that he should become an artilleryman and a good artilleryman, a sort of ascetic in the service of his fatherland, *etwas* ασκησις *zu treiben,* he wrote in his German, mottled with Greek.

"This life is full of inconvenience," he wrote again, "but, tasted as one would an *entremets,* it impresses me as altogether profitable. It is a constant appeal to the energy of man which has a value above all as an antidote against that paralysing scepticism the effects of which we have observed together. In the barracks one learns to know one's nature, to know what it has to give among strange men, the greater part of whom are very rough.... Hitherto it has appeared to me that all have felt kindly towards me, captain and privates alike; moreover, everything that I must do, I do it with zeal and interest. Has one not reason to be proud, if one be noted, among thirty recruits, as the best rider? In truth, that is worth more than a philological diploma."

Whereupon he cites in full the fine Latin and Ciceronian testimonial written by old Ritschl in praise of his memoir, *De fontibus Laertii Diogenii.* He is happy in his success and does not conceal his pleasure at it. The fact amuses him. "Thus are we made," he writes; "we know what such praise is worth, and, in spite of everything, an agreeable chuckle puts a grimace on our countenance."

This valiant mood lasted only a short time. Nietzsche was soon to avow that an artilleryman on horseback is a very unhappy animal when he has literary tastes, and reflected in the mess-room on the problems of Democritus.

He deplored his slavery, and was delivered from it by an accident. He fell from his horse and injured his side. He suffered, but he was able to study and meditate at leisure, which was what he liked in life. However, when the exquisite May days arrived and he had been laid up for a long month, he grew impatient and sighed for the hours of exercise. "I who used to ride the most difficult mounts!" he wrote to Gersdorff. To distract himself he undertook a short work on a poem of Simonides, *The Complaint of Danaë*. He corrected the doubtful words in the text and wrote to Ritschl about a new study: "Since my schooldays," he wrote, "this beautiful song of *Danaë* has remained in my memory as an unforgettable melody: in this time of May can one do better than become a trifle lyrical oneself? provided that on this occasion at least you do not find in my essay too 'lyrical' a conjecture."

Danaë occupied him, and the complaints of the goddess, abandoned with her child to the caprice of malevolent billows, mingled in his letters with his own complaints. For he was suffering; his wound remained open, and a splinter of a bone appeared one day with the discharge of matter. "I had a queer impression at the sight," he wrote, "and little by little it became clear to me that my plans for the examination, for a voyage to Paris, might very easily be thwarted. The frailty of our being never appears so plainly *ad oculos* as at the moment when one has just seen a little piece of one's own skeleton."

The voyage to Paris, here mentioned, was the last conceived, and the dearest of his dreams. He caressed the idea of it, and, as he was never able to keep a joy to himself alone, he must write to Gersdorff and then to Rohde, and to two other comrades, Kleimpaul and Romundt: "After the last year of our studies," he said to them, "let us go to Paris together and spend a winter there: let us forget our learning: let us dispedantise ourselves (*dépédantisons-nous*); let us make the acquaintance of the *divin cancan*, the green absinthe: we will drink of it; let us go to Paris and live *en camarades*, and, marching the boulevards, let us represent Germanism and Schopenhauer down there; we shall not be altogether idle: from time to time we will send a little copy to the newspapers, casting a few Parisian anecdotes athwart the world; after a year and a half, after two years [he never ceased to prolong the imaginary period], we will come back to pass our examination." Rohde having promised his company, Nietzsche bore less impatiently the weariness of a convalescence which lasted until the summer.

At last he was cured. In the first days of October, feeling a lively need for the pleasures which Naumburg had not to offer—music, society, conversation, the theatre—he reinstalled himself at Leipsic. Both masters and comrades gave him a warm welcome. His re-entry was happy. He had scarcely completed his twenty-third year and a glorious dawn already preceded him. An important review in Berlin asked him for some historical studies, and he gave them. In Leipsic itself he was offered the editorship of a musical review: this he refused, although importuned. *"Nego ac pernego,"* wrote he to Rohde, now in residence in another University city.

He interested himself in everything, except politics. The din and confusion of men in public meeting assembled was insupportable to him. "Decidedly," said he, "I am not a ζῶον πολιτικόν." And he wrote to his friend Gersdorff, who had been giving him some information about Parliamentary intrigues in Berlin:

"The course of events astonishes me; but I cannot well understand them, nor take them in, unless I draw out of the crowd and consider apart the activity of a determined man. Bismarck gives me immense satisfaction. I read his speeches as though I were drinking a strong wine; I hold back my tongue that it may not swallow too quickly and that my enjoyment may last. The machinations of his adversaries, as you relate them to me, I conceive without difficulty; for it is a necessity that everything that is small, narrow, sectarian and limited should rebel against such natures and wage an eternal war upon them."

Then to so many satisfactions, new and old, was added the greatest of joys: the discovery of a new genius, Richard Wagner. The whole of Germany was making the same discovery about this time. Already she knew and admired this tumultuous man, poet, composer, publicist, philosopher; a revolutionary at Dresden, a "damned" author at Paris, a favourite at the Court of Munich; she had discussed his works and laughed over his debts and his scarlet robes. It was by no means easy to pass a clear judgment on this life which was a mixture of faith and insincerity, of meanness and greatness; on this thought which was sometimes so strong and often so wordy. What kind of man was Richard Wagner? An uneasy spirit? a genius? One scarcely knew, and Nietzsche had remained for a long time in a state of indecision. *Tristan and Isolde* moved him infinitely; other works disconcerted him. "I have just read the *Valkyrie*," he wrote to Gersdorff, in October, 1866, "and I find myself impressed so confusedly that I can reach no judgment. Its great beauties and *virtutes* are counterbalanced by so many defects and deformities equally great; $0 + a + (-a)$ gives 0, all calculations made." "Wagner is an insoluble problem," he said on another occasion. The musician whom he then preferred was Schumann.

Wagner had the art of imposing his glory on the world. In July, 1868, he produced at Munich the *Meistersinger*, that noble and familiar poem in which the German people, heroes of the action, filled the stage with their arguments, their sports, their labours, their loves, and themselves glorified their own art, music. Germany was then experiencing the proud desire of greatness. She had the confidence and the *élan* which dare recognise the genius of an artist. Wagner was acclaimed; he passed during the last months of 1868 that invisible border-line above which a man is transfigured and exalted, above glory itself, into a light of immortality.

Friedrich Nietzsche heard the *Meistersinger*. He was touched by its marvellous beauty and his critical fancies vanished. "To be just towards such a man," he wrote to Rohde, "one must have a little enthusiasm.... I try in vain to listen to his music in a cold and reserved frame of mind; every nerve vibrates in me...." This miraculous art had taken hold of him; he wished that his friends should share his new passion; he confided his Wagnerian impressions to them: "Last night at the concert," he wrote, "the overture to the *Meistersinger* caused me so lasting a thrill that it was long since I had felt anything like it." Wagner's sister, Madame Brockhaus, was living in Leipsic. She was a woman out of the ordinary; and her friends affirmed that they recognised in her a little of the genius of her brother. Nietzsche wanted to approach her. This modest desire was soon satisfied.

"The other evening," he writes to Rohde, "on returning home I found a letter addressed to me, a very short note: 'If you would care to meet Richard Wagner come to the Café zum Theater at a quarter to four.—W. ... SCH.' The news, if you will forgive me, positively turned my head, and I found myself as if tossed about by a whirlwind. It goes without saying that I went out at once to seek the excellent Windisch, who was able to give me some further information. He told me that Wagner was at Leipsic, at his sister's, in the strictest incognito; that the Press knew nothing about his visit, and that all the servants in the Brockhaus household were as mute as liveried gravediggers. Madame Brockhaus, Wagner's sister, had presented to him only one visitor, Madame Ritschl, whose judgment and penetration of mind you know, thus allowing herself the pleasure of being proud of her friend before her brother and proud of her brother before her friend, the happy creature! While Madame Ritschl was in the room Wagner played the *Lied* from the *Meistersinger,* which you know well; and the excellent lady informed him that the music was already familiar to her, *mea opera.* Thereupon pleasure and surprise on the part of Wagner: he expresses a keen desire to meet me incognito. They decide to invite me for Friday evening. Windisch explains that that day is impossible to me on account of my duties, my work, my engagements: and Sunday afternoon is suggested. We went to the house, Windisch and I, and found the professor's family there, but not Richard: he had gone out with his vast skull hidden under some prodigious headdress. I was presented to this very distinguished family, and received a most cordial invitation for Sunday evening, which I accepted.

"I spent the next few days, I assure you, in a highly romantic mood: and you must admit that this *début,* this unapproachable hero, have something about them bordering on the world of legend.

"With such an important function before me I decide to dress in my best. It so chanced that my tailor had promised to deliver me on Sunday a black coat: everything promised well. Sunday was a frightful day of snow and rain. One shuddered at the idea of leaving the house. So I was far from displeased to receive a call during the afternoon from R——, who babbled about the Eleatics and the nature of God in their philosophy—because as *candidandus* he is going to take the thesis prescribed by Abrens, *The Development of the Idea of God down to Aristotle,* while Romundt proposes to solve the problem *Of the Will,* and thereby to win the University prize. The evening draws on, the tailor fails to arrive and Romundt departs. I go with him as far as my tailor's, and entering the shop, I find his slaves very busy on my coat: they promise that it will be delivered in three hours. I leave, more content with the course of things; on my way home I pass Kintschy, read the *Kladderadatsch,* and find with satisfaction a newspaper paragraph to the effect that Wagner is in Switzerland, but that a beautiful house is being built for him at Munich. As for me, I know that I am about to see him, and that a letter arrived for him yesterday from the little King, bearing the address: To the great German composer, Richard Wagner.

"I return home; no tailor. I read very comfortably a dissertation on the *Eudocia,* a little distracted from time to time by a troublesome though distant noise. At last I hear the sound of knocking at the old iron grille, which is closed ..."

It was the tailor; Nietzsche tried on the suit, which fitted him well; he thanked the journeyman, who, however, stayed on, and asked to be paid. Nietzsche, being short of money, was of another opinion; the journeyman repeated his demand, Nietzsche reiterated his refusal; the journeyman would not yield, went off with the suit, and Nietzsche, left abashed in his room, considered with displeasure a black frock-coat, greatly doubting whether it would "do for Richard." Finally he put it on again:

"Outside the rain is falling in torrents. A quarter past eight! At half past Windisch is to meet me at the Café zum Theater. I precipitate myself into the dark and rainy night, I too a poor man, all in black, without a dress coat, but in the most romantic of humours. Fortune favours me; there is something mysterious and unusual in the very aspect of the streets on this night of snow.

"We enter the very comfortable parlour of the Brockhaus's; there is no one there but the closest relations of the family, and we two. I am introduced to Richard, to whom I express my veneration in a few words; he asks me very minutely how I became a faithful disciple of his music, bursts out in invectives against all the productions of his work, those of Munich, which are admirable, alone excepted; and gibes of the orchestra conductors who counsel paternally: 'Now, if you please, a little passion, gentlemen, a little more passion, my friends!' He imitates the accent of Leipsic very well.

"How I would like to give you an idea of the pleasures of the evening, of our enjoyments, which have been so lively, so peculiar, were it not that even to-day I have not yet recovered my old equilibrium, and cannot do better than tell you as I chatter along a 'fairy tale.' Afterwards, before dinner, Wagner played all the principal passages from the *Meistersinger;* he himself imitated all the voices: I can leave you to imagine that much was lost. As a talker he is incredibly swift and animated, and his abundance and humour are enough to convulse with gaiety a circle of intimates such as we were. Between whiles I had a long conversation with him about Schopenhauer. Ah, you wall understand what a joy it was for me to hear him speak with an indescribable warmth, explaining what he owes to our Schopenhauer, and telling me that Schopenhauer, alone among the philosophers, understood the essence of music. Then he wanted to know what is the present attitude of the philosophers with regard to Schopenhauer; he laughed very heartily at the Congress of Philosophers at Prague, and spoke of philosophical *domesticity.* Afterwards he read us a fragment of his Memoirs, which he is now writing, a scene from his student-life at Leipsic, overwhelmingly funny, of which I cannot think even now without laughing. His mind is amazingly supple and witty.

"At last, as we were preparing to leave, Windisch and I, he gave me a very warm handshake, and invited me, in the most friendly fashion, to pay him a visit, to talk of music and philosophy. He also entrusted me with the mission of making his music known to his sister and his parents: a mission which I shall discharge with enthusiasm. I will write you of the evening at greater length when I am able to review it from a little further off, and more objectively. To-day, a cordial greeting and, for your health, my best wishes."

That day of calm appreciation, which Nietzsche was waiting for, did not come. He had come in contact with a godlike man. He had felt the shock of genius, and his soul remained shaken by it. He studied the theoretical writings of Wagner, which he had hitherto neglected, and meditated seriously on the idea of the unique work of art which was to be a synthesis of the scattered beauties of poetry, the plastic arts, and harmony. He saw the German spirit renovated through the Wagnerian ideal, and his swift mind went off in that direction.

Ritschl said to him one day: "I am going to surprise you. Would you like to be appointed a Professor in the University of Basle?" Nietzsche's surprise was, in fact, extreme. He was in his twenty-fourth year, and had not obtained his final degrees. The astonishing proposition had to be repeated to him Ritschl explained that he had received a letter from Basle; he was asked what sort of man was Herr Friedrich Nietzsche, author of the fine essays published in the *Rheinisches Museum;* could he be entrusted with a Chair of Philology? Ritschl had answered that Herr Friedrich Nietzsche was a young man who had ability enough to do anything he chose to do. He had even dared to write that Herr Nietzsche had genius. The matter, though suspended for the moment, had already gone pretty far.

Nietzsche listened to the news with infinite anxiety. It made him proud and yet left him broken-hearted. The whole year of liberty which he had thought to be still before him suddenly vanished, and with it his projects of study, of vast reading, of travel. He was losing a happy life swollen with dreams. How could he reject so flattering an offer? He had, it appears, contrary to all good sense, a certain hesitation against which Ritschl had to fight. The old savant felt a real tenderness for this singular pupil of his, this sagacious philologist, metaphysician and poet; he loved him and believed in him. But he had one anxiety: he feared lest Nietzsche, under the incessant solicitation of instincts almost too numerous and too fine, should disperse his energy on too many objects and waste his gifts. For four years he had been iterating in his ears the same counsel: *Restrict yourself in order to be strong;* and he now repeated it in pressing terms. Nietzsche understood, and gave way. He wrote at once to Erwin Rohde: "As to our Parisian voyage, think of it no longer; it is certain that I am to be appointed to this Professorship at Basle; I who wished to study Chemistry! Henceforward I must learn how to renounce. Down there how much alone I shall be—without a friend whose thought resounds to mine like beautiful thirds, minor or major!"

He obtained his final diploma without examination, in consideration of his past performances and of the unique circumstance. The professors of Leipsic did not like the notion of examining their colleague of Basle.

Friedrich Nietzsche remained some weeks at Naumburg with his own people. The family were full of joy and pride: so young and a University professor! "What great matter is it?" retorted Nietzsche impatiently; "there is an usher the more in the world, that is all!" On April 13th he writes to his friend Gersdorff:

"Here I am at the last term, the last evening that I shall spend beside my hearth; to-morrow morning I strike out into the great world; I enter a profession which is new to me, in an atmosphere heavy and oppressive with duties and obligations. Once more I must say adieu: the golden time in which one's activities are free and unfettered; in which every instant is sovereign; in which art and the world are spread out before our eyes as a pure spectacle in which we hardly participate—that time is past beyond recall. Now begins the reign of the harsh goddess of daily duty. *Bemooster Bursche zieh? ich aus.* ... You know that poignant student-song. Yes, yes! now comes my turn to be a philistine!

"One day or another, here or there, the saying always comes true. Offices and dignities are not to be accepted with impunity. The whole thing is to know whether the chains which you are forced to carry are of iron or of thread. And I still have courage enough to break some link on occasion, and to risk some plunge or other into the perilous life. Of the compulsory gibbosity of the professor I do not as yet discern in myself any trace. To become a philistine, a man of the crowd, ἄνθρωπος ἄμουσος— Zeus and the Muses preserve me from such a fate! Moreover, I find it hard to see how I could contrive to become what I am not. I am more afraid of another kind of philistinism, the professional species. It is only too natural that a daily task, an incessant concentration on certain facts and certain problems, should hang like a weight on the free sensibility of the mind, and strike at the roots of the philosophic sense. But I imagine that I can confront this peril more calmly than most philologists: philosophical seriousness is too deeply rooted in me: the true and essential problems of life and thought have been too clearly revealed to me by the great mystagogue Schopenhauer to permit me to be ever guilty of shameful treachery to the 'Idea.' To vivify my science with this new blood; to communicate to my hearers that Schopenhauerian earnestness which glitters on the brow of that sublime thinker—such is my desire, my audacious hope: I want to be more than a pedagogue to honest savants. I am thinking of the duties of the masters of our time; I look forward, and my mind is filled with the thought of that next generation which follows at our heels. Since we must endure life, let us at least endeavour so to use it as to give it some worth in the eyes of others when we are happily delivered from it."

Friedrich Nietzsche disquieted himself needlessly. If he could have guessed what the approaching days held for him, his joy would have been immense. Richard Wagner lived not far from Basle, and was to become his friend.

CHAPTER III

FRIEDRICH NIETZSCHE AND RICHARD WAGNER—TRIEBSCHEN

Nietzsche installed himself at Basle, selected his domicile, and exchanged visits with his colleagues. But Richard Wagner was constantly in his thoughts. Three weeks after his arrival some friends joined with him in an expedition to the shores of the lake of the Four Cantons. One morning he left them and set off on foot by the river bank towards the master's retreat, Triebschen. Triebschen is the name of a little cape which protrudes into the lake; a solitary villa and a solitary garden, whose high poplars are seen from afar, occupy its expanse.

He stopped before the closed gate and rang. Trees hid the house. He looked around, as he waited, and listened: his attentive ear caught the resonance of a harmony which was soon muffled up in the noise of footsteps. A servant opened the door and Nietzsche sent in his card; then he was left to hear once more the same harmony, dolorous, obstinate, many times repeated. The invisible master ceased for a moment, but almost at once was busy again with his experiments, raising the strain, modulating it, until, by modulating once more, he had brought back the initial harmony. The servant returned. Herr Wagner wished to know if the visitor was the same Herr Nietzsche whom he had met one evening at Leipsic. "Yes," said the young man. "Then would Herr Nietzsche be good enough to come back at luncheon time?" But Nietzsche's friends were awaiting him, and he had to excuse himself. The servant disappeared again, to return with another message. "Would Herr Nietzsche spend the Monday of Pentecost at Triebschen?" This invitation he was able to accept and did accept.

Nietzsche came to know Wagner at one of the finest moments of the latter's life. The great man was alone, far from the public, from journalists, and from crowds. He had just carried off and married the divorced wife of Hans von Bülow, the daughter of Liszt and of Madame d'Agoult, an admirable being who was endowed with the gifts of two races. The adventure had scandalised all the Pharisees of old-fashioned Germany. Richard Wagner was completing his work in retreat: a gigantic work, a succession of four dramas, every one of which was immense: a work which was not conceived for the pleasure of men, but for the trouble and salvation of their souls; a work so prodigious that no public was worthy to hear it, no company of singers worthy to sing it, no stage, in short, vast enough or noble enough to make its representation possible. What matter! The world must stoop to Richard Wagner; it was not for him to yield to it. He had finished *Rhinegold,* and the *Valkyries; Siegfried* was soon to be completed; and he began to know the joy of the workman who has mastered his work, and is able at last to view it as a whole.

Restlessness and anger were mixed with his joy, for he was not of those who are content with the approbation of an élite. He had been moved by all the dreams of men, and he wished in his turn to move all men. He needed the crowd, wanted to be listened to by it, and never ceased to call to the Germans, always heavy and slow-footed in following him. "Aid me," he cries out in his books, "for you begin to be strong. Because of your strength do not disdain, do not neglect those who have been your spiritual masters, Luther, Kant, Schiller and Beethoven: I am the heir of these masters. Assist me. I need a stage where I may be free; give me it! I need a people who shall listen to me; be that people! Aid me, it is your duty. And, in return, I will glorify you."

We may picture this first visit: Nietzsche with his soft manners, his nervous voice, his fiery and veiled look; his face which was so youthful in spite of the long, drooping moustache; Wagner in the strength of the fifty-nine years that he carried without sign of weakness, overflowing with intuitions and experiences, desires and expectations, exuberant in language and gesture. What was their first interview like? *We* have no record of it, but no doubt Wagner repeated what he was writing in his books, and said imperiously: "Young man, you too must help me."

The night was fine and conversation spirited. When it was time for Nietzsche to go, Wagner desired to accompany his guest on his way home along the river. They went out together. Nietzsche's joy was great. The want from which he had long suffered was now being supplied; he had needed to love, to admire, to listen. At last he had met a man worthy to be his master; at last he had met him for whom no admiration, no love could be too strong. He gave himself up entirely and resolved to serve this solitary and inspired being, to fight for him against the inert multitude, against the Germany of the Universities, of the Churches, of the Parliaments, and of the Courts. What was Wagner's impression? No doubt he too was happy. From the very beginning he had recognised the extraordinary gifts of his young visitor. He could converse with him; and to converse means to give and to receive. And so few men had been able to afford him that joy.

On the 22nd of May, eight days after this first visit, a few very intimate friends came from Germany to Triebschen to celebrate the first day of their master's sixtieth year. Nietzsche was invited, but had to decline, for he was preparing his opening lecture and did not like to be distracted at his task. He was anxious to express straightway the conception that he had formed of his science and of its teaching. For his subject he took the Homeric problem, that problem which is an occasion of division between scholars who analyse antiquity and artists who delight in it. His argument was that the scholars must resolve this conflict by accepting the judgment of the artists. Their criticism, fecund in useful historical results, had restored the legend and the vast frame of the two poems. But it had decided nothing, and could have decided nothing. After all, the *Iliad* and the *Odyssey* were there before the world in clear shapes, and if Goethe chose to say: "The two poems are the work of a single poet "—the scholar had no reply. His task was modest, but useful and deserving of esteem. Let us not forget, said Nietzsche at the conclusion of his inaugural lecture, how but a few years ago these marvellous Greek masterpieces lay buried beneath an enormous accumulation of prejudices. The minute labour of our students has saved them for us.

Philology is neither a Muse nor a Grace; she has not created this enchanted world, it is not she who has composed this immortal music. But she is its virtuoso, and we have to thank her that these accents, long forgotten and almost indecipherable, resound again, and that is surely a high merit. "And as the Muses formerly descended among the heavy and wretched Bœotian peasants, this messenger comes to-day into a world filled with gloomy and baneful shapes, filled with profound and incurable sufferings, and consoles us by evoking the beautiful and luminous forms of the Gods, the outlines of a marvellous, an azure, a distant, a fortunate country...."

Nietzsche was highly applauded by the bourgeois of Basle, who had come in great numbers to hear the young master whose genius had been announced. His success pleased him, but his thoughts went otherwhere, towards another marvellous, azure, and distant land—Triebschen. On the 4th of June he received a note:

"Come and sleep a couple of nights under our roof," wrote Wagner. "We want to know what you are made of. Little joy I have so far from my German compatriots. Come and save the abiding *faith* which I still cling to, in what I call, with Goethe and some others, German liberty."

Nietzsche was able to spare these two days and henceforward was a familiar of the master's. He wrote to his friends:

"Wagner realises all our desires: a rich, great, and magnificent spirit; an energetic character, an enchanting man, worthy of all love, ardent for all knowledge. ... But I must stop; I am chanting a pæan....

"I beg you," he says further, "not to believe a word of what is written about Wagner by the journalists and the musicographers. No one in the world knows him, no one can judge him, since the whole world builds on foundations which are not his, and is lost in his atmosphere. Wagner is dominated by an idealism so absolute, a humanity so moving and so profound, that I feel in his presence as if I were in contact with divinity...."

Richard Wagner had written, at the request of Louis II., King of Bavaria, a short treatise on social metaphysics. This singular work, which had been conceived to fascinate a young and romantic prince, was carefully withheld from publicity, and lent only to intimates. Wagner gave it to Nietzsche, and few things surely that the latter ever read went home more deeply. As traces of the impression he received from it are to be discovered in his work down to the very end, it will be worth our while to give some idea of its nature.

Wagner starts by explaining an old error of his: in 1848 he had been a Socialist. Not that he had ever welcomed the ideal of a levelling of men; his mind, avid of beauty and order, in other words, of superiorities, could not have welcomed a notion of the kind. But he hoped that a humanity liberated from the baser servitudes would rise with less effort to an understanding of art. In this he was mistaken, as he now understood.

"My friends, despite their fine courage," he wrote, "were vanquished; the emptiness of their effort proved to me that they were the victims of a basic error and that they had asked from the world what the world could not give them."

His view cleared and he recognised that the masses are powerless, their agitations vain, their co-operation illusory. He had believed them capable of introducing into history a progress of culture. Now he saw that they could not collaborate towards the mere maintenance of a culture already acquired. They experience only such needs as are gross, elementary, and short-lived. For them all noble ends are unattainable. And the problem which reality obliges us to solve is this: how are we to contrive things so that the masses shall serve a culture which must always be beyond their comprehension, and serve it with zeal and love, even to the sacrifice of life? All politics are comprised within this question, which appears insoluble, and yet is not. Consider Nature: no one understands her ends; and yet all beings serve her. How does Nature obtain their adhesion to life? She deceives her creatures. She puts them in hope of an immutable and ever-delayed happiness. She gives them those instincts which constrain the humblest of animals to lengthy sacrifices and voluntary pains. She envelops in illusion all living beings, and thus persuades them to struggle and to suffer with unalterable constancy.

Society, wrote Wagner, ought to be upheld by similar artifices. It is illusions that assure its duration, and the task of those who rule men is to maintain and to propagate these conserving illusions. Patriotism is the most essential. Every child of the people should be brought up in love of the King, the living symbol of the fatherland, and this love must become an instinct, strong enough to render the most sublime abnegation an easy thing.

The patriotic illusion assures the permanence of the State but does not suffice to guarantee a high culture. It divides humanity, it favours cruelty, hatred, and narrowness of thought. The King, whose glance dominates the State, measures its limits, and is aware of purposes which extend beyond it. Here a second illusion is necessary, the religious illusion whose dogmas symbolise a profound unity and a universal love. The King must sustain it among his subjects.

The ordinary man, if he be penetrated with this double illusion, can live a happy and a worthy life: his way is made clear, he is saved. But the life of the prince and his counsellors is a graver and a more dangerous thing. They propagate the illusions, therefore they judge them. Life appears to them unveiled, and they know how tragic a thing it is. "The great man, the exceptional man," writes Wagner, "finds himself practically every day in the same condition in which the ordinary man despairs of life, and has recourse to suicide." The prince and the aristocracy which surrounds him, his nobles, are forearmed by their valour against so cowardly a temptation. Nevertheless, they experience a bitter need to "turn their back on the world." They desire for themselves a restful illusion, of which they may be at the same time the authors and the accessories. Here art intervenes to save them, not to exalt the naïve enthusiasm of the people, but to alleviate the unhappy life of the nobles and to sustain their valour.

"Art," writes Richard Wagner, addressing Louis II., "I present to my very dear friend as the promised and benignant land. If Art cannot lift us in a real and complete manner above life, at least it lifts us in life itself to the very highest of regions. It gives life the appearance of a game, it withdraws us from the common lot, it ravishes and consoles us."

"Only yesterday"—wrote Nietzsche to Gersdorff on the 4th of August, 1869—"I was reading a manuscript which Wagner confided to me, *Of the State and Religion,* a treatise full of grandeur, composed in order to explain to 'his young friend,' the little King of Bavaria, his particular way of understanding the State and Religion. Never did any one speak to his King in a tone more worthy, more philosophical; I felt myself moved and uplifted by that ideality which the spirit of Schopenhauer seems constantly to inspire. Better than any other mortal, the King should understand the tragic essence of life."

In September, Friedrich Nietzsche, after a short stay in Germany, returned to a life divided between Basle and Triebschen. At Basle he had his work, his pupils, who listened to him with attention, the society of amiable colleagues. His wit, his musical talent, his friendship with Richard Wagner, his elegant manners and appearance, procured him a certain prestige. The best houses liked his company, and he did not refuse their invitations. But all the pleasures of society are less acceptable than the simplest friendship, and Nietzsche had not a single friend in this honest bourgeois city; at Triebschen alone was he satisfied.

"Now," he writes to Erwin Rohde, who was living at Rome, "I, too, have my Italy, but I am able to visit it only on Saturdays and Sundays. My Italy is called Triebschen, and I already feel as if it were my home. Recently I have been there four times running, and into the bargain a letter travels the same road almost every week. My dear friend, what I see and hear and learn there I find it impossible to tell you. Schopenhauer and Goethe, Pindar and Æschylus are, believe me, still alive."

Each of his returns was an occasion of melancholy. A feeling of solitude depressed him. He confided in Erwin Rohde, speaking at the same time of the hopes he had in his work.

"Alas, dear friend," he said, "I have very few satisfactions, and solitary, always solitary, I must ruminate on them all within myself. Ah! I should not fear a good illness, if I could purchase at that price a night's conversation with you. Letters are so little use! ... Men are constantly in need of midwives, and almost all go to be delivered in taverns, in colleges where little thoughts and little projects are as plentiful as litters of kittens. But when we are full of our thought no one is there to aid us, to assist us at the difficult accouchement: sombre and melancholy, we deposit in some dark hole our birth of thought, still heavy and shapeless. The sun of friendship does not shine upon them."

"I am becoming a virtuoso in the art of solitary walking," he says again; and he adds: "My friendship has something pathological about it." Nevertheless he is happy in the depths of his being; he says so himself one day, and warns his friend Rohde against his own letters:

"Correspondence has this that is vexatious about it: one would like to give the best of oneself, whereas, in fact, one gives what is most ephemeral, the accord and not the eternal melody. Each time that I sit down to write to you, the saying of Hölderlin (the favourite author of my schooldays) comes back to my mind: 'Denn liebend giebt der Sterbliche *vom Besten!* And, as well as I remember, what have you found in my last letters? Negations, contrarieties, singularities, solitudes. Nevertheless, Zeus and the divine sky of autumn know it, a powerful current carries me towards positive ideas, each day I enjoy exuberant hours which delight me with full perceptions, with real conceptions—in such instants of exalting impressions, I never miss sending you a long letter full of thoughts and of vows; and I fling it athwart the blue sky, trusting, for its carriage towards you, to the electricity which is between our souls."

And we can get a glimpse of these positive ideas, these precious impressions, because we are in possession of all the notes and the blunders of the young man who was acquiring, at the price of constant effort, strength and mastery.

"My years of study," he wrote to Ritschl, "what have they been for me? A luxurious sauntering across the domains of philology and art; hence my gratitude is especially lively at this moment that I address you who have been till now the 'destiny' of my life; and hence I recognise how necessary and opportune was the offer which changed me from a wandering into a fixed star, and obliged me to taste anew the satisfaction of galling but regular work, of an unchanging but certain object. A man's labour is quite another thing, when the holy *anangkei* of his profession helps him; how peaceful is his slumber, and, awakening, how sure is his knowledge of what the day demands. There, there is no philistinism. I feel as if I were gathering a multitude of scattered pages in a book."

The Origin of Tragedy proves to be the book the guiding ideas of which Nietzsche was now elaborating. Greek thought remains the centre round which his thought forms, and he meditates, in audacious fashion, on its history. A true historian, he thinks, should grasp its ensemble in a rapid view. "All the great advances in Philology," he writes in his notes, "are the issue of a creative gaze." The eyes of a Goethe discovered a Greece clear and serene. Being still under the domination of his genius, we continue to perceive the image which he has put before us. But we should seek and discover for ourselves. Goethe fixed his gaze on the centuries of Alexandrine culture. Nietzsche neglects these. He prefers the rude and primitive centuries, whither his instinct, since his eighteenth year, had led him when he elected to study the distiches of the aristocrat, Theognis of Megara. There he inhales an energy, a strength of thought, of action, of endurance, of infliction; a vital poetry, vital dreams which rejoice his soul.

Finally, in this very ancient Greece, he finds again, or thinks that he finds again, the spirit of Wagner, his master. Wagner wishes to renew tragedy, and, by using the theatre, as it were, as a spiritual instrument, to reanimate the diminished sense of poetry in the human soul. The "tragic" Greeks had a similar ambition; they wished to raise their race and ennoble it again by the most striking evocation of myths. Their enterprise was a sublime one, but it failed, for the merchants of the Piræus, the democracy of the towns, the vulgar herd of the market-place and of the port, did not care for a lyrical art which stipulated a too lofty manner of thought, too great a nobleness in deed. The noble families were vanquished and tragedy ceased to exist. Richard Wagner encounters similar enemies—they are the democrats, insipid thinkers, and base prophets of well-being and peace.

"Our world is being judaised, our prattling *plebs,* given over to politics, is hostile to the idealistic and profound art of Wagner," writes Nietzsche to Gersdorff. "His chivalrous nature is contrary to them. Is Wagner's art, as, in other times, Æschylus's art, to suffer defeat?" Friedrich Nietzsche is always occupied with a like combat.

He unfolds these very new views to his master. "We must renew the idea of Hellenism," he says to him; "we live on commonplaces which are false. We speak of the 'Greek joy,' the 'Greek serenity'; this joy, this serenity, are tardy fruits and of poor savour, the graces of centuries of servitudes. The Socratic subtlety, the Platonic sweetness, already bear the mark of the decline. We must study the older centuries, the seventh, the sixth. Then we touch the naïve force, the original sap. Between the poems of Homer, which are the romance of her infancy, and the dramas of Æschylus, which are the act of her manhood, Greece, not without long effort, enters into the possession of her instincts and disciplines. It is the knowledge of these times which we should seek, because they resemble our own. Then the Greeks believed, as do the Europeans of to-day, in the fatality of natural forces; and they believed also that man must create for himself his virtues and his gods. They were animated by a tragic sentiment, a brave pessimism, which did not turn them away from life. Between them and us there is a complete parallel and correspondence; pessimism and courage, and the will to establish a new beauty...."

Richard Wagner interested himself in the ideas of the young man, and associated him more and more intimately in his life. One day, Friedrich Nietzsche being present, he received from Germany the news that the *Rhinegold* and the *Valkyries,* badly executed far from his advice and direction, had had a double failure. He was sad and did not hide his disappointment; he was afflicted by this depreciation of the immense work which he had destined for a non-existent theatre and public, and which now crumbled before his eyes. His noble suffering moved Nietzsche.

Nietzsche took part in his master's work. Wagner was then composing the music of the *Twilight of the Gods.* Page after page the work grew, without haste or delay, as though from the regular overflowing of an invisible source. But no effort absorbed Wagner's thought, and, during these same days, he wrote an account of his life. Friedrich Nietzsche received the manuscript with directions to have it secretly printed, and to supervise the publication of an edition limited to twelve copies. He was asked to oblige with more intimate services. At Christmas, Wagner was preparing a Punch and Judy show for his children. He wanted to have pretty figurines, devils and angels. Madame Wagner begged Nietzsche to purchase them in Basle. "I forget that you are a professor, a doctor, and a philologist," she said graciously, "and remember only your five-and-twenty years." He examined the figurines of Basle, and, not finding them to his liking, wrote to Paris for the most frightful devils, the most beatific angels imaginable. Friedrich Nietzsche, admitted to the solemnity of the Punch and Judy show, spent the Christmas festival with Wagner, his wife and family, in the most charming of intimacies. Cosima Wagner made him a present; she gave him a French edition of Montaigne, with whom, it seems, he was not acquainted, and of whom he soon became so fond. She was imprudent that day. Montaigne is perilous reading for a disciple.

"This winter I have to give two lectures on the æsthetic of the Greek tragedies," wrote Nietzsche, about September, to his friend the Baron von Gersdorff; "and Wagner will come from Triebschen to hear them." Wagner did not go, but Nietzsche was listened to by a very large public.

He described an unknown Greece, vexed by the mysteries and intoxications of the god Dionysius, and through its trouble, through this very intoxication, initiated into poetry, into song, into tragic contemplation. It seems that he wished to define this eternal romanticism, always alike to him, whether in Greece of the sixth century B.C. or in Europe of the thirteenth century; the same, surely, which inspired Richard Wagner in his retreat at Triebschen. Nietzsche, however, abstained from mentioning this latter name.

"The Athenian coming to assist at the tragedy of the great Dionysos bore in his heart some spark of that elementary force from which tragedy was born. This is the irresistible outburst of springtime, that fury and delirium of mingled emotions which sweeps in springtime across the souls of all simple peoples and across the whole life of nature. It is an accepted thing that festivals of Easter and Carnival, travestied by the Church, were in their origin spring festivals. Every such fact can be traced to a most deep-rooted instinct: the old soil of Greece bore on its bosom enthusiastic multitudes, full of Dionysos; in the Middle Ages in the same way the dances of the Feast of Saint John and of Saint Vitus drew out great crowds who went singing, leaping and dancing from town to town, gathering recruits in each. It is, of course, open to the doctors to regard these phenomena as diseases of the crowd: we content ourselves with saying that the drama of antiquity was the flower of such a disease, and if that of our modern art does not fountain forth from that mysterious source, that is its misfortune."

In his second lecture Nietzsche studied the end of tragic art. It is a singular phenomenon; all the other arts of Greece slowly and gloriously declined. Tragedy had no decline. After Sophocles it disappeared, as though a catastrophe had destroyed it. Nietzsche recounts the catastrophe, and names the destroyer, Socrates.

He dared to denounce the most revered of men. It was he, the poor Athenian, a man of the people, an ugly scoffer, who suppressed the ancient poetry. Socrates was neither an artist nor a philosopher; he did not write, he did not teach, he scarcely spoke; seated in the public place, he stopped the passers-by, astonished them by his pleasant logic, convinced them of their ignorance and absurdity, laughed, and obliged them to laugh at themselves. His irony dishonoured the naïve beliefs which gave strength to the ancestors of the race, the myths which upheld their virtues. He despised tragedy, and made open declaration of his contempt for it; that was enough. Euripides was troubled, and suppressed his inspiration, while the young Plato, who perhaps would have surpassed Sophocles himself, listened to the new master, burnt his verses, and renounced art. He disconcerted the old instinctive lyrical humanity of Greece; and, by the voice of Plato, whom he had seduced, he imposed the illusion, unknown to the ancients, of Nature as accessible to the reason of man, altogether penetrated by it, and always harmonious. Friedrich Nietzsche was to insert these pages in his book upon *The Birth of Tragedy.*

This charge pronounced against Socrates surprised his audience in Basle. Wagner knew it, and in September, 1870, wrote to Nietzsche an enthusiastic but extremely shrewd letter.

"As for me, I cry out to you: That's it! you have got hold of the truth, you touch the exact point with keen accuracy. I await with admiration the series of work in which you will combat the errors of popular dogmatism. But none the less you make me anxious, and I hope with all my heart that you are not going to come a cropper. I would also like to advise you not to expound your audacious views, which must be so difficult to establish, in short brochures of limited range. You are, I feel, profoundly penetrated with your ideas: you must gather them together into a larger book of much wider scope. Then you will find and will give us the *mot juste* on the divine blunders of Socrates and Plato, those creators so wonderful as to exact adoration even from us who forswear them! Our words, my dear friend, swell into hymns when we consider the incomprehensible harmony of those essences, so strange to our world! And what pride and hope animate us when, returning on ourselves, we feel strongly and clearly that we can and should achieve a work, outside the reach even of those masters!"

None of the letters addressed by Nietzsche to Wagner have been published. Have they been lost? Were they destroyed? Or are they merely refused by Madame Cosima Wagner, who is perhaps not incapable of rancour? The facts are unknown. However, we may be certain that Nietzsche begged Wagner to ally himself with him, to aid him in rendering clear those difficult views of his. Wagner replied:

"MY DEAR FRIEND,—How good it is to be able to exchange such letters! There is no one to-day with whom I can talk as seriously as with you—the Unique [2] excepted.

---

[2] Cosima Wagner.

God only knows what would happen to me but for that! But I should be able to give myself up to the pleasure of fighting with you against "Socratism" only on one condition, that of having an enormous deal of time at my disposal, free from the temptation of any better project—to speak quite plainly, I should have to abandon all creative work. Division of labour is a good thing in this connection. You can do much for me: you can take on your shoulders a full half of the task assigned to me by fate. And so doing, you will perhaps achieve the whole of your own destiny. I have never had much success in my essays in Philology: you have never had much success in your essays in music: and it is well that things should be so. As a musician you would have come to much the same end to which I should have come had I stuck obstinately to Philology. But Philology remains in my blood; it directs me in my work as a musician. As for you, remain a philologist, and keeping to Philology, allow yourself to be directed by music. I mean what I say in a very serious spirit. You have taught me within what base preconceptions a professional philologist is to-day expected to imprison himself—I have taught you in what an unspeakable den a genuine 'absolute' musician must to-day waste himself. Show us what Philology ought to be, and help me to prepare the way for that great 'Renaissance' in which Plato will embrace Homer, and in which Homer, penetrated by the ideas of Plato, will be at last and for the first time the sublime Homer ..."

At this instant Nietzsche had conceived his work, and was making ready to write it at a spurt. "Science, art, and philosophy grow so intimately within me," he said in February to Rohde, "that I am about to give birth to a centaur."

Professional duties, however, interrupted this flight. In March he was appointed titular professor. The honour flattered him, the duties kept him occupied. At the same time he was given the care of a class of higher rhetoric; then he was asked to draw up in the noblest Latin an address of congratulation to Professor Baumbrach, of Fribourg, who had taught for fifty years in the University of that town. Nietzsche, who never shirked anything, applied himself to the preparation of his class and the composition of his discourse. In April, more work. Ritschl founded a review, the *Acta societatis philologic? Lipsi?*, and desired that his best pupil should contribute to it. Nietzsche did not haggle over the help asked of him. He promised his copy, and wrote to Rohde to ask for his collaboration also.

"Personally, I feel most strongly that I am under an obligation," he wrote. "And, notwithstanding that this work will put me out at the moment, I am quite committed to it. We must collaborate for the first number. You are aware that certain persons will read it with curiosity, with malevolence. Therefore, it *must* be good. I have promised my faithful help—answer me."

May and then June, 1870, came. Friedrich Nietzsche seems to have been occupied, above all else, with his work for the *Acta*. During the holidays at Pentecost, Rohde, on his way back from Italy, stopped at Basle. Nietzsche was delighted, he wished Wagner to make his friend's acquaintance, and brought him to Triebschen. They spent a fine day together, on the brink of an abyss which none of them apparently perceived.

Rohde, continuing on his road to Germany, left Basle. Nietzsche remained alone, the victim of a foolish accident. He had given himself a strain and was forced to be up.

Had he given any attention to the rumours of war which troubled Europe in 1870? It seems not. He was little curious of news, and scarcely read the newspapers. Not that he was indifferent to his country, but he conceived it, in the manner of Goethe, as a source of art and moral grandeur. One of his thoughts, one alone, is perhaps inspired by the public unrest. "No war," he writes; "the State would become too strong thereby." No doubt we have here, besides one of Nietzsche's own impressions, an echo of the conversations of Triebschen: Wagner recruited his most ardent admirers in Southern Germany, in the Rhineland, in Bavaria, where his protector Louis II. reigned; the Germans of the North appreciated him badly, the Berliners worst of all, and he had no wish for a warlike crisis which would certainly have the effect of adding to the weight of Prussian dictation. The State to which Nietzsche pointed in his short note was the Prussian State. He foresaw, and like his master dreaded, the imminent hegemony of Berlin, that despised town of bureaucrats and bankers, of journalists and Jews.

On July 14th, a convalescent, stretched out on his long chair, he wrote to his comrade, Erwin Rohde. He spoke to him of Richard Wagner and of Hans von Bülow, of art and of friendship. Suddenly he stops in the middle of a phrase, marking with a blank line the interruption of his thought.

"Here is a terrible thunderclap," he wrote. "The Franco-German war is declared; a demon alights upon all our culture, already worn threadbare. What are we about to experience?

"Friend, dear friend, we met once more in the twilight of peace. To-day what do all our aspirations signify? Perhaps we are at the beginning of the end! What a gloomy sight. Cloisters will become necessary. And we shall be the first friars."

He signed himself *The Loyal Swiss.* This unexpected signature may be explained in a literal manner. In order to be appointed a professor at Basle, Friedrich Nietzsche had had to renounce his nationality. But assuredly it indicated more than this. It announced his detachment of mind: he had decided on the rôle of the contemplator.

What a misunderstanding of himself! He was too young, too brave, too much enamoured of his race, to adopt the part of spectator only in the imminent drama. As "a loyal Swiss," and as such dispensed from military duties, he quietly took up his abode with his sister Lisbeth in a mountain inn, where he wrote out some pages on Greek lyricism. It was then that he formulated for the first time his definition of the Dionysian and Apollonian spirits. Nevertheless, the German armies were crossing the Rhine and gaining their first victories, and it was not without emotion that Nietzsche heard the news. The thought of lofty deeds in which he had no part, of perils from which he was preserved, troubled his meditations.

On July 20th, writing to Madame Ritschl, he expressed the thoughts which occupied his solitude. First he gave expression to a fear which, as it seemed, the memory of a Greece ruined by the conflict of Sparta and Athens inspired in him. "Unhappy, historical analogies teach us that the very traditions of culture may be destroyed by the bitterness of such a war of nations." But he also expressed the emotion which had begun to seize him. "How I am ashamed of this inactivity in which I am kept, now that the instant has come when I might be applying what I learned in the artillery. Naturally I make myself ready for an energetic course of action, in case things should take a bad turn; do you know that the students of Kiel have enlisted together, with enthusiasm?" On the morning of August 7th he read in his paper the dispatches from Wörth: *German victory: Enormous losses.* He could no longer remain in his retreat. He returned to Basle, asked and obtained from the Swiss authorities permission to serve in the ambulance corps, and proceeded at once to Germany to enlist for the war which allured him.

He crossed conquered Alsace: he saw the charnel houses of Wissembourg and of Wörth: on August 29th he bivouacked not far from Strassburg, where conflagrations lit up the horizon; then he made his way, by Lunéville and Nancy, towards the country around Metz, now converted into an immense ambulance, where the wounded of Mars-la-Tour, Gravelotte and Saint-Privat, so numerous that it was difficult to nurse them, were dying of their wounds and of infectious illnesses. Some unfortunates were given into his charge: he did his duty with kindness and courage, but experienced a singular emotion, a sacred and almost enthusiastic horror. For the first time he considered without repulsion the labour of the masses. He watched those millions of beings, some struck down and marked by death, others marching the roads or standing under arms: he considered them without contempt, he esteemed their destiny. Under the menaces of war, these men have something momentous about them. They forget their vain thoughts; they march, they sing, they obey their chiefs; they die. Friedrich Nietzsche was recompensed for his pains; a fraternal impulse uplifted his soul, he no longer felt his solitude, he loved the simple people who surrounded him. "All my military passions awake," he writes, "and I cannot satisfy them! I would have been at Rezonville, at Sedan, actively, passively perhaps. This Swiss neutrality always ties my hands."

His passage through France was rapid. He received orders to convey the wounded in his care to the hospital at Carlsruhe.

He set out and was shut up, for three days and three nights, with eleven men, lying in a market cart closed fast against the cold and the rain. Two of the wounded who accompanied him were attacked by diphtheria, all had dysentery. "To reach truth," says a German mystic, "the most rapid mount is Affliction." Friedrich Nietzsche recalled this maxim of which he was so fond. He tried his courage, verified his thoughts. He dressed the sores of his wounded, he listened to their complaints, their appeals, and did not interrupt his meditation. Till now he had known only his books; now he knew life. He relished this bitter ordeal, always discerning some far-off beauty. "I, also, I have my hopes," he was to write; "thanks to them I was able to look on at the war and to pursue my meditations without pause, in presence of the worst horrors.... I recall a solitary night during which I lay stretched out in a market van with the wounded men confided to me and never ceased to explore in thought the three abysses of tragedy which have for names: *Wahn, Wille, Wehe*—Illusion, Will, Affliction. Whence then did I draw the confident certitude that he should undergo in birth a similar ordeal, the hero to come of tragic knowledge and Greek gaiety?"

He arrived at Carlsruhe with his sick and wounded; he had contracted their illness and was attacked by dysentery and diphtheria. An unknown who had been his ambulance companion nursed him devotedly. As soon as he was well again, Nietzsche went to his home at Naumburg, there to seek not repose, but an entire leisure from work and thought.

"Yes," he wrote to his friend Gersdorff, who was fighting in France—"Yes, that conception of things which is common to us has undergone the ordeal by fire. I have had the same experience as you. For me, as for you, these weeks will remain in my life as an epoch in which each one of my principles re-affirmed itself in me; I would have risked death with them.... Now I am at Naumburg again, but poorly restored to health so far. The atmosphere in which I have lived has been long over me like a dark cloud; I heard an incessant lamentation."

Once already, in July, 1865, during the campaign at Sadowa, he had known war, and undergone its allurement. A simple and great aspiration had laid hold of him; and for a moment he had felt himself in accord with his race. "I feel a patriotic emotion," he wrote; "it is a new experience for me." He grasped at this sudden exaltation and cultivated it.

Indeed, his is a changed soul. He is no longer the "loyal Swiss" of another time; he is a man among men, a German proud of his Germany. A war has transformed him; he glorifies war. War awakes the energy of men; it even troubles their spirits. It obliges them to seek in an ideal order, an order of beauty and duty, the ends of a life which is too cruel. The lyric poet, the sage, misunderstood in ages of peace, are heard with respect in ages of war. Then men have need of them, and are conscious of their need. The same necessity which ranges them behind their chiefs renders them attentive to genius. Humanity is made truly one, and is drawn towards the heroic and the sublime, only under the pressure of war.

Friedrich Nietzsche, though still very weak and suffering, again took up the notes of his book that he might record in it his new ideas. In Greece, he argues, art was the visible form of a society, disciplined by struggle, from the workshop, where the captive slave laboured, up to the gymnasium and the agora, where the free man played with arms. Such was that winged figure, that goddess of Samothrace, that had for companion of her flight a bloody trireme.

The Greek genius emanated from war, it sang war, it had war for its comrade. "It is the people of the tragic mysteries," wrote Friedrich Nietzsche, "who strike the great blow of the Persian battles; in return, the people who have maintained these wars need the salutary beverage of tragedy." We follow in his notes the movement of a mind which wishes to grasp the very idea of the tragic, athwart a vaguely-known Greece. Again and again we find this word *tragic* brought in as if it were a fundamental strain which the young thinker trains himself to repeat, like a child trying to learn a new word:—"Tragic Greece conquers the Persians.... Tragic man is nature itself in its highest strength of creation and knowledge: he trifles with sorrow...." Three formulas satisfy his research for a moment. "The tragic work of Art—the tragic Man—the tragic State." Thus he determined the three essential parts of his book, which he would entitle as a whole: *The Tragic Man.*

Let us not misunderstand the real object of his meditations: this society, this discipline which he discerned in the past, were in reality the ideal forms of the Fatherland which he desired and for which he dared to hope. He saw on the one hand Latin Europe, weakened by utilitarianism and the softness of life, on the other Germany, rich in poets, in soldiers, in myths, in victories. She was suzerain of those races which were in process of decay. How would she exercise this suzerainty? Might not one augur from her triumph a new era, warlike and tragic, chivalrous and lyric? One could conceive it; and therefore one should hope for it, and this was enough to dictate one's duty. How glorious this Germany would be, with Bismarck as its chief, Moltke as its soldier, Wagner as its poet—its philosopher, too, existed, and was called Friedrich Nietzsche. This belief, though he expressed it nowhere, he surely had: for he had not a doubt as to his genius.

He was elated, but did not let his dreams lead him astray: he imagined an ideal Fatherland, yet never lost from sight the Fatherland, human, too human, which actually existed.

During October and the first days of November, alone with his own people in that Naumburg whose provincial virtues he did not love, he bore hardly with the vulgarity of the little people, of the functionaries with whom he mixed. Naumburg was a small Prussian town; Friedrich Nietzsche did not care for this robust and vulgar Prussia. Metz had capitulated; the finest army of France was taken captive: a delirium of conceit swept all Germany off its feet. Friedrich Nietzsche resisted the general tendency. The sentiment of triumph was a repose which his exacting soul might not know. On the contrary, he was disgusted and alarmed.

"I fear," he wrote to his friend Gersdorff, "that we shall have to pay for our marvellous national victories at a price to which I, for my part, will never consent. In confidence—I am of opinion that modern Prussia is a Power highly dangerous to culture.... The enterprise is not easy, but we must be philosophers enough to keep our sang-froid in the midst of all this smoke, we must keep watch so that no robber may come and steal any part of what, in my opinion, is commensurable with nothing beside, not even the most heroic of military actions, not even our national exaltation."

Then a document appeared which deeply moved Friedrich Nietzsche. It was the date of the centenary of Beethoven. The Germans, occupied with their war, had neglected to commemorate it. Richard Wagner's voice was raised, it alone was strong enough to recall to the conquerors the memory of another glory: "Germans, you are brave," he cried; "remain brave in peace.... In this marvellous year 1870 nothing is better suited to your pride in being brave than the memory of the great Beethoven.... Let us celebrate that great pioneer and path-hewer, let us celebrate him worthily, not less worthily than the victory of German courage: for he who gives joy to the world is raised higher among men than he who conquers the world."

Germans, you are brave; remain brave in peace—no saying could move Friedrich Nietzsche more deeply. He desired to be near the master again, and, though not yet restored to health, he left Naumburg.

He saw Richard Wagner again and was not entirely satisfied. This man, who had been so splendid in misfortune, seemed to have lost stature. There was a vulgar quality in his joy. Well had the German victory avenged him for those Parisian cat-calls and railleries which he had had to endure; now he "ate Frenchmen" with an enormous and peaceable relish. Nevertheless he declined certain offers; he was promised the highest office and honours if he accepted residence in Berlin. He refused, being unwilling to let himself be enthroned as poet-laureate of a Prussian Empire; and his disciple was thankful for the refusal.

Friedrich Nietzsche found at Basle an even better confidant of his anxieties. The historian Jacob Burckhardt, a great scholar of arts and civilisations, was melancholy; all brutality was odious to him, and he detested war and its destruction. A citizen of the last city in Europe which maintained its independence and its old customs, proud of this independence and of these customs, Jacob Burckhardt disliked those nations of thirty or forty millions of souls which he saw establishing themselves. To the designs of Bismarck and of Cavour he preferred the counsel of Aristotle—"So arrange that the number of citizens does not exceed ten thousand; otherwise they would not be able to meet together on the public square."

He had studied Athens, Venice, Florence, and Sienna. He held in high esteem the ancient and Latin disciplines, in very moderate esteem the German disciplines: he dreaded German hegemony. Burckhardt and Nietzsche were colleagues. They often met in the intervals between two lectures. Then they would talk and, on fine days, stroll together along that terrace over which all European travellers lean, that is between the cathedral of red sandstone and the Rhine, here so young still but already so strong, as it passes with a long murmur of ruffled waters. The simply-built University is situated quite near, on the slope, between the river and the Museum.

The two colleagues were eternally examining their common thought. How should that tradition of culture and beauty be continued, that fragile and oft-broken tradition which two tiny States, Attica and Tuscany, have transmitted to our care? France had not deserved censure; she had known how to maintain the methods and a school of taste. But had Prussia the qualities fitting her heritage? Friedrich Nietzsche repeated the expression of his hope. "Perhaps," said he, "this war will have transformed our old Germany; I see her more virile, endowed with a firmer and more delicate taste." Jacob

Burckhardt listened. "No," said he, "you are always thinking of the Greeks, for whom war had no doubt an educative virtue. But modern wars are superficial; they do not reach, they do not correct the bourgeois, *laissez-aller* style of life. They are rare; their impressions are soon effaced; they are soon forgotten; they do not exercise people's thought." What did Nietzsche answer? A letter to Erwin Rohde enables us to divine the ill-assured accent of his observations. "I am very anxious," he writes, "as regards the immediate future. I seem to recognise there the Middle Ages in disguise.... Be careful to free yourself from this fatal Prussia, with its repugnance to culture! Flunkeys and priests sprout from its soil like mushrooms, and they are going to darken all Germany with their smoke!"

Jacob Burckhardt, long a recluse amid his memories and his books, had the habit of melancholy and made the best of it. By way of discreet protest against the enthusiasms of his contemporaries, he delivered a lecture upon *Historical Greatness.* "Do not take for true greatness," said he to the students of Basle, "such and such a military triumph, such and such an expansion of a State. How many nations have been powerful who are forgotten and merit their oblivion! Historical greatness is a rarer thing; it lies wholly in the works of those men whom we call great men, using that vague term because we cannot truly fathom their nature. Some unknown genius leaves us *Notre Dame de Paris;* Goethe gives us his Faust; Newton his law of the Solar System. This is greatness, and this alone." Friedrich Nietzsche listened and applauded. "Burckhardt," wrote he, "is becoming a Schopenhauerian...." But a few wise words do not satisfy his ardour. Nor can he so quickly renounce the hope which he has conceived; he wishes to act, to save his Fatherland from the moral disaster which in his judgment menaces her.

How act? Here was a sluggish people, not easily aroused, lacking in sensitiveness, a people stunted by democracy, a people in revolt against every noble aspiration: by what artifice could one sustain among them the imperilled ideal, the love of heroism and of the sublime? Nietzsche formed a project which was so audacious and so advanced that he meditated long upon it without confiding in any one. Richard Wagner was then working to establish that theatre of Bayreuth in which he hoped to realise his epic creation in complete freedom. Nietzsche dared to imagine a different institution, but one of the same order; a kind of seminary where the young philosophers, his friends, Rohde, Gersdorff, Deussen, Overbeck, Romundt should meet, live together and, free from duties, liberated from administrative tutelage, meditate, under the guidance of certain masters, on the problems of the hour. A double home of art and of thought would thus maintain at the heart of Germany, above the crowd and apart from the State, the traditions of the spiritual life. "Cloisters will become necessary," he had written to Erwin Rohde in July; six months' experience brought back this idea. "Here assuredly is the strangest thing which this time of war and victory has raised up; *a modern anchoritism*—an impossibility of living in accord with the State."

Friedrich Nietzsche let himself be drawn away by this dream, the unreality of which he failed to recognise. He was imagining a reunion of solitaries, similar to the

Port Royal des Champs. He knew that such a society did not accord with the manners and tastes of his times, but he judged it to be necessary and believed that he had strength enough to establish or impose it.

A profound instinct inspired and directed him. That old college of Pforta had been monachal in its origins, in its buildings and in its very walls, in the lasting gravity and ordered rule of life. Thus he had, as a child, received the impress of what was almost the life of a religious. He kept the memory of it, and the nostalgia. During his years at the University he had constantly sought to isolate himself from the world by surrounding himself with friends. He studied Greece, and the antique wisdom nourished his soul: he loved Pythagoras and Plato, the one the founder, the other the poet, of the finest brotherhood that man had ever conceived, the close and sovereign aristocracy of sages armed, of meditative knights. Thus did Christian humanity and Pagan humanity, united by a remote harmony, concur with his thoughts and his aspirations.

He wished to write an open letter to his friends, known and unknown; but he would only call them at the favourable moment, and till then would keep his secret. "Give me two years," he wrote to his friend Gersdorff enthusiastically and mysteriously, "and you will see a new conception of antiquity diffuse itself, which must bring a new spirit into the scientific and moral education of the nation!" Towards mid-December he believed that the moment had come. Erwin Rohde wrote him a melancholy letter, a very feeble echo of the passionate letters which Nietzsche had addressed to him. "Soon we shall need cloisters ..." he said, repeating the same idea expressed six months earlier by his friend. It was but a word; Friedrich Nietzsche saw in it a sign of spontaneous agreement, a presage of enthusiastic collaboration, and he wrote in a joyous transport:

"DEAR FRIEND,—I received your letter and I answer it without losing a minute. Above all I wish to tell you that I feel *altogether* like you, and that we shall be, in my opinion, very weak, if, abandoning our feeble complaints, we do not deliver ourselves from ennui by an energetic act.... I have at last understood the bearing of Schopenhauer's judgments on the philosophy of the universities. No radical truth is possible there. No revolutionary truth can come out from there.... We shall reject this yoke; to me that is certain. And we shall then form a new Greek academy: Romundt will be of our company.

"You know, since your visit to Triebschen, the projects of Bayreuth. For a long time, without confiding in any one, I have been considering whether it would not be suitable for us to break with philology and *its perspectives of culture.* I am preparing a great *adhortatio* for all those who are not yet completely captured and stifled by the manners of this present time. What a pity that I must write to you, and that for long we have not been able to examine in conversation each of my thoughts! To you who know not their turnings and their consequences, my plan will perhaps appear as an eccentric caprice. That, it is not; it is a necessity.

"... Let us try to reach a little island on which there will be no longer need to close one's ears with wax. Then we shall be one another's masters. Our books, from now till then, are but hooks to catch our friends, a public for our æsthetic and monachal association. Let us live, let us work, let us enjoy for one another's sake; in that manner only, perhaps, shall we be able to work for the *whole*. I may tell you (see how serious is my design) that I have already commenced to reduce my expenses in order to constitute a little reserve fund. We shall gamble in order to try our 'luck'; as to the books which we shall be able to write, I shall demand the highest honorarium as a provision for coming times. In brief, we shall neglect no lawful means of success in founding our cloister. We also have our duty for the next two years!

"May this plan seem to you worthy of meditation! Your last letter, moving as it was, signified to me that the time had come to unveil it for you.

"Shall we not be able to introduce a new form of Academy into the world?

> 'Und sollt' ich nicht, sehnsuchtigster Gewalt,
> In's Leben ziehn die einzigster Gestalt?'

"Thus Faust speaks of Helen. No one knows anything of my project, and now it depends upon you to see that Romundt is advised of it.

"Assuredly, our school of philosophy is neither an historical reminiscence nor an arbitrary caprice; is it not a *necessity* that pushes us on to that road? It seems that the plan of our student days, that voyage which we were to make together, returns in a new form, symbolic now and vaster than it was. On this occasion, I won't leave you in the lurch as I then did. That memory always annoys me.

"With my best hopes, your faithful

"FRATER FRIEDRICH.

"From the 23rd of December till the 1st of January I go to Triebschen, near Lucerne."

On the 22nd of December Friedrich Nietzsche left Lucerne: he had received no reply from Rohde. He found the house at Triebschen in high festival with children's games and the preparations for Christmas. Madame Wagner gave him a volume of Stendhal, *Les Promenades dans Rome*. He offered Wagner the famous woodcut of Dürer's of *The Knight, the Dog, and Death,* on which he had written a commentary for the book he was then preparing, *The Origin of Tragedy:* "A spirit which feels itself isolated, desperate and solitary," he wrote, "could choose no better symbol than that rider of Dürer's, who, unperturbed by his gruesome companions and yet wholly without hope, pursues his terrible path alone with dog and horse. This rider of Dürer's is our Schopenhauer: he was without hope, but he desired the truth. His like does not exist." Nietzsche would have been happy in the master's house if he had not been expecting Rohde's reply: the waiting worried him. He stopped for a week at Triebschen. Wagner was never done talking about Bayreuth and his vast projects.

Nietzsche, too, had his thought which he would have joyfully uttered; but first he wanted his friend's approbation, and that approbation did not come. He left without having received a word or spoken one on the subject.

At last, at Basle, he received the too long-desired letter: an honest, affectionate, but negative reply. "You tell me that cloisters are necessary to-day," wrote Rohde. "I believe it. But there are necessities for which no remedy exists. How can we find the money? And even when we shall have found the money, I do not know that I shall follow you; I do not feel in me a creative force which renders me worthy of the solitude whither you call me. For a Schopenhauer, a Beethoven, a Wagner, the case is different, as it is for you, dear friend. But, as I am in question, no! I must hope for a different life. Still let us entertain the wish for such a retreat, among certain friends, in a cloister of the muses; I agree to that. Deprived of desires, what would we become?"

If Rohde refused to follow him, who would follow him? He did not write his *Adhortatio;* Romundt was not advised, and even Wagner, it seems, knew nothing of the proposal.

Nietzsche made no vain complaints, but set to work to elaborate alone those revolutionary truths for which he would have wished to contrive a kindlier manner of birth. He turned his back upon Germany, upon those modern States which have it as their mission to flatter the servilities, soften the conflicts, and favour the idleness of men. He considered anew primitive Greece, the city of the seventh and the sixth centuries; thither a mysterious attraction ever drew him back. Was it the seduction of a perfect beauty? Doubtless, but it was also the seduction of that strength and cruelty which a modern conceals as he conceals a stain, and which the old Greeks practised with joy. Nietzsche loved strength; on the battlefield of Metz he had felt within him the appetite and instinct.

"If," he wrote, "genius and art are the final ends of Greek culture, then all the forms of Greek society must appear to us as necessary mechanisms and stepping-stones towards that final end. Let us discover what means were utilised by the will to act which animated the Greeks...." He discerns and names one of these means: slavery. "Frederick Augustus Wolf," he notes, "has shown us that slavery is necessary to culture. There is one of the powerful thoughts of my predecessor." He grasped it, held it to him, and forced it to disclose its whole meaning. This idea, suddenly discovered, inspired him; it was profound and moved him to the depths of his being; it was cruel, almost monstrous, and satisfied his romantic taste. He shuddered before it, he admired its sombre beauty.

"It may be that this knowledge fills us with terror," he wrote; 'I such terror is the almost necessary effect of all the most profound knowledge. For nature is still a frightful thing, even when intent on creating the most beautiful forms. It is so arranged that culture, in its triumphal march, benefits only a trivial minority of privileged mortals, and it is necessary that the slave service of the great masses be maintained, if one wish to attain to a full joy in becoming *(werde lust)*.

"We moderns have been accustomed to oppose two principles against the Greeks, the one and the other invented to reassure a society of an altogether servile kind which anxiously avoids the world, *slave:* we talk of the 'dignity of man' and the 'dignity of labour.'

"The language of the Greeks is other. They declare in simple terms that work is a disgrace, for it is impossible that a man occupied with the labour of gaining a livelihood should ever become an artist....

"So let us avow this cruel sounding truth: slavery is necessary to culture; a truth which assuredly leaves no doubt as to the absolute value of being.

"The misery of those men who live by labour must be made yet more vigorous, in order that a very few Olympian men may create a world of art.... At their expense, by the artifice of unpaid labour, the privileged classes should be relieved from the struggle for life, and given such conditions that they can create, and satisfy a new order of needs.... And if it is true to say that the Greeks were destroyed by slavery, this other affirmation is, most certainly, even truer: for lack of slavery, we are perishing."

But what was the origin of this very institution of slavery? How was the submission of the slave, that "blind mole of culture," secured? The Greeks teach us, answered Nietzsche: "The conquered belongs to the conqueror," they say, "with his wives and his children, his goods and his blood. Power gives the first *right*, and there is no right which is not at bottom appropriation, usurpation, power." Thus Nietzsche's thought was brought back towards its first object. The war had inspired him in the first instance. Now he rediscovers that solution. In sorrow and in tragedy, men had invented beauty; into sorrow and into tragedy they must be plunged, and there retained that their sense of beauty might be preserved. In pages which have the accent and rhythm of a hymn, Friedrich Nietzsche glorifies and invokes war:

"Here you have the State, of shameful origin; for the greater part of men, a well of suffering that is never dried, a flame that consumes them in its frequent crises. And yet when it calls, our souls become forgetful of themselves; at its bloody appeal the multitude is urged to courage and uplifted to heroism. Yes, the State is to the blind masses, perhaps, the highest and most worthy of aims; it is, perhaps, the State which, in its formidable hours, stamps upon every face the singular expression of greatness.

"Some tie, some mysterious affinity, exists between the State and art, between political activity and artistic production, the battlefield and the work of art. What is the rôle of the State? It is the tenaille of steel which binds society together. Without the State, in natural conditions—*bellum omnium contra omnes*—society would remain limited by the family, and could not project its roots afar. By the universal institution of States, that instinct which formerly determined the *bellum omnium contra omnes* has been concentrated; at certain epochs terrible clouds of war menace the peoples and discharge themselves at one great clap, in lightnings and thunders, fiercer as they are less frequent. But these crises are not continual; between one and another of them society breathes again; regenerated by the action of war, it breaks on every side into blossom and verdure, and, when the first fine days come, puts forth dazzling fruits of genius.

"If I leave the Greek world and examine our own, I recognise, I avow it, symptoms of degeneration which give me fears both for society and for art. Certain men, in whom the instinct of the State is lacking, wish, no longer to serve it, but to make it serve them, to use it for their personal ends. They see nothing of the divine in it; and, in order to utilise it, in a sure and rational manner, they are concerned to evade the shocks of war: they set out deliberately to organise things in such a manner that war becomes an impossibility. On the one hand they conjure up systems of European equilibrium, on the other hand they do their best to deprive absolute sovereigns of the right to declare war, in order that they may thus appeal the more easily to the egoism of the masses, and of those who represent them. They feel it incumbent on them to weaken the monarchical instinct of the masses, and do weaken it, by propagating among them the liberal and optimistic conception of the world, a conception which has its roots in the doctrines of French rationalism and the Revolution; that is, in a philosophy altogether foreign to the German spirit, a Latin platitude, devoid of any metaphysical meaning.

"The movement, to-day triumphant, of nationalities, the extension of universal suffrage which runs parallel to this movement, seem to me to be determined above all by *the fear of war*. And behind these diverse agitations, I perceive those who are chiefly moved by this alarm, the solitaries of international finance, who, being by nature denuded of any instinct for the State, subordinate politics, the State and society to their money-making and speculative ends.

"If the spirit of speculation is not thus to debase the spirit of the State, we must have war and war again—there is no other means. In the exaltation which it procures, it becomes clear to men that the State has not been founded to protect egoistical individuals against the demon of war; quite the contrary: love of country, devotion to one's prince, help to excite a moral impulse which is the symbol of a far higher destiny.... It will not therefore be thought that I do ill when I raise here the pæan of war. The resonance of its silver bow is terrible. It comes to us sombre as night: nevertheless Apollo accompanies it, Apollo, the rightful leader of states, the god who purifies them.... Let us say it then: war is necessary to the State, as the slave is to society. No one will be able to avoid these conclusions, if he have sought the causes of the perfection which Greek art attained, and Greek art alone."

War and yet again war which exalts the peoples: such was the cry of the solitary. He had but to drop his pen, to listen and look around him, and he saw the pedantic empire and repressed his hopes. "We follow the trouble of his thought. He hesitates, he records at the same moment the abiding illusion and the inevitable disillusion:

"I could have imagined," he writes, "that the Germans had embarked on this war to save Venus from the Louvre, like a second Helen. It would have been the spiritual interpretation of their combat. The fine antique severity inaugurated by this war—for the time to be grave has come—we think that is the time for *art* also."

He continued to write; his thought becomes clearer and more melancholy: "The State, when it cannot achieve its highest aim, grows beyond measure. The World Empire of the Romans, in face of Athens, has nothing of the sublime. This sap, which should all run to the flowers, resides now in the leaves and stalks, which swell to an immense size."

Rome troubled him; he disliked it; he judged it a slur upon antiquity. That city, warlike, but ever plebeian, victorious, but ever vulgar, filled him with gloomy fore-thought:

"Rome," he wrote, "is the typical barbaric state: the will cannot there attain to its noble ends. The organisation is more vigorous, the morality more oppressive ... who venerates this colossus?"

Who venerates this colossus? Let us give a modern and pressing application to these interrogatory words. The colossus is not Rome, it is Prussia and her empire. Narrow was the soil of Athens or of Sparta, and brief their day; but what did that matter if the object, which was spiritual strength and beauty, was attained? Friedrich Nietzsche was haunted by this vision of Greece with its hundred rival cities, raising between mountains and sea their acropoles, their temples, their statues, all resounding with the rhythm of pæans, all glorious and alert.

"The sentiment of Hellenism," he wrote, "as soon as it is awakened, becomes aggressive and translates itself into a combat against the culture of the present day."

Friedrich Nietzsche suffered from the wounds which life inflicted upon his lyrical dream. His friends listened to him, but followed him imperfectly. The professor, Franz Overbeck, who lived in his house and saw him every day, was a man of distinction, with a strong and acute mind. A German by birth, a Frenchman by education, he understood the problems of the day, and joined in the anxieties and intentions of Nietzsche; but his ardour could not equal Nietzsche's. Jacob Burckhardt was a man of noble intellect and character, but he was without hope, and Friedrich Nietzsche passionately desired to hope. No doubt, there was Wagner, whom neither passion nor hope ever could surprise, but he had just published an Aristophanic buffoonery directed against the conquered Parisians. Friedrich Nietzsche read this gross work, and condemned it. Overbeck and Burckhardt lacked ardour; Wagner lacked delicacy; and Nietzsche confided in no one. A chair of philosophy had just been vacated in the University of Basle. Nietzsche took fire at once. He wrote to Erwin Rohde, and told him that he should apply for this chair, and that he would assuredly secure it. Thus the two friends were to meet again. Vain hope! Erwin Rohde presented himself as a candidate, but was not accepted. Nietzsche reproached himself for having lured on his friend. He grew melancholy. He felt himself drawn "like a little whirlpool into a dead sea of night and oblivion."

He had never recovered entirely from the ordeals of the war. Neither sleep nor sure and certain health were ever at his call again. In February the nervous force which had sustained him suddenly gave way, and his disorders assumed an acute form. Violent neuralgias, insomnia, troubles and weaknesses of the eyesight, stomach ills, jaundice represented the nature of the crisis which had been tormenting him for five months. The doctors, quite at a loss, advised him to give up work and to take a voyage. Friedrich Nietzsche sent for his sister, who came to Naumburg. He brought her to pay a farewell visit to Triebschen, and left for Lugano.

At that time the railway did not cross the Alps. Travellers went by diligence over the ridge of the St. Gothard. Chance furnished Nietzsche with a remarkable companion, an old man of a talkative humour, and with no desire to conceal his identity: it was Mazzini. The old humanitarian and the young apostle of slavery hit it off wonderfully well. Mazzini cited Goethe's phrase:

"*Sich des halben zu entwohnen und im Ganzen, Vollen, Schönen resolut zu leben*" (To abjure half-measures, and to live resolutely in the Whole, the Full, the Beautiful). Friedrich Nietzsche never forgot the energetic maxim, nor the man who had transmitted it to him, nor this day of rapid and healthful travel, not far from those summits which he was afterwards to love so much.

The fine mountain crossing amid the snow and silence of the Alps had sufficed. He was almost cured on his arrival at Lugano. His nature was still supple and youthful; his returns to life were prompt and radiant; a naïve gaiety re-animated all his being. He spent two happy months in Italian Switzerland. A Prussian officer, a relation of General von Moltke, was staying at his hotel. He lent him his manuscripts and often talked to him of the destinies of the new German Empire and of the aristocratic warrior's mission which the victory had conferred upon it. It was a fine springtide for the numerous Germans who had come to rest at the place: they liked to gather round their young philosopher and listen to him. February began, the war was over, and these happy people, freed from all anxieties, abandoned themselves for the first time to the pleasure of their triumph. They sang; they danced in public up to the Market-place, and Nietzsche was not the least prompt to rejoice with them, to dance and sing. "When I recall these days," writes Madame Förster-Nietzsche, who gives us a sad and gracious account of the time, "it seems to me that I am having a veritable dream of Carnival."

From Lugano, Friedrich Nietzsche wrote to Erwin Rohde:

"I have very often suffered from a heavy and depressed mood. But more than once inspiration has returned to me; my manuscript has benefited from it. I have given the go-by to philology in the most cavalier fashion. They may praise me, they may blame me, they may promise me the highest honours, they may talk as they choose; I turn my back upon it. Every day I go deeper into my philosophic domain, and I begin to have confidence in myself; better still, if I am ever to be a poet, from to-day I feel myself disposed towards it. I do not know, I have no means of knowing, whither my destiny guides me. And nevertheless, when I examine myself, everything is in perfect accord within me, as though I had followed some good genius. My ends are extremely hidden from me; no concern for office, for hierarchic honours, directs my efforts; and none the less I live in a surprising condition of clarity, of serenity. What a sensation it is to see one's world before one, a fine globe, round and complete! Now it is some fragment of a new metaphysic, now it is a new æsthetic which grows up within me, now another idea claims me, a new principle of education which entails the complete rejection of our Universities and gymnasia. I never learn any fact but it immediately finds a good place in some corner that has been long prepared for it. This sentiment of an interior world which springs up within me I feel in all its force when I think not coldly, but quietly and without exaggerated enthusiasm, on the history of these last ten months, on these events which I consider as the instruments of my noble designs. Pride, folly, are words that feebly express my condition of mental 'insomnia.'

"Ah, how I desire health! As soon as one has something in view which must last longer than oneself—how one gives thanks for every good night, for every mild ray of sun, even for every occasion on which one digests aright!"

On the 10th of April, Nietzsche had returned to Basle. He gathered his notes together, re-read them for the last time, and fixed definitely the plan of his work. He allowed those digressions upon war, slavery, the city, of which we have already given some extracts, to drop, and—Wagner, it is said, desired it—limited himself to his first subject: ancient tragedy, the model and precursor of German musical drama. Wagner's advice, Madame Förster-Nietzsche insinuates, was not altogether disinterested; it suited him that his disciple's first work should be consecrated to his fame. This has an air of probability; still it certainly seems that Nietzsche had let himself be captured and seduced by too many ideas, that he had not so much amassed the matter for one book as begun, rather at hazard, a whole series of studies in æsthetics, history, and politics. He needed to restrict himself, and yet could not make up his mind to it. If Wagner helped him here, he did well. Perhaps we owe the happy completion of this book to him—the only real book which Nietzsche ever completed.

What was it that he had to say? He was to analyse the origin and the essence of the Greek lyric spirit; he was to set the two Greeces over against one another, the one intoxicated by its myths and Dionysian chants, strong in illusions—Æschylus's Greece, tragic and conquering Greece; the other impious, rational, anæmic—Socratic Greece, Alexandrine Greece, which in dying corrupted the peoples who had remained young around her, the pure blood of primitive humanity. Then he was to display the two Germanys in conflict in a like manner, the Germany of the Democrats and the savants, the Germany of the soldiers and the poets; between these two one had to choose. Nietzsche declared his choice: beholden to Wagner, as he was, for all his tranquillity of thought, for all his joys, he indicated Wagner to his compatriots. While the peace was being signed at Frankfort between the nations, Friedrich Nietzsche, thus establishing peace within himself, ended the rough draft of his work. He remarked upon this coincidence of dates, for his internal conflicts and the revolutions of his thought did not appear to him less important events than external conflicts and the revolutions of races.

But the Peace of Frankfort did not terminate all the conflicts of this terrible year. A civil war now broke out in France, and its calamities stirred Europe even more profoundly than the battles of Frœschwiller or Sedan. On the morning of the 23rd of May, the newspapers of Basle announced the destruction of Paris and the burning of the Louvre. Nietzsche learnt the news with a feeling of dismay: the most beautiful works, the flower of human labour, were ruined; human hands, an unhappy people, had dared this profanation. All Nietzsche's alarms were thus confirmed. Without discipline, without an hierarchy, culture, he had written, cannot subsist. All have not the right to share in beauty; the immense majority should live humbly, work for their masters and revere their lives. Such is the economy which assures strength to societies, and, in return for their strength, delicacy, grace, beauty; and this is the order which Europe hesitates to maintain. Nietzsche might now have boasted of the correctness of his judgment; it was far from him to do so. It was with alarm that he considered his perspicacity, his solitude, and his responsibility. His thoughts suddenly turned to Jacob Burckhardt; what melancholy must be his! He wished to see him, to talk to him, to listen to him, to make his desolation his own. He hurried to Burckhardt's house; but Burckhardt, though the hour was early, had gone out. Nietzsche walked the roads like a desperate man. Finally he went back. Jacob Burckhardt was in his study, and awaited him. He had gone to seek his friend, as his friend had gone to seek him. The two men remained for long together, and Fräulein Nietzsche, alone in the next room, heard their sobs through the closed door.

"Let us avow it," he writes to his friend, the Baron von Gersdorff, "we are all, with all our past, responsible for the terrors which menace us to-day. We shall do wrong, if we consider with a peaceful conceit the unchaining of a war against culture, and if we impute the fault merely to the unfortunates who do the deed. When I heard of the firing of Paris, I was for some days utterly powerless, lost in tears and doubts; the life of science, of philosophy and of art appeared to me as an absurdity when I saw a single day suffice for the ruin of the finest works of art; what do I say?—of entire periods of art. I profoundly deplored the fact that the metaphysical value of art could not manifest itself to the lower classes; but it has a higher mission to fulfil. Never, however lively my affliction were, would I have cast the stone at the sacrilegious, who in my eyes are only carriers of the mistake of all—a mistake which gives cause for much thought...."

In the autobiographical notes written in 1878 these words may be read: "The War: my profoundest affliction, the burning of the Louvre."

Friedrich Nietzsche had gone back to his old way of life; almost every week he was Wagner's guest. But soon he perceived that since the German victory Triebschen had changed. Too many intimates made haste to the master's house, too many unknown people invaded the abode whose peaceful seclusion he had loved. They were not all of the sort that Nietzsche would have desired; but Wagner talked, discoursed, overflowed with them all. Judging that the favourable moment had come, he had set out to rouse Germany and secure at last the construction and gift of the hall which he needed, the theatre, or the temple, of Bayreuth.

Friedrich Nietzsche heard and took part in these discussions with an uneasy ardour. Wagner's idea exalted him. But he had the soul of a solitary, and could not help being worried, and sometimes shocked, by these noises from the world which had to be tolerated. Wagner did not suffer: on the contrary, he seemed elated by the joy of feeling the crowd nearer to him; and Nietzsche, a little surprised, a little disappointed, sought, without precisely finding again, his hero. "To sway the people," he had written in his student notebooks, "is to put passions in the service of an idea." Wagner adapted himself to work of this kind. In the service of his art and of his fame he accepted all the passions. A Chauvinist with the Chauvinists, an idealist with the idealists, as much of a Gallophobe as was desired; restoring the Æschylian tragedy for some, for others re-animating the old German myths; willingly a pessimist, a Christian if it pleased, sincere moreover from moment to moment, this prodigious being, a great leader of men as well as a great poet, handled his compatriots most dexterously.

No one could resist the impulse which he gave: every one had to yield and to follow. He fixed the very details of the plans of the theatre whose site had just been chosen. He studied the practical organisation of the work, and laboured to create those *Vereine* in which propagandists and subscribers were to be grouped. He set himself out to procure rare and unexpected delights for the faithful. One day he surprised them with a performance for their benefit alone, in the gardens of Triebschen, of the *Siegfried-Idyll,* a gracious interlude written for the churching of his wife, a noble echo of the most intimate times. He gave Nietzsche his rôle, for he could not allow that voice, so passionate and hard to control, and yet so eloquent, to be lost. The young man offered to set out on a mission. He would stir up those circles in Northern Germany, so slow and heavy in its emotions. Bus proposal was not accepted; Wagner, no doubt, feared the violence of his apostolate: "No," he said to him, "finish and publish your book." Nietzsche felt somewhat melancholy at the refusal. Henceforth, it seems, difficulties began to arise between the two.

Moreover, the advice of the master was less easy to follow than it seemed. *The Origin of Tragedy* did not find a publisher. Nietzsche's applications failed, and his summer was spoilt by the check. He decided to print certain chapters of it in the reviews. "I put my little book into the world bit by bit," he wrote in July to Erwin Rohde; "what a childbirth! what tortures!"

At the beginning of October he was staying at Leipsic. Here he saw again his master Ritschl, and his friends Rohde, Gersdorff, who had come to meet him, and spent with them some happy days of conversation and comradeship. But the fate of his book remained uncertain: all the publishers of scientific and philological works bowed the author out. They were not tempted by a bizarre work, in which learning was allied with lyricism and the problems of ancient Greece with the problems of modern Germany. "The book is a centaur," said Nietzsche. This mythological assurance did not satisfy the book-sellers. Finally he had to address himself, not without regret—for he maintained that his work was a scientific work—to Richard Wagner's publisher, from whom he received, after a month's delay, a favourable reply. He wrote to his friend Gersdorff, in a free and relieved tone, which helps us to measure the vexation from which he had suffered.

"BASLE, *November* 19, 1871.

"Pardon me, dear friend, I ought to have thanked you sooner. I had felt in your last letter, in every one of your words, your strong intellectual life. It seemed to me that you remained a soldier at soul and brought your military nature to art and philosophy. And that is good, for we have no right to live to-day, if we are not militants, militants who prepare a *sæculum* to come, something of which we can guess at in ourselves, across our best instants. For those instants, which are what there is of best in us, draw us away in spirit from *our* time; nevertheless, in some manner, they need to have their hearthstone somewhere: whence I infer that at such instants we feel a confused breath of coming times pass over us. For instance, take our last meeting at Leipsic; has it not left in your memory the impression of such instants, as seemed to be strangers to everything, linked with another century? Whatever may be, this remains, '*Im Ganzen, Vollen, Schönen, resolut zu leben.*' But it needs a strong will, such as is not given to the first comer!... To-day, only to-day, the excellent publisher Fritzsch replies to me."

Fritzsch proposed to him that he should give his book the format and character of a recent work of Wagner's: *Die Bestimmung der Oper.* Nietzsche rejoiced at the idea, and he wrote five concluding chapters which accentuated the Wagnerian tendency of the work. This rapid composition and the correction of the proofs did not deter him from another enterprise.

The Origin of Tragedy was about to appear. He did not doubt for a moment that it would be read, understood, acclaimed. His comrades, his masters, had always acknowledged the strength of his thought. Apparently, it never occurred to him that a vaster public remained callous; but he wished to affect it profoundly, at the first blow, and he formed new projects by which he might make the most of his success. He wanted to talk: speech was a livelier weapon. He recalled the emotions which he had experienced when, as a young professor, he was given the singular task of teaching the most delicate language, the most difficult works, to chance audiences; he remembered his perhaps fanciful design: that seminary of philologists, that house of study and retreat, of which he was always dreaming. He wanted to denounce the schools, the gymnasia, the Universities, the heavy apparatus of pedantry which was stifling the German spirit, and define the new and necessary institutions, destined, no longer for the emancipation of the masses, but for the culture of the State. He had written to Erwin Rohde as early as the month of March: "A new idea claims me, a new principle of education which points to the entire rejection of oar Universities, of our gymnasia...." In December, he announced at Basle, for January, 1872, a series of lectures upon *The Future of our Educational Institutions.*

Towards mid-December, he accompanied Richard Wagner to Mannheim, where a two days' festival was being devoted to the works of the master.

"Oh, what a pity you were not there!" he wrote to Erwin Rohde. "All the sensations, all the recollections of art, what are they compared to these? I am like a man whose ideal has been realised. It is Music, and Music alone! ... When I say to myself that a certain number of men of the generations to come—at least some hundreds among them—will be moved by this music as I am myself, I cannot augur for less than an entire renewal of our culture!"

He returned to his house in Basle: but the impression of his days in Mannheim remained with him. The details of his everyday life caused him a strange and tenacious disgust. "All that cannot be translated into music," he wrote, "is repulsive and repugnant to me.... I have a horror of reality. Or, rather, I no longer see anything of the real, it is only a phantasmagoria." Under the stress of this emotion he acquired a clearer view of the problem which occupied him, he formulated more clearly the principle for which he was seeking. To "teach," to "uplift" men, what does that mean? It is to dispose their minds in such sort that the productions of genius will be assured, not of the understanding of all, for that cannot be, but of the respect of all.

As in the preceding years, Richard and Cosima Wagner invited him to spend Christmas at Triebschen. He excused himself; the work of his lectures occupied all his time. He offered Cosima Wagner, by way of homage, a musical fantasy on Saint Sylvester's Night, composed some weeks earlier. "I am very impatient to know what they will think of it down there," he wrote to Rohde. "I have never been criticised by any competent person." In reality, good judges had already often discouraged his musical enterprises, but he soon forgot their vexatious advice.

On the last day of 1871, his book appeared: *Die Gebürt der Tragödie aus dem Geiste der Musik (The Birth of Tragedy from the Spirit of Music)*. The sub-title which the current editions give, *Hellenism and Pessimism*, was added in 1885 on the issue of the second edition. Friedrich Nietzsche sent the first copy to Richard Wagner, from whom he received almost at once a frenzied letter.

"DEAR FRIEND,—I have never read a finer book than yours. It is all splendid! At this moment, I write to you very hurriedly because the reading has profoundly moved me, and I expect that I wait for the return of my sang-froid to re-read you methodically. I said to Cosima: After you, he it is whom I love most; and then, at a long distance, Lenbach, who has made so striking and so true a portrait of me.... Adieu! Come soon to see us!

"Yours,

"R. W."

On the 10th of January Wagner wrote again:

"You have just published a book which is incomparable. All the influences which you may have undergone are reduced to nothing by the character of your book: what distinguishes it from every other, is the complete confidence with which a penetrating individuality displays itself. It is here that you satisfy the ardent desire of myself and of my wife: in short, a strange voice might have been talking of us, and we would have fully approved it! Twice we have read your book from the first line to the last—in the daytime, separately—at night, together—and we were lamenting that we had not at our disposal that second copy which you had promised. We deliver battle over that sole copy. I am constantly in need of it; between my breakfast and my working hours, it is it that sets me going; for since I have read you, I have begun again to work on my last act. Our readings, whether together or separately, are constantly interrupted by our exclamations. I am not yet recovered from the emotion which I experienced. There is the condition we are in!"

And Cosima Wagner wrote, for her part: "Oh, how fine your book is! How beautiful it is and how profound, how profound it is and how audacious!" On January 16th he delivered his first lecture. His joy, his sense of security, were extreme. He knew that Jacob Burckhardt read and approved him; he knew that he had the admiration of Rohde, Gersdorff, Overbeck. "What they say of my book is incredible," he wrote to a friend. "... I have concluded an alliance with Wagner. You cannot imagine how we are bound to one another, and how identical are our views." He conceived his second work without delay; he would publish his lectures. It would be a popular book, an exoteric translation of his *Tragedy*. But the idea of an even more decisive action at once supervened. Germany was preparing to inaugurate the new University of Strassburg; and an apotheosis of professors on a soil that had been conquered by soldiers awoke the indignation of Friedrich Nietzsche. He wished to address a pamphlet to Bismarck, "under the form of an interpellation in the Reichstag." Have our pedants, he would ask, the right to go in triumph to Strassburg? Our soldiers have conquered the French soldiers, and that is glorious. But has our culture humiliated French culture? Who would dare to say so?

Some days went by. Whence came the less happy tone of his letters? Why was it that he did not write his interpellation, that he gave up the idea of it? We know: except for a few friends who had understood his book, no one read it, no one bought it; not a review, not a newspaper deigned to take notice of it. Ritchsl, the great philologist of Leipsic, kept silent. Friedrich Nietzsche wrote to him: "I want to know what you think." He received in reply a severe criticism and a reproof. Erwin Rohde offered an article for the *Litterarische Centralblatt;* it was not inserted. "It was the last chance of a serious voice being upraised for me in a scientific sheet," he wrote to Gersdorff; "now I expect nothing more—except spite or idiocy. But, as I have told you, I count upon the peaceful journey of my book through the centuries with perfect confidence. For in it certain eternal verities are said for the first time: they must resound...."

Certainly Friedrich Nietzsche had not foreseen his ill-success: it astonished and disconcerted him. A sore throat obliged him to interrupt his lectures, and he found pleasure in the contretemps. He had let himself be drawn towards ideas which were very lofty and delicate, and difficult even to himself. He wished to show that two sorts of schools should be instituted, the one professional, for the majority; the other, classical and truly superior, for an infinitesimal number of chosen individuals, whose course would be extended as far as their thirtieth year. How was this isolated circle, aloof from the common herd, to be formed, and how was it to be taught? Friedrich Nietzsche recurred to his most intimate and familiar thought, to that aristocratic ideal to which his meditations always led him. He had often studied its problems. But to examine them in public he needed his whole strength, and also a sympathetic audience. He felt that he had been weakened by the failure of his book. His very slight indisposition did not last long: nevertheless he did not return to his lectures. It was vain to ask him to do so: he refused. It was vain to press him to have them published; Richard Wagner strongly insisted: he eluded this insistence. His notes have come to us in a sorry condition of incompleteness and disorder. They are the echoes, the vestiges of a dream.

"The aristocracy of the mind must conquer its entire liberty in respect of the State, which is now keeping Science in curb.

"Later, men will have to raise the tables of a new culture ... then destruction of the gymnasia, destruction of the University ... an areopagus, for the justice of the mind.

"*The culture of the future: its ideal of social problems.* The imperative world of the beautiful and the sublime ... the only safeguard against Socialism ..."

Finally these three interrogatory words, which sum up his doubts, his desires, and perhaps his whole work: "*Ist Veredlung möglich?*" (Is ennoblement possible?)

Friedrich Nietzsche courageously renounced his hope and was silent. He had lost his country: Prussia would not be the invincible framework of a lyrical race; the German Empire would not realise the "imperative world of the beautiful and the sublime." On April 30th the new University of Strassburg was inaugurated. "I hear from here the patriotic rejoicings," he wrote to Erwin Rohde. In January he had refused an offer of employment which would have withdrawn him from Basle. In April he spoke of leaving Basle and of going to Italy for two or three years. "The first review of my book has at last appeared," he wrote, "and I find it very good. But where has it appeared? In an Italian publication, *La Rivista Europea!* That is pleasant and symbolical!"

He had a second reason for melancholy: Richard Wagner was leaving to make his home at Bayreuth. A letter of Cosima Wagner announced the departure: "Yes, Bayreuth!... Adieu to dear Triebschen, where the *Origin of Tragedy* was conceived, and so many other things which perhaps will never begin again!"

Three years before, in this spring season, Nietzsche had hazarded his first visit to Triebschen; he wished to return again. He did return, and found the house desolate. A few pieces of furniture, covered over with horse-cloths and dispersed from room to room, seemed like flotsam and jetsam from another time. Every small object, all the family knick-knacks, had disappeared. The light entered, hard and crude, through the curtainless windows. Wagner and his wife were completing then-last packages, throwing the last of the books into the last of the baskets. They welcomed the faithful

Nietzsche, asked his aid; he gave it at once. He wrapped up in packets the letters, the precious manuscripts; then more books and scores. Suddenly his heart failed him. So it was all over, Triebschen was done with! Three years of his life, and what years they had been! How unexpected, how moving, how delicious, and they were to escape in a day! Now he must renounce the past, and follow the master without regret. Now he must forget Triebschen and, for the future, think only of Bayreuth. No sooner was this magical name pronounced than it fascinated Nietzsche and troubled him. His hours at Triebschen had been so fine, hours of repose and meditation, hours of work and silence. A man, a woman of genius; a nest of children; an infinity of happy conversations, of beauty—Triebschen had given all that. What would Bayreuth give? The crowd would come there, and what would it bring with it? Friedrich Nietzsche left the books which he was engaged in packing. The grand piano had remained in the middle of the salon. He opened it, preluded, then improvised. Richard and Cosima Wagner, leaving aside all their affairs, listened. A harrowing, unforgettable rhapsody resounded through the empty salon. It was the adieu.

In November, 1888, Friedrich Nietzsche, already stricken with madness, set himself to recount his history. "Since I am here recalling the consolations of my life, I ought to express in a word my gratitude for what was by far my most profound and best-loved joy—my intimacy with Richard Wagner. I wish to be just with regard to the rest of my human relationships; but I absolutely cannot efface from my life the days at Triebschen, days of confidence, of gaiety, of sublime flashes—days of *profound* perceptions. I do not know what Wagner was for others: our sky was never darkened by a cloud."

CHAPTER IV

FRIEDRICH NIETZSCHE AND RICHARD WAGNER—BAYREUTH

Bayreuth has had a strange destiny. This little German town, so long obscure, scintillates in the eighteenth century, shines with a somewhat flickering brilliance, but becomes celebrated at last throughout all Europe. An intelligent Margravine— Frederick's sister, the friend of Voltaire and of French elegance—lives there, beautifies it, enlivens the barren country with castles, and lavishes on its façades the singular volutes of the "rococo" style. The Margravine dies and Bayreuth is again forgotten. A century passes and suddenly its fame returns; the little town that the Margrave adorned becomes the Jerusalem of a new art and a new religion. A strange destiny, but a factitious one. It is a poet who has regulated the antitheses. The history of Bayreuth ought to be included among Wagner's works.

He wished to set up his theatre in a quiet and secluded town. It suited him, not to go to his audience, but rather to force his audience to come to him. He chose, from many others, this town; the two Germanys would be thus confronted, the one, that of the past, a slave to French customs, mean and shabby; the other, that of the future, his own, an emancipating and innovating Germany. The work was started without delay. The master decided that the foundation-stone of his theatre should be laid with pomp on the 22nd of May, 1872, the anniversary of his birth.

"So we shall see one another again," wrote Nietzsche to his friend Rohde. "Our meetings are ever becoming more grandiose, more historical, are they not?"

They were present together at the ceremony, one of them coming from Basle, the other from Hamburg. Two thousand people were assembled in the little town. The weather was appalling. But the unceasing rain, the threatening sky, made the ceremony still more imposing. Wagnerian art is a serious thing and has no need of smiling heavens. The faithful disciples, standing in the open air at the mercy of the winds, saw the stone laid. In the hollow block Wagner deposited a piece of poetry written by himself, and then threw the first spadeful of plaster. In the evening he invited his friends to hear an execution of the "Symphony" with chorus, the orchestration of which he had in parts slightly strengthened. He personally conducted. Young Germany, assembled in the Margrave's theatre, listened piously to this work in which the nineteenth century declared its need, and when the final chorus struck up— "Millions of men embrace each other"—it really seemed, said a spectator, as if the sublime wish was about to be realised.

"Ah! my friend," wrote Nietzsche, "through what days we have lived! No one can rob us of these grave and sacred memories. We ought to go forth into life inspired to battle on their behalf. Above all, we ought to force ourselves to regulate all our acts, with as much gravity and force as is possible, so as to prove that we are worthy of the unique events at which we have assisted."

Nietzsche wanted to fight for Wagner, for he loved Wagner and he loved battle. "To arms, to arms!" he writes to Rohde; "war is necessary to me, *ich brauche den Krieg.*" But he had already proved many a time, what he now began sadly to understand, that his nature did not lend itself to reticence and to the prudence necessary in such a contest, in which public opinion was the stake. There was no instant but a word, an attitude ran foul of his radical idealism. He felt the instinctive constraint that he had already known at Triebschen. Wagner disturbed him. He hardly recognised the grave and pure hero whom he had loved so much. He saw another man, a powerful workman, brutal, vindictive, jealous. Nietzsche had thought of making a tour in Italy, with a relation of Mendelssohn's; he was obliged to give up this idea in order to humour the master, who detested the race, even to the very name of Mendelssohn.

"Why is Wagner so distrustful?" Nietzsche wrote in his diary; "it excites distrust."

Wagner was as dictatorial as he was distrustful. The days had become rare when he could converse at leisure with nobleness and freedom as he had done at Triebschen. He spoke briefly, he commanded.

Nietzsche was still ready to go on a mission to Northern Germany to speak, write, and found *Vereine,* and to "thrust under the noses of the German savants the things which their timid eyes failed to perceive." Wagner would not accept this proposal; he wished Nietzsche to publish his lectures on *The Future of our Educational Systems.* Nietzsche resisted a desire in which he thought he detected a certain egotism.

"Our Herr Nietzsche only wants to do what he likes," exclaimed the irritable Wagner.

His anger saddened and humiliated Nietzsche both on his own account and on his master's. He thought, "Ill, weighed down with work, have I no right to respect? Am I under any one's orders? Why is Wagner so tyrannical?" We read in his diary, "Wagner has not the strength to make those around him free and great. Wagner is not loyal; he is, on the contrary, suspicious and haughty."

At the same time there appeared a pamphlet, *The Philology of the Future, a reply to F. Nietzsche.* The author was Willamowitz, who had been Nietzsche's comrade at the school of Pforta.

"DEAR FRIEND," he wrote to Gersdorff, who informed him of the pamphlet, "Don't worry over me. I am ready. I will never entangle myself in polemics. It is a pity it should be Willamowitz. Do you know that he came last autumn to pay me a friendly visit? Why should it be Willamowitz?"

Wagner, at whom the title itself of the pamphlet, *The Philology of the Future,* was aimed—it parodied his famous formula, *The Music of the Future*—wrote a reply, and profited by the occasion to renew his invitation to Friedrich Nietzsche.

"What must one think of our schools of culture?" he concludes. "It is for you to tell us what German culture ought to be, so as to direct the regenerated nation towards the most noble objects." Once again Nietzsche was firm in his determination. He was by no means satisfied with these lectures, being discontented with their form and uncertain even of their thought. "I do not wish to publish anything as to which my conscience is not as pure as that of the seraphim." He tried to express his Wagnerian faith in another style.

"I should have so much pleasure," he wrote to Rohde, "in writing something for the service of our cause, but I don't know what. All that I advance is so wounding, such an irritant, and more likely to hurt than to serve. Why should my poor book, naïve and enthusiastic as it was, have been received so badly? Singular! Now, what shall we do, we others?"

He began to write *Reden eines Hoffenden (Words of a Man of Hope)*, which he soon gave up.

Friedrich Nietzsche re-opened his Greek books, so invariably beautiful and satisfying. He explained—before very few pupils, because the evil fame of the *Gebürt* withdrew young philologists from him—the *Choephores of Æschylus* and some passages of ante-Platonic philosophy.

Across a gulf of twenty-five centuries that clear radiance descended upon him, scattering all doubts and shadows. Nietzsche often heard with misgiving the fine words which it pleased his Wagnerian friends to use. "Millions of men embrace each other," the chorus sang at Bayreuth in the work of Wagner. It sang well, but, after all, men did not embrace each other; and here Nietzsche suspected a certain extravagance, a certain falsehood. Look at the ancient Greeks, those ambitious and evil men. They do not embrace each other much, their hymns never speak of embraces. They desire to excel, and are devoured by envy; their hymns glorify these passions. Nietzsche liked their naïve energy, their precise speech. He refreshed himself at this source and wrote a short essay: *Homer's Wettkampf (The Homeric Joust)*. We find ourselves driven at the very beginning far away from the Wagnerian mysticism.

"When you speak of *Humanity*," he writes, "you imagine an order of sentiment by which man distinguishes himself from nature, but such a separation does not exist; these qualities called 'natural' and those called 'human' grow together and are blended. Man in his noblest aspirations is still branded by sinister nature.

"These formidable tendencies which seem inhuman are perhaps the fruitful soil which supports all humanity, its agitations, its acts, and its work.

"Thus it is that the Greeks, the most human of all men, remain cruel, happy in destruction."

This rapid sketch was the occupation of a few days. Nietzsche undertook a long work. He studied the texts of Thales, Pythagoras, Heraclitus, Empedocles. He tried to approach those philosophers who were truly worthy of the name which they themselves had invented, those masters of life, scornful of argument and of books; citizens and at the same time thinkers, and not *déracinés* like those who followed them—Socrates and his school of mockers, Plato and his school of dreamers, philosophers of whom each one dares to bring a philosophy of his own, that is to say, an individual point of view in the consideration of things, in the deliberation of acts. Nietzsche, in a few days, filled a copybook with notes.

All the same, he continued to be interested in the successes of his glorious friend. In July *Tristan* was played at Munich. He went, and met many other disciples; Gersdorff, Fräulein von Meysenbug, whom he had met at the May festivals of Bayreuth. She had preserved, despite her fifty years, that tender charm that never left her, and the physical grace of a frail and nervous body. Friedrich Nietzsche passed some pleasant days in the company of his comrade and his new friend. All three regretted them when they were gone, and at the moment of departure expressed a hope of meeting each other soon again. Gersdorff wished to return in August to hear *Tristan,* and once more Nietzsche promised to be there, but at the last moment Gersdorff was unable to be present, and Nietzsche had not the courage to return alone to Munich. "It is insupportable," he wrote to Fräulein von Meysenbug, "to find yourself face to face with an art so serious and profound. In short, I remain at Basle." Parmenides, on whom he was meditating, consoled him for the loss of *Tristan.*

Fräulein von Meysenbug kept Nietzsche advised of all news, whether trivial or important, in connection with the Wagnerian campaign. The master had just terminated *The Twilight of the Gods,* the last of the four dramas of the Tetralogy. He had at last finished his great work. Fräulein von Meysenbug was informed in a note written to her by Cosima Wagner. "In my heart I hear sung 'Praise be to God,'" wrote the wife. "Praise be to God," repeated Fräulein von Meysenbug, and she adds—these few words indicate the tone of the place and of the time: "The disciples of the new spirit need new mysteries by which they may solemnise together their instinctive knowledge. Wagner creates them in his tragic works, and the world will not have recovered its beauty until we have built for the new Dionysian myth a Temple worthy of it." Fräulein von Meysenbug confided to Nietzsche the measures she was taking to win Marguerite of Savoy, the Queen of Italy, to the cause, and to make her accept the Presidency of a small circle of noble patronesses. A few women of the highest aristocracy, friends of Liszt's, initiated by him into the Wagnerian cult, composed this sublime *Verein.*

In all this there was an irritating atmosphere of snobbery and excessive religiosity. Yet Fräulein von Meysenbug was an exquisite woman with irreproachable intentions, pure with that purity which purifies all that it touches: Nietzsche did not practise his criticism on this friend's letters. He soon felt the fatigue of continuous work. He lost his sleep and was obliged to rest. Travel had often lightened his mind. He set out, at the end of summer, for Italy, and went as far as Bergamo but no further. This country, which he was afterwards to love so much, displeased him. "Here reigns the Apollonian cult," Fräulein von Meysenbug, who was staying at Florence, told him; "it is good to bathe in." Nietzsche was very little of an Apollonian. He perceived only voluptuousness, excessive sweetness, harmony of line. His German tastes were disconcerted and he returned to the mountains, where he became, as he wrote, "more audacious and more noble." There, in a poor village inn at Splügen, he had a few days of happiness.

"Here, on the extreme border of Switzerland and Italy," he wrote in August, 1872, to Gersdorff, "I am alone, and I am very well satisfied with my choice. A rich and marvellous solitude, with the most magnificent roads in the world, along which I go meditating for hours, buried in my thoughts, and yet I never fall over a precipice. And whenever I look around me there is something new and great to see. No sign of life except when the diligence arrives and stops for relays. I take my meals with the men, our one contact. They pass like the Platonic shadows before my cave."

Until now Nietzsche had not cared much for high mountains; he preferred the moderate valleys and woods of the Jura, which reminded him of his native country, the hills of the Saale and Bohemia. At Splügen a new joy was revealed to him; the joy of solitude and of meditation in the mountain air. It was like a flash of lightning. He went down to the plains and forgot; but six years later, with the knowledge of his eternal loneliness on him, he found, sheltered in mean inns like this one, once again the same lyrical élan that he had discovered in October, 1872.

He soon left his sanctuary and returned without vexation to Basle, whither his professional duties drew him. There he had made friendships and established a way of life. He liked the town, and tolerated the inhabitants. Basle had truly become his centre. "Overbeck and Romundt, my companions of table and of thought," he writes to Rohde, "are the best society in the world. With them I cease my lamentations and my gnashing of teeth. Overbeck is the most serious, the most broad-minded of philosophers, and the most simple and amiable of men. He has that radical temper, failing which I can agree with no one."

His first impression on his return was trying. All his pupils left him. He was not at a loss to understand the reason of this exodus; the German philologists had declared him to be "a man scientifically dead." They had condemned him personally, and put an interdict upon his lectures. "The Holy Vehmgericht has done its duty well," he wrote to Rohde. "Let us act as if nothing had happened. But I do not like the little University to suffer on my account, it hurts me. We lose twenty entries in the last half-year. I can hardly as much as give a course on Greek and Latin rhetoric. I have two pupils, one is a Germanist, the other a Jurist."

At last he received some comfort. Rohde had written in defence of his book an article which no review would accept. Weary of refusal, he touched up his work and published it under the form of a letter addressed to Richard Wagner. Nietzsche thanked him. "Nobody dared to print my name," he wrote to Rohde.

"... It was as if I had committed a crime, and now your book comes, so ardent, so daring a witness to our fraternal combat! My friends are delighted with it. They are never tired of praising you, for the details and the whole; they think your polemics worthy of a Lessing. ... What pleases me most is the deep and threatening clamour of it, like the sound of a waterfall. We must be brave, dear, dear friend. I always have faith in progress, in our progress. I believe that we will always go on increasing in loyal ambitions, and in strength. I believe in the success of our advance towards ends more noble yet, and more aspiring. Yes, we will reach them, and then as conquerors, who discover goals yet further off, we shall push on, always brave! What does it matter to us that they will be few, so few, those spectators whose eyes can follow the path we are pursuing? What does it matter if we have for spectators only those who have the necessary qualities for judging this combat? All the crowns which my time might give me I sacrifice to that unique spectator, Wagner. The ambition to satisfy him animates me more, and more nobly, than any other influence. Because he is difficult and he says everything, what pleases him and what displeases him; he is my good conscience, to praise and to punish."

At the commencement of December, Nietzsche was lucky enough to find his master again for a few hours, and to live with him in the intimate way that reminded him of the days at Triebschen. Wagner, passing through Strassburg, called to him; and he went at once. The meeting was untroubled by any discord, a harmony now, no doubt, rare enough; for Cosima Wagner, after having remarked this in one of her letters, expressed the hope that such perfect hours would suffice to dissipate all misunderstandings and to prevent their recrudescence.

Nietzsche worked a great deal during these last months of 1872. His studies on the tragic philosophies of the Greeks were well advanced; he left them over. Those wise men had restored his serenity, and he profited by the help which they had given him to contemplate once more the problems of his century. The problems—this is hardly a correct expression, for he knew of only one. He questioned himself how a culture should be founded, that is to say, a harmony of traditions, of rules, of beliefs, by submission to which a man may become nobler. Actual modern societies have for their end the production of certain comforts; how should different societies be substituted which would not only satisfy men, but benefit them? Let us know our wretchedness; we are stripped of culture. Our thoughts and our acts are not ruled by the authority of any style; the idea even of such an authority is lost to us. We have perfected in an extraordinary manner the discipline of knowledge, and we seem to have forgotten that others exist. We succeed in describing the phenomena of life, in translating the Universe into an abstract language, and we scarcely perceive that, in writing and translating thus, we lose the reality of the Universe of Life. Science exercises on us a "barbarising action," wrote Nietzsche. He analysed this action.

"The essential point of all science has become merely accessory, or else it is entirely absent.

"The study of languages—without the discipline of style and rhetoric.

"Indian studies—without philosophy.

"Classical antiquity—without a suspicion of how closely everything in it is bound up with practical efforts.

"The sciences of nature—without that beneficent and serene atmosphere which Goethe found in them.

"History—without enthusiasm.

"In short, all the sciences without their practical uses, that is to say, studied otherwise than as really cultivated men would study them. Science as a means of livelihood."

It is necessary, therefore, that the sense of beauty, of virtue, and of strong and regulated passions should be restored. How can a philosopher employ himself in this task? Alas! the experience of antiquity teaches and discourages us. The philosopher is a hybrid being, half logician, half artist, a poet, an apostle, who constructs his dreams and his commandments in a logical manner. Men listen willingly enough to poets and apostles, they do not listen to philosophers, they are not moved by their analyses and their deductions. Consider that long line of genius, the philosophers of tragic Greece. What did they realise? Their lives were given in vain to their race. Empedocles alone moved the mob, but he was as much a magician as philosopher; he invented myths and poems; he was eloquent, he was magnificent; it was the legend, and not the thought of Empedocles, that was effective. Pythagoras founded a sect, a philosopher cannot hope for more: his labour grouped together a few friends, a few disciples, who passed over the human masses like a ripple on the ocean; not one of the great philosophers has swayed the people, writes Nietzsche. Where they have failed, who will succeed? It is impossible to found a popular culture on philosophy.

What is then the destiny of these singular souls? Is their force, which is at times immense, lost? Will the philosopher always be a paradoxical being, and useless to men? Friedrich Nietzsche was troubled; it was the utility of his own life that he questioned. He would never be a musician, that he knew at last; never a poet, he had ceased to hope for it. He had not the faculty of conceiving the uniformities, of animating a drama, of creating a soul. One evening he confessed this to Overbeck with such sadness that his friend was moved. He was therefore a philosopher, moreover, a very ignorant one, an amateur of philosophy, an imperfect lyrical artist; and he questioned himself: Since I have for weapons only my thoughts, the thoughts of a philosopher, what can I do? He answered: I can help. Socrates did not create the truths that error kept prisoners in the souls of his interlocutors, he only aspired to the title of accoucheur. Such is the task of a philosopher. He is an inefficient creator, but a very efficient critic. He is obliged to analyse the forces which are operative around him, in science, in religion, and in art; he is obliged to give the directions, to fix the values and the limits. Such shall be my task. I will study the souls of my contemporaries, and I shall have every authority to say to them: Neither science nor religion can save you; seek refuge in art, the power of modern times, and in the artist who is Richard Wagner. "The philosopher of the future," he wrote, "he must be the supreme judge of an æsthetic culture, a censor of every digression."

Nietzsche went to Naumburg for the Christmas holidays. Wagner sent him word to ask him to stop at Bayreuth on his way home to Basle, but he was hard pressed by work and perhaps a little ill, and no doubt a secret instinct warned him that solitude would be best for the meditation of the problems which he had to determine for himself. He made his apologies. Besides, he had had for some weeks many opportunities of proving his attachment. He had written an article (the only one in all his work) in answer to an alienist who had undertaken to prove that Wagner was mad. He had offered a sum of money to help in the propaganda. This anonymous and distant manner was the only one that suited him at the time. Even at Basle he tried to found a Wagnerian Verein. He was therefore astounded when he discovered that the master was displeased at his absence. Already in the past year an invitation, also declined, had helped to provoke a mild lecture.

"It is Burckhardt who is keeping you at Basle," wrote Cosima Wagner. Nietzsche wrote and remedied things, but the painful impression remained.

"Everything is quieted," he told the friend who had informed him; "but I cannot quite forget. Wagner knows that I am ill, absorbed in work, and in need of a little liberty. I shall be, henceforth, whether I wish it or no, more anxious than in the past. God knows how many times I have wounded him. Each time I am astonished, and I never succeed in precisely locating the point in which we have clashed."

This annoyance did not affect his thought; we can follow it to its smallest shades of meaning, thanks to the notes published in the tenth volume of his complete works. It is quite active and fecund. "I am the adventurer of the spirit," he was to write. "I wander in my thought. I go to the idea that calls me...."

He was never to wander so audaciously as in the first weeks of 1876.

He completed a finer and sober essay, *Ueber Wahrheit und Lüge im ausser moralischen Sinne (On Truth and Falsehood in an Extra-Moral Sense.)* (It is a pity that it is necessary to translate these high-sounding expressions, and we render them word for word.) Nietzsche always liked high-sounding words; he does not recoil here from using the word "untruth," and essays for the first time a "reversal of values." To the true he opposes the false and prefers it. He exalts the imaginary worlds which poets add to the real world. "Dare to deceive thyself and dream," Schiller had said; Friedrich Nietzsche repeats this advice. It was the happy audacity of the Greeks; they intoxicated themselves with their divine histories, their heroic myths, and this intoxication set their souls on high adventures. The loyal Athenian, persuaded that Pallas dwelt in his city, lived in a dream. More clear-sighted, would he have been stronger; more passionate, braver? Truth is good in proportion to the services which it assures, and illusion is preferable if it performs its duty better. Why deify the truth? It is the tendency of the moderns; *Pereat vita, fiat veritas!* they say readily. Why this fanaticism? It is an inversion of the sane law for men: *Pereat Veritas, fiat vita!*

Nietzsche wrote down these dogmatic formulas, but did not stop at them. He went on writing. It was thus that he worked and advanced in his researches. Let us not forget that these thoughts, firm though they were in manner, were only indications, steps on the road. He would give birth to other and perhaps contrary thoughts. Friedrich Nietzsche had in him two instincts, opposed to each other; the one, that of the philosopher, and the other, that of the artist; the one was bent on truth, the other was ready to fabricate. He hesitated at the moment when he had to sacrifice one or the other. The instinct for the true protested within him. He did not abandon his formulas; he took them up again, he essayed new definitions, he indicated the difficulties, the hiatus. His thoughts had no disguise, and we can follow his researches. Let us translate this significant disorder:

"*The philosopher of the tragic knowledge*. He binds the disordered instinct of knowledge, but not by a new metaphysic. He does not establish new beliefs. He sees with a tragic emotion that the ground of metaphysics opens under him, and he knows that the many-coloured whirlwind of science can never satisfy him. He builds for himself a new life; to art he restores its rights.

"*The philosopher of the desperate knowledge* abandons himself to blind science: knowledge at any price.

"Even if metaphysics be only an anthropomorphic appearance, for the tragic philosopher that achieves the *image of being*. He is not sceptical. Here there is an idea to create; for scepticism is not the end. The instinct of knowledge forced to its extreme limits turns against itself to transform itself into a criticism of the faculty of knowledge. Knowledge in the service of the best kind of life. One should even *will illusion*, therein lies the tragic."

What is then this philosopher of the desperate knowledge whose attitude Nietzsche defines in two lines. Must he not love him, having found for him already such a beautiful name? *There is an idea to create*, writes Nietzsche; what then is this idea? It seems that in many passages Nietzsche is pleased to contemplate, without its veils, that terrible reality, whose aspect alone, says the Hindu legend, means death.

"How," he writes, "do they dare talk of a destiny for the earth? In infinite time and space there are no ends: *what is there, is eternally there*, whatever the forms. What can result from it for a metaphysical world one does not see.

"Without support of this order humanity should stand firm; a terrible task for the artist!

"The terrible consequences of Darwinism, in which, moreover, I believe. We respect certain qualities which we hold as eternal, moral, artistic, religious, &c, &c, &c. The spirit, a production of the brain, to consider it as supernatural! To deify it, what folly!

"To speak of an unconscious end of humanity, to me, that is false. Humanity is not a whole like an ant-hill. Perhaps one may speak of the unconscious ends of an ant-hill—but of all the ant-hills of the world!

"Our duty is not to take shelter in metaphysics, but actively to sacrifice ourselves to the *birth of culture*. Hence my severity against misty idealism."

At that instant Nietzsche had almost reached the term of his thought, but with great labour and consequent suffering. Headaches, pains in the eyes and stomach, laid hold of him once more. The softest light hurt him, he was obliged to give up reading. Nevertheless, his thought never halted. He was again occupied with the philosophers of tragic Greece; he listened to the words which come down to us diminished by the centuries, but always firm. He heard the concert of the everlasting responses—

Thales. Everything derives from a unique element. *Anaximander.* The flux of things is their punishment. *Heraclitus.* A law governs the flux and the institution of things.

Parmenides. The flux and the institution of things is illusion. The One alone exists.

Anaxagoras. All qualities are eternal; there is no becoming.

The Pythagoreans. All qualities are quantities. *Empedocles.* All causes are magical. *Democritus.* All causes are mechanical. *Socrates.* Nothing is constant except thought.

Friedrich Nietzsche is moved by these opposing voices, by these rhythms of thought which accuse nature in their eternal collisions. "The vicissitudes of the ideas and systems of man affect me more tragically than the vicissitudes of real life," said Hölderlin. Nietzsche's feeling was the same. He admired and envied those primitives who discovered nature and who found the first answers. He threw aside the devices of art, he confronted life as Œdipus confronted the Sphinx, and under this very title *Œdipus* he wrote a fragment to the mysterious language of which we may open our ears.

Œdipus. I call myself the last philosopher because I am the last man. I speak alone and I hear my voice sounding like that of a dying man. With thee, dear voice, whose breath brings to me the last memories of all human happiness, with thee let me speak yet a moment more: thou wilt deceive my solitude; thou wilt give me back the illusion of society and love, because my heart will not believe that love is dead. It cannot endure the terror of the most solitary solitude, and forces me to speak as if I were two. Is it thou that I hear, my voice? Thou murmurest, and thou cursest? Yet—thy malediction should rend the entrails of the world! Alas, in spite of everything it subsists, more dazzling and colder than ever; it looks at me with its stars pitilessly; it exists blind and deaf as before, and nothing dies but man. And yet, you still speak to me, beloved voice! I die not alone in this universe. I, the last man: the last plaint, your plaint, dies with me. Misery, misery! pity me, the last man of misery, Œdipus!

It seems that Nietzsche, now at the extreme limits of his thought, experiences a sudden need of rest. He wants to speak to his friends, to feel himself surrounded by them and diverted. The Easter holidays in 1873 gave him a fortnight's release. He left for Bayreuth, where he was not expected.

"I leave this evening," he writes to Fräulein von Meysenbug. "Guess where I am going? You've guessed, and, height of bliss, I shall meet the best of men, Rohde, to-morrow at half-past four. I shall be staying with Wagner, and then see me quite happy! We shall speak much of you, much of Gersdorff. He has copied my lectures, you say? It touches me, and I will not forget it. What good friends I have! It is really shameful.

"I hope to bring back from Bayreuth courage and gaiety, and to strengthen myself in everything that is good. I dreamt last night that I was having my *Gradus ad*

Parnassum carefully rebound. This mixture of bookbinding and symbolism is comprehensible; moreover, very insipid. But it is a truth! It is necessary from time to time to rebind ourselves by frequenting men more valorous and stronger than ourselves or else we lose a few of our pages, then a few more, still a few more, until the last page is destroyed. And that our life should be a *Gradus ad Parnassum,* that also is a truth that we must often repeat to ourselves. The future to which I shall attain if I take plenty of trouble, if I have a little happiness and much time, is to become a more sober writer, and from the first and ever better to pursue my calling as a man of letters more soberly. From time to time I feel a childish repugnance to printed paper, I think that I see soiled paper. And I can very well picture a period when reading was not much liked, writing even less so; but one far preferred to think a lot, and to act still more. For everything to-day awaits that efficacious man, who, condemning in himself and us our millenarian routines, will live better and will give us his life to imitate."

Friedrich Nietzsche left for Bayreuth.

He there learnt a piece of unexpected news. Money was lacking. Of the twelve hundred thousand francs needed, eight hundred thousand only had been realised with great difficulty. The enterprise was compromised and perhaps ruined. Everyone was losing heart. The master alone was confident and calm. Since he had attained his manhood, he had desired to possess a theatre. He knew that a constant will prevails over chance, and a few months of crisis did not alarm him after forty years of waiting. Capitalists from Berlin, Munich, Vienna, London, and Chicago were making proposals to him which Richard Wagner invariably refused to entertain. He wished his theatre to belong to himself alone, and to be near him: "It is not a question of the success of the affair," he said, "but of awakening the hidden forces of the German soul." But his remarkable serenity failed to reassure his friends. A panic was engendered at Bayreuth, and no one again dared to hope.

Friedrich Nietzsche looked on, listened, observed, and then fled to Naumburg. "My despair was deep," he has written; "there was nothing that did not seem criminal to me." He was rediscovering the world after ten months of solitude, and finding it even more cowardly and more miserable than he had ever judged it to be. There was worse to endure, for he was discontented with himself. He recalled his last meditations. "I call myself the last philosopher, because I am the last man." And he questioned himself: Was he really "the last philosopher"? "the last man"? Had he not flattered himself in assigning himself a rôle so difficult and magnificent? Had he not been ungrateful, cowardly, and vile, like the others, in abandoning the struggle at the decisive moment to shut himself up in his solitude and his selfish dreams? Had he not forgotten his master? He accused himself; remorse accentuated his despair. "I should not think of myself," was his reproach—"Wagner alone is a hero—Wagner, so great in misfortune, great as of old at Triebschen. It is he whom we must serve. I must henceforth be vowed to help him."

It had been his intention to publish a few chapters of his book on *The Philosophers of Tragic Greece*. He abstained from this delight; put away in a drawer— not without a pang—his almost finished manuscript. He wished to "spit out lava," to insult Germany and treat her like a brute, since, imbecile brute that she was, she would only yield to brutality.

"I return from Bayreuth in such a state of persistent melancholy," he wrote to Rohde, "that the only hope for me is holy wrath."

Friedrich Nietzsche looked for no joy in the work which he was about to undertake. To attack is to recognise, to condescend, to lower oneself. He would have preferred to have had no traffic with base humanity. But here was Richard Wagner; was it to be borne that he should be tormented and trammelled? that the Germans should sadden him as they saddened Goethe, and break him, as they broke Schiller? To-morrow other men of genius would be born: was it not necessary to fight from to- day to assure them their liberty and the freedom of their lives? It is impossible to ignore the masses that beset us. It is a bitter destiny, but one that may not be eluded. It is the destiny of the best-born, and above all of the best Germans, heroes begotten and misunderstood by a race insensible to beauty.

Friedrich Nietzsche remembered what Goethe had said of Lessing: "Pity this extraordinary man, pity him that he lived in such a pitiable era, that he was forced to act ceaselessly by polemics." He applied this to himself, but polemics seemed to be a duty to him, as in other times they had been to Lessing. He looked round for an adversary. The illustrious D. F. Strauss now represented official philosophy; he was its heavy pontiff. Having renounced the critical researches, in which he was a real master, he was affecting, in his old age, the attitude of a thinker, and was elaborating his *Credo* with sham elegances borrowed from Voltaire and About.

"I simply propose," he wrote in *The Old Faith and the New*, "to say how we live—how for long years past we have been wont to direct our lives. By the side of our professions—for we belong to the most diverse professions; we are not all artists or scholars, but also officials, soldiers, artisans, or proprietors, and, I have already said and I repeat it, our number is not small, we are many thousand, and not of the worst, in every country—by the side of our professions, I say, we try, as far as possible, to keep our minds open to the highest interests of humanity; our hearts are exalted by these new destinies, as unforeseen as they are magnificent, assigned by Fate to our country which formerly endured so much. The better to understand these things, we study history, to which easy access is opened to the first comer by a number of both popular and attractive works. And then we try to extend our knowledge of nature by the aid of manuals which are within reach of everybody. Finally we find in reading our great poets, in hearing our great musicians, stimulants for spirit and feeling, for the imagination and the heart, stimulants which in truth leave nothing to be desired. Thus we live, thus we march forward in happiness."

So the Philistines are happy and very rightly, thought Nietzsche: this is the era of their power. Assuredly the species is not new. Even Attica had its abettors of "banausia." But the Philistine formerly lived under humiliating conditions. He was merely tolerated. He was not talked of, nor did he talk. Then a more indulgent period arrived, in which he was listened to, his follies flattered; he appeared droll. This was enough: he became a fop, proud of his *prudhommerie.* To-day he triumphs; it is impossible to hold him back. He becomes a fanatic, and founds a religion: it is the new faith, of which Strauss is the prophet. Friedrich Nietzsche would have assuredly approved of that classification of the ages which Gustave Flaubert suggested about this time: "*Paganisme, christianisme, muflisme*" (Paganism, Christianity, Snout-ism). The Philistine dictates his tastes, and imposes his mannerisms. A war breaks out: he reads his paper, the telegrams interest him, and contribute to his happiness. Great men have suffered, and have left us their works: the Philistine knows these works, and appreciates them—they add to his well-being. Moreover, he appreciates with discernment. The Pastoral Symphony ravishes him, but he condemns the exaggerated uproar of the Symphony with chorus. David Friedrich Strauss says it distinctly: and that clear mind of his is not to be deceived.

Friedrich Nietzsche sought no further; he had found the man whom he wished to destroy. In the first days of May he had all his notes in hand, his work was ready. His strength suddenly gave out: his aching head, his eyes that could not bear the light without pain, played traitor to his desire to work; in a few days he was all but an invalid, almost blind. Overbeck and Romundt did their best to help him. But they had, both of them, other work; their time was measured by their professional duties. A third friend came to give assistance to the invalid. The Baron von Gersdorff, a man of leisure and a devoted friend, was travelling in Italy. He had been Friedrich Nietzsche's comrade at the college of Pforta, and since those already distant days had scarcely seen him again, but his friendship had remained intact. He hastened to Basle. He was a younger son of good family. His elder brothers having died, one in 1866 in the Austrian campaign, the other in 1871 in the French campaign, he had been obliged to sacrifice his tastes, to renounce philosophy and learn farming so as to be able to manage the family estate in North Germany. He was the only one of Nietzsche's friends who was not a slave to paper and books. "He is a fine type of the reserved and dignified gentleman, although extremely simple in his manners," wrote Overbeck; "at bottom the best fellow imaginable, and at the first glance you are left with the impression of a man who is entirely trustworthy." A friend of Romundt's, Paul Rée, also came to help or distract the invalid, who, thanks to so many kindnesses, was able to resist his sufferings. Lying always in semi-darkness, he dictated: the faithful Gersdorff wrote down what he had to say, and by the end of June the manuscript was sent to the publisher.

Friedrich Nietzsche's condition improved when he had finished his work. He felt a great need of fresh air and of solitude. His sister, who had come from Naumburg, took him to the mountains of the Grisons. His headaches grew less severe, his eyesight became stronger. He rested for a few weeks, correcting his proofs, rejoicing in his new-found strength, but always haunted by his angers and his aspirations.

One day, while walking with his sister on the outskirts of Flimms, he came on a little *château* in a sequestered site. "What a beautiful retreat," he said; "what a beautiful spot in which to establish our lay convent." The *château* was for sale. "Let us visit it," said the young girl. They went in, and were delighted with everything: the garden, the terrace from which a wide view stretched out before them, the big hall with its chimney-piece of sculptured stone. The rooms were few, but why should there be more? This would be given to Richard Wagner, that to Cosima Wagner, this other would be at the disposal of friends of passage, Fräulein von Meysenbug or Jacob Burckhardt. Gersdorff, Deussen, Rohde, Overbeck, Romundt, would often reside there. "Here," declared Nietzsche, "we will build a covered walk, a sort of cloister. Thus, in every kind of weather, we can walk as we talk. For we shall talk much, we shall read but little, and write hardly at all."

He returned to his familiar dream once again, fraternal intercourse between disciples and masters. Fräulein Nietzsche grew very excited. "You will need a woman to keep house," she said. "It will be I." She enquired about the price and wrote to the proprietor, but matters were not arranged.

"I looked too young," wrote Fräulein Nietzsche, who tells the anecdote, "and the gardener did not take us seriously." What are we to think of this affair? It is hard to know. Was it only the chatter of a young girl to which Friedrich Nietzsche had hearkened for an instant? Or was it, on the contrary, a serious notion? Probably the latter. His spirit, hospitable to chimeras, ill knew what the world admits and what it does not admit. He came back to Basle. His pamphlet had provoked a good deal of discussion. "I read it, and re-read it," wrote Wagner, "and I swear to the great gods that I hold you to be the only one who knows what I want." "Your pamphlet is a thunderbolt," wrote Hans von Bülow. "A modern Voltaire ought to write: *écr.... l'inf....* This international æsthetic is for us a far more odious adversary than red or black bandits."

Other good judges, elderly men in many cases, approved of the young polemist; Ewald (of Gottingen), Bruno Bauer, Karl Hildebrandt, *"dieses letzten humanen Deutschen,"* said Nietzsche—"this last of the human Germans"—declared for him. "This little book," wrote the critic, "may mark a return of the German spirit towards serious thought and intellectual passion."

But these friendly voices were few.

"The German Empire," he had written, "is extirpating the German spirit." He had wounded the pride of a conquering people. In return, he suffered many an insult, many an accusation of scurviness and treachery. He rejoiced over it. "I enter society with a duel," he said; "Stendhal gave that advice." Complete Stendhalian that he was (or at least he flattered himself that he was), Nietzsche was, notwithstanding, accessible to pity. David Strauss died but a few weeks after the publication of the pamphlet, and Nietzsche, imagining that his work had killed the old man, was sorely grieved. His sister and his friends tried in vain to reassure him; he did not wish to abandon a remorse which was, moreover, so glorious.

Stimulated by this first conflict, he dreamt of vaster conflicts. With extraordinary rapidity of conception he prepared a series of treatises which he wished to publish under a general title: *Unzeitgemässe Betrachtungen* ("Thoughts Out of Season"). D. F. Strauss had furnished the subject of the first of the series. The second was to be entitled *The Use and Abuse of History*. Twenty others were to follow. His friends, ever the associates of his dreams, would contribute, he thought, to the work.

Franz Overbeck had just published a little book entitled *The Christianity of our Modern Theology*. He attacked the German savants and their too modernist tendencies, which attenuated Christianity, and allowed the irrevocable and serious doctrine, which was that of the early Christians, to fall into oblivion. Nietzsche had Overbeck's *Christlichkeit* and his *D. F. Strauss* bound together. On the outside page he wrote six lines of verse.

"Two twins of the same house enter joyfully into the world—to devour the dragons of the world. Two fathers, one work. Oh, miracle! The mother of these twins is called Friendship."[3]

Friedrich Nietzsche hoped for a series of similar volumes, the work of many hands but inspired by one spirit.

"With a hundred men bred up to the conflict of modern ideas, inured to heroism," he then wrote, "all our noisy and lazy culture would be reduced to eternal silence. A hundred men of that stamp carried the civilisation of the Renaissance on their shoulders." A double hope and a vain one: his friends failed him, and he himself did not write his twenty pamphlets. Only their titles, and a few pages of rough outline, are left to us. On *The State, The City, The Social Crisis, Military Culture*, on *Religion*, what had he to tell us? Let us moderate our regrets; little perhaps; little, at all events, that could be called precious, as distinct from his desires and his complaints.

He was also busy with another work, and announced it to Gersdorff in mysterious terms: "Let it be enough for you to know that a danger, a terrible and unexpected one, menaces Bayreuth, and that the task of digging the countermine has fallen to me." In fact, Richard Wagner had begged him to write a supreme appeal to the Germans, and he applied himself to the task of drawing it up with all the gravity, all the profundity, all the solemnity of which he was capable. He demanded Erwin Rohde's assistance and advice. "Can I count on it that you will send me soon," he wrote, "a fragment drawn up in the Napoleonic style?" Erwin Rohde, a prudent man, declined. "One would have

---

[3] "Ein Zwillingspaar von einem Haus,
Gieng muthig in die Welt hinaus,
Welt—Drachen zu zerreissen.
Zwi'r Väter—Werk! Ein Wunder war's!
Die Mutter doch des Zwillingpaars
Freundschaft ist sie geheissen."

to be polite," he said, "when the only true thing for the rabble is insult." Friedrich Nietzsche did not embarrass himself with politeness.

At the end of October the presidents of the Wagner Vereine, assembled united at Bayreuth, invited Friedrich Nietzsche to read his manifesto, *A Summons*[4] *to the Germans.*

"We wish to be listened to, for we speak in order to give a warning; and he who warns, whoever he be, whatever he says, always has the right to be heard.... We lift our voices because you are in danger, and because, seeing you so mute, so indifferent, so callous, we fear for you.... We speak to you in all sincerity of heart, and we seek and desire our good only because it is also yours: the salvation and the honour of the German spirit, and of the German name...."

The manifesto was developed in the same menacing and rather emphatic tone, and the reading was received in an embarrassing silence. There was no murmur of approval, no look of encouragement for the writer. He was silent. At last some voices made themselves heard. "It is too serious; it is not politic enough, there must be changes, a great many changes." Some opined, "It is a monk's sermon." He did not wish to argue, and withdrew his draft of a summons. Wagner alone had supported him with a great deal of energy. "Wait," said he; "in a little time, a very little time, they will be obliged to return to your challenge, they will all conform to it."

Nietzsche remained very few days at Bayreuth. The situation, which had been serious at Easter, was now desperate. The public, who for some months had gibed at the great enterprise, now forgot all about it. A formidable indifference stood in the way of the propagandists, and every day it seemed more difficult to collect the necessary money. All idea of a commercial loan, of a lottery, had been set aside. An appeal written in haste to replace that of Nietzsche was spread all over Germany; ten thousand copies were printed, an infinitesimal number were sold. A letter was addressed to the directors of one hundred German theatres. Each was asked to give as a subscription to Bayreuth its receipts at a single benefit performance. Three refused, the others did not reply.

Friedrich Nietzsche returned to Basle. He succeeded, with the aid of Gersdorff, in drawing up his second "Thoughts Out of Season," *The Use and Abuse of History.* But he wrote few letters, few notes, he formed no new project, and for the moment almost entirely escapes from our study. The double hope of his youth, that he might assist at the triumph of Wagner, and have a share in achieving this triumph, was ruined. His help had been refused. He had been told: "Your text is too grave, too solemn." And he asks himself, What does this mean? Is not the art of Wagner a matter of supreme gravity and solemnity? He is unhappy, humiliated, wounded in his *amour propre* and in his dreams. During these last weeks of 1873 he lived like an earthworm in his room at Basle.

---

[4] *Mahnruf.*

He went to spend the New Year holidays at Naumburg. There, alone with his own people, he picked up some strength. He had always liked the repose of anniversaries, which was so favourable to reflection, and, as a young man, never allowed the feast of Saint Sylvester to pass without putting on paper a meditation on his life, his memories, and his views of the future. On December 31, 1873, he wrote to Erwin Rohde; the tone of his letter recalls his former habit.

"The *Letters of an Heretical Æsthete,* by Karl Hildebrandt, have given me inordinate pleasure," he wrote. "What a refreshment! Read, admire, he is one of ours, he is of the society of those who hope. May it prosper in the New Year, this society, may we remain good comrades! Ah! dear friend, one has no choice, one must be either of those who hope, or of those who despair. Once and for all I have decided on hope. Let us remain faithful and helpful to one another in this year 1874 and until the end of our days.

"Yours,

"FRIEDRICH NIETZSCHE.

"NAUMBURG, *Saint Sylvester's,* 1873-74."

The first days of January came, and Friedrich Nietzsche applied himself to work once more. Since the strange misadventure at Bayreuth (no doubt the irritation of an author, whose aid has been rejected, accounts for these unforeseen changes), he has been tormented by anxieties and by doubts; he wished to clear them up. In two lines, which are like an introduction to his thoughts of the time, he brings the Wagnerian art into history. "Every thought that is great," he writes, "is dangerous, and dangerous, above all, in its newness. The impression is that of an isolated phenomenon which justifies itself by itself." Then, having posited this general principle, he approached the definitive questions: "What kind of man is Wagner? What does his art signify?"

It was a catastrophe in fairyland. The modern Æschylus, the modern Pindar vanished; the beautiful metaphysical and religious decorations fell in, and the art of Wagner appeared as it really was—an art, the late, magnificent, and often sickly flower of a humanity fifteen centuries old.

"Let us really ask ourselves," wrote Nietzsche in his notes, of which his friends did not know—"Let us really ask ourselves what is the value of the time which adopts the art of Wagner as its art? It is radically anarchical, a breathless thing, impious, greedy, shapeless, uncertain of its groundwork, quick to despair—it has no simplicity, it is self-conscious to the marrow, it lacks nobility, it is violent, cowardly. This art unites pell mell in one mass all that still attracts our modern German souls; aspects, ways of feeling, all comes pell mell. A monstrous attempt of art to affirm and dominate itself in an anti-artistic period. It is a poison against a poison."

The demi-god was gone, and in his place was a stage-player. Nietzsche recognised despairingly that he had allowed himself to be captured by the gambols of a giant. He had loved with simplicity and with the ardour of his youth, and had been deceived. There was jealousy in his anger, and a little of that hatred which is never far from love.

His heart, his thought, of which he was so proud, he had given to a man: this man had trifled with these sacred gifts.

We may pass over these personal sorrows; others, even more profound, humiliated Friedrich Nietzsche. He was humiliated because he had betrayed Truth. He had desired to live for her; he now perceived that for four years he had lived for Wagner. He had dared to repeat after Voltaire, "It is necessary to tell the truth and sacrifice oneself;" he now saw that he had neglected her, that perhaps he had shunned her, in seeking consolation from the beauties of Wagner's art. "If you seek for ease, believe," he had written some years before to his young sister: "if you desire the truth, search"; and the duty which he had indicated to this child he had himself failed to observe. He had suffered himself to be seduced by images, by harmonies, by the magic of words; he had fed on lies.

His fault was graver yet, for he had consented to this abasement. The universe is evil, he had written in *The Origin of Tragedy*—cruel like a dissonance of notes, and the soul of man, dissonant like the universe, suffering from itself, would detach itself from life if it did not invent some illusion, some myth which deceives but appeases it and procures it a refuge of beauty. In truth, if we thus draw back, if we create our consolations for ourselves, whither will we not let ourselves be led? One hearkens to one's weakness; there is no cowardice that is not thus authorised. To accept is to deliver oneself over to the illusionist. Is it a noble or a vile illusion? How can we know if we are deceived, if we ask to be deceived? Nietzsche felt his memories degraded, and his hopes discouraged by the bitterness of remorse.

The *Use and Abuse of History* appeared in February. It is a pamphlet directed against that science, history, the invention and pride of the moderns; it is a criticism of the faculty, recently acquired by men, by which they reanimate within themselves the sentiments of past centuries, at the risk of lessening the integrity of their instincts and perplexing their rectitude. A brief indication gives the spirit of the book.

"The man of the future: eccentric, energetic, hot-blooded, indefatigable, an artist, and an enemy of books. I should desire to hunt from my ideal State the self-styled 'cultivated' men, as Plato did the poets: it would be my terrorism."

Thus Nietzsche affronted the ten thousand "Herr Professors" to whom history is their daily bread and who guide the public. He was punished by their hatred and their silence. No one spoke of his book. His friends tried to find him some readers. Overbeck wrote to his student friend, Treischke, the political writer, the Prussian historiographer. "I am sure," he said to him, "that you will discern in these contemplations of Nietzsche's the most profound, the most serious, the most instinctive devotion to German greatness." Treischke refused his assent; Overbeck wrote again. "It is Nietzsche, my suffering friend, of whom I will and above all must talk to you." Treischke showed temper in his reply and the dispute became bitter. "Your Basle," he wrote, "is a boudoir, from which German culture is insulted!" "If you saw the three of us, Nietzsche, Romundt, and myself," said Overbeck, "you would see three good companions. Our difference strikes me as a painful symbol. It is so frequent an accident, so unfortunate a feature in our German history, this misunderstanding between political men and men of culture." "How unlucky for you," retorted Treischke, "that you met this Nietzsche, this madman, who tells us so much about his inactual thoughts, and who has nevertheless been bitten to the marrow by the most actual of all vices, the *folie des grandeurs.*"

Overbeck, Gersdorff and Rohde wretchedly watched the failure of this book which they admired. "It is another thunderbolt," wrote Rohde; "it will have no more effect than fireworks in a cellar. But one day people will recognise it and will admire the courage and precision with which he has put his finger on our worst wound. How strong he is, our friend." And Overbeck: "The sensation of isolation that our friend experiences is growing in a painful manner. Ever and ever to sap the branch of the tree on which one supports oneself cannot be done without grievous consequences." And Gersdorff: "The best thing for our friend would be for him to imitate the Pythagoreans: five years without reading or writing. When I am free, which will be in two or three years, I shall return to my property: that asylum will be at his disposal."

These men, with their touching solicitude concerning their friend's lot, did not suspect either the true cause or the intensity of his distress. They pitied his solitude, they did not know how profound it was, or how lonely he was even with them. What mattered to him the failure of a book from which he was separated by a revolution of thought? "As to my book," he wrote to Rohde, "I can hardly think that I wrote it." He had discovered his error and his fault. Hence his sorrow, hence the agony which he dared not confess. "At the present moment," he announced to Gersdorff, "many things ferment within me, many extreme and daring things. I do not know in what measure I may communicate them to my best friends, but in any case I cannot write them." One evening, however, passion carried him away. He was alone with Overbeck; the conversation happened to turn on *Lohengrin,* and, with a sudden fury, Nietzsche pulled to pieces this false and romantic work. Overbeck listened to him in amazement. Nietzsche became silent, and from that moment was more careful to practise the pretence which shamed him and disgusted him with himself.

"Dear, true friend," he wrote to Gersdorff in April, 1874 "if only you could have a far lower opinion of me! I am almost sure you will lose those illusions that you have about me, and I would wish to be the first to open your eyes, by explaining fully and conscientiously that I *deserve nothing.* If you could understand how radically I am discouraged, and from what melancholy I suffer on my own account. I do not know if I shall ever be capable of production. Henceforward I seek only a little liberty, a little of the real atmosphere of life, and I am arming myself against the numerous, the unspeakably numerous, revolting slaveries that encompass me. Shall I ever succeed? Doubt upon doubt. The aim is too distant, and if I ever succeed in reaching it, then I shall have consumed the better part of myself in long and trying struggles. I shall be free and languishing like an ephemeron at dusk. I express my lively fear! It is a misfortune to be so conscious of one's struggles, so clairvoyant...."

This letter was written on the 1st April On the 4th of April he sent Fräulein von Meysenbug a letter which was quite melancholy and yet less hopeless.

"Dear Fräulein, what pleasure you give, and how deeply you touch me! This is the first time that I have had flowers sent to me, but I know now that these numberless living colours, voiceless though they be, can speak plainly to us. These heralds of spring are blooming in my room, and I have been able to enjoy them for more than a week. It needs must be that, in our grey and painful lives, these flowers should come and lay bare to us a mystery of nature. They prevent our forgetting that it always is, and always must be, possible for us to find, somewhere in the world, life and hope and light and colour. How often do we lose this faith! And how beautiful and happy a thing it is when those who are battling confirm themselves and one another in courage, and by sending those symbols of flowers or books, recall their common pledge.

"My health (forgive a word on this subject) has been satisfactory since the new year, save that I have to be careful of my sight. But, as you know, there are states of physical suffering that are almost a blessing, for they produce forgetfulness of what one suffers *elsewhere.* Rather one tells oneself that there are remedies for the soul, as there are for the body. That is my philosophy of illness, and it gives hope for the soul. And is it not a work of art, still to hope?

"Wish me strength to write my eleven 'Unseasonable Thoughts' that still remain to be done. Then at last I shall have said everything that weighs upon us; and it may be that after this general confession, we shall feel ourselves liberated, in however slight a degree.

"My heartfelt wishes are with you, dear Fräulein."

At last Friedrich Nietzsche began to work. His instinct brought him back to the philosopher who had helped his first years. He wished to consecrate to Schopenhauer his third "Unseasonable Thought." Ten years before, he had led a miserable existence at Leipsic; Schopenhauer saved him. His strange gaiety, his lyricism, the irony with which he expresses his harshest thoughts, had restored to him the power of life. If Schopenhauer "troubles you, burdens you," he wrote at that time to a friend, "if he has not the power to raise you, and guide you, through the keenest sorrows of external life, to that sorrowful, but happy state of mind that takes hold on us when we hear great music, to that state in which the surroundings of the earth seem to fall away from us—then I do not claim to understand his philosophy."

Once more he experienced the impressions of his youth. He remembered that the most productive crises of his life had been the most sorrowful, and as a disciple in the school of his former master he recovered his courage. "I have eleven fine melodies yet to sing," he writes to Rohde, in announcement of the work which was to follow. And his Schopenhauer is a melody, a hymn to Solitude, to the daring of a thinker. His heart was full of music at that time. He rested from writing and composed a hymn to Friendship. "My song is for all of you," he wrote to Erwin Rohde.

His sister joined him, and the two left Basle and settled together in the country, near the falls of the Rhine. Friedrich Nietzsche recovered the gaiety of his most childish days, partly, no doubt, to amuse the girl who had come so tenderly to join him—*aliis lætus, sibi sapiens,* according to the maxim that is found written in his diary of the time—but also because he was truly happy, despite his sorrow: happy to be himself, free and unspotted before life. "My sister is with me," he writes to Gersdorff. "Every day we make the finest plans for our future life, which is to be idyllic, hard-working, and simple. All is going well: I have put well away, far from me, all weakness and melancholy."

He used to walk with his sister and talk, laugh, dream, and read. What did he read? Schopenhauer, no doubt, and Montaigne, in that small and elegant edition which became a sad reminder: Cosima Wagner had given it to him in former days at Triebschen in gratitude for the dolls he used to bring to the little girls. "Because that man wrote," he used to say, "the pleasure of life on earth has been intensified. Since I have had to do with this free and brave spirit I like to repeat what he himself said of Plutarch—'Je ne le puis si peu raccointer que je n'en tire cuisse ou aile.' If the duty were laid upon me, it would be in his company that I would attempt to live on earth as at home." Schopenhauer and Montaigne: these two ironists, one confessing his despair, the other hiding it, are the men with whom Nietzsche elects to try to live. But he read at the same time with deepest appreciation the work of a younger thinker, one less unfavourable to his aspirations—the trustful Emerson, the young prophet of a young people, one who in his slightest expressions so happily renders the pure emotion that lightens the eighteenth year of a man's life and passes away with that year.

Friedrich Nietzsche had read Emerson at Pforta, and he discovered him again in the spring of 1874, and recommended him to his friends.

"The world is young," wrote Emerson at the end of his *Representative Men.* "The former great men call to us affectionately. We too must write Bibles, to unite again the heavens and the earthly world. The secret of Genius is to suffer no fiction to exist for us; to realise all that we know in the high refinement of modern life, in arts, in sciences, in books, in men; to exact good faith, reality, and a purpose: and first, last, midst, and without end, to honour every truth by use."

Nietzsche had need of the comfort of such words and loved them.

Friedrich Nietzsche finished the manuscript of his *Schopenhauer as Educator* at the beginning of June. Intellectually he was almost cured, but he had other sufferings. Madame Förster-Nietzsche tells how one day, when her brother had expressed his disgust of novels and their monotony of love, some one asked him what other sentiment could have the power of inspiring passion. "Friendship," he said quickly. "It produces absolutely the same crises as love, but in a purer atmosphere. First of all, attraction brought about on both sides by common convictions, mutual admiration and glorification: then, distrust on one side, and on the other doubts as to the excellence of the friend and his ideas: the certainty that a rupture is inevitable and yet will be painful. In friendship there are all these sufferings, and others too many to tell." Nietzsche had knowledge of every one from June, 1871, onwards.

He loved Wagner; he had never ceased to love him. He had been able to correct himself of his intellectual error. Richard Wagner was not a philosopher or an educator of Europe. True enough, none the less he was a wonderful artist, the source of all beauty and of all happiness, and Nietzsche desired him still, as one desires a woman, because she gives joy. Any idea of rupture was unbearable, and to none did he confess his thoughts.

The situation was false and awkward. In January, at the worst moment of the crisis, he had to write to Wagner to congratulate him on a truly extraordinary and unexpected piece of news: the King of Bavaria, the poor madman, had suddenly stepped in and rescued the enterprise of Bayreuth by promising the necessary money. At the same time Nietzsche despatched his pamphlet on *The Use and Abuse of History*. Now, there was not one mention in it of the master's name. This created rather a shock at Bayreuth, and Madame Cosima Wagner took upon herself the task of delicately calling him to order.

"It has been given to you to take part in the sufferings of genius," she wrote, "and it is this that has made you capable of pronouncing a general judgment on our culture and has lent to your works the marvellous warmth which, I am convinced, will last long after our stars of petroleum and gas have been extinguished. Perhaps you would not have penetrated with so sure a look the colour-medley of Appearance if you had not mingled so deeply in our lives. From this same source has sprung your irony and humour, and this background of sufferings shared has given them a far greater power than if they were simply a play of the intellect."

"Alas!" said Nietzsche to his sister, "see what they think of me at Bayreuth." On the 22nd of May, the anniversary of Wagner's birthday, Nietzsche paid him his tribute of homage; Wagner answered him at once, and asked him to come and spend a few days in "his room." Nietzsche made some excuse and declined the invitation. A few days later he wrote to Wagner—his letters have been lost or destroyed. He received the following answer:

"DEAR FRIEND,—Why do you not come to see us?

"Do not isolate yourself so, or I shall be able to do nothing for you.

"Your room is ready.

"I have just received your last letter; I shall say more of it another time.

"Yours cordially,

"R. W.

"WAHNFRIED, *the 9th June,* 1874."

It is probable that Wagner liked Nietzsche as far as he was capable of liking any man. From among all the admirers and too submissive disciples who surrounded him he distinguished this zealous young man, eager to give himself, eager for freedom. He was often impatient and forgave quickly. He guessed, though he did not precisely understand, that crises of tragedy shook this troubled life: so he wrote kindly. But Nietzsche only suffered the more: he felt more keenly the value of what he was going to lose. His courage failed him, and for the second time he refused the master's invitation. An echo reached him of the irritation caused at Bayreuth.

To a friend he wrote: "I hear that they are again worried about me there, and that they consider me unsociable and ill-humoured as a sick dog. Really, it is not my fault if there are some people whom I prefer seeing at a distance to near at hand."

The faithful Gersdorff—faithful to both parties, master and disciple—wrote to Nietzsche begging and pressing him to come; Nietzsche resisted his insistence and revolted at it.

"DEAR FRIEND,—Where did you get this strange idea of compelling me by a threat to spend a few days this summer at Bayreuth? We know, both of us, that Wagner is naturally disposed to distrust, but I do not think it wise to kindle this distrust further; besides, consider that I have duties towards myself, and that they are difficult to discharge with my health shattered as it is. Really, it is not right for any one to lay constraint of any kind on me."

These revolts were only momentary. Nietzsche had not the strength to break with Wagner. He longed with his whole being to preserve the friendship. Certainly he had refused to go to Bayreuth. But he had given excuses. He had asked for time, given urgent work as a pretext; he had made arrangements for the future. And towards the end of July, receiving a new invitation, tired at last of denying himself, he set out.

Meanwhile a curious idea had occurred to him.

Did he merely wish to affirm his independence? or did he wish to *correct* Wagner? It may be that he conceived the fantastic dream of influencing his master, purifying him, lifting him up to the height of the devotion which he inspired. He took a score of Brahms, whom he admired, and whom Wagner pursued with a jealousy that was comic at times, slipped it in his trunk, and, early in the first evening, put it well in view on the piano. It was bound in the most beautiful red. Wagner perceived it, and, without doubt, understood; he had the sense to say nothing. Next day, however, Nietzsche repeated the manœuvre. Then the great man exploded; he screamed, raged, and foamed; then dashed off, banging the doors behind him. He met Nietzsche's sister, who had come with her brother, and, suddenly laughing at himself, gaily related the anecdote.

"Your brother had again thrust that red score on the piano, and the first thing I see on entering the room is it! Then I fell into a fury, like a bull before a red rag. Nietzsche, as I knew well, wanted me to understand that that man, too, had composed beautiful music. I exploded—what is called exploding!"

And Wagner laughed noisily. The bewildered Fräulein Nietzsche sent for her brother.

"Friedrich, what have you done? What has happened?"

"Ah! Lisbeth. Wagner has not been great...." Wagner had laughed; he was appeased. That same evening, he made friends again with the *enfant terrible*. But Nietzsche, as he shook hands with the master, allowed himself no illusion: the gulf between them was deeper, the definitive separation more menacing.

He left Bayreuth. His health, tolerable in the month of August, was bad in September; well or ill, he worked, correcting the proofs of his *Schopenhauer*, which he published in October.

"You will know enough from my book," he wrote to Fräulein von Meysenbug, "of the ordeals of my year, ordeals in reality more cruel and more serious even, than you will be able to guess in reading me. Still, *in summa*, all's well, my life is bereft of sunshine, but *I advance*, and that is assuredly a great happiness, to advance in one's duty.... At the moment, I want to make myself clear as regards the system of antagonistic forces on which our 'modern world' rests. Happily I have neither political nor social ambitions. No danger menaces me, no considerations hinder me, nor am I inclined or forced to compromise. In short, I have a free field, and I will know one day in what degree our contemporaries, proud as they are of their liberty of thought, tolerate free thoughts.... What will be my ardour when at last I shall have thrown off all that mixes in me of negation and refractoriness! And yet, I dare to hope that in about five years this magnificent aim will be ready to be achieved."

It was a hope well charged with shadows. Friedrich Nietzsche, greedy to possess, longing to act, had to look forward to five years of waiting, of arid work, of criticism. "Thirty years," he put down in a note-book. "Life becomes a difficult affair. I see no motive to be gay; but there ought always to be a motive to be gay."

He returned to Basle and recommenced his course. This duty, which had always been a burden, became heavier still: he was entrusted with the charge of a Greek class for quite young men. He was conscious of the value of his time, and knew that every hour given to the University added to the delay, already so long, of the five years. He suffered from each of them as from a remorse, as though he were failing in his duty as a man of letters.

"I have before me work enough for fifty years," he wrote to his mother in autumn, "and I must mark time under the yoke, and it is with difficulty that I can throw a look to right or left. Alas! (a sigh). The winter has quickly come, very quickly, a very hard one. It will probably be cold at Christmas. Would I bother you if I went to see you? I delight so much in the thought of being once more with you, free for ten days of this cursed University work. So prepare me for Christmas a little corner in the country, where I might end my life in peace and write beautiful books.

"Alas! (a sigh)."

In these moments of depression he was always seized by memories of Wagner, and of the almost serene existence that he had tasted in his intimacy. The glory of the master, a moment faded, went on increasing; the public bowed before success, and Nietzsche, who had fought in the difficult times, had now to stand aside in the hour of triumph. The idea that the art of Wagner was within his reach, always offering the miracle of its "fifteen enchanted worlds "; the idea that Wagner himself was there, offering himself also, ever genial, abundant, laughing, tender, sublime, caressing, and like a god creating life around him: the idea that he had possessed so much beauty, and that, with a little cowardice, he could possess it again, and that never, never again would he possess it; this was an everlasting sadness to Nietzsche.

Finally, giving way to his need of an outlet, he wrote to the one comforter, to Wagner. Like all his other letters to Wagner, this letter is lost, or destroyed; but the tone of the letter which we are about to quote, the tone of Wagner's reply, helps us to imagine its eloquence.

Wagner answered:

"DEAR FRIEND,—Your letter has again made us most anxious on your account. Presently, my wife will write more fully than I. But I have just a quarter of an hour's rest, and I want—to your great annoyance possibly—to devote it to posting you up in what we say of you here. It seems to me, amongst other things, that never have I had in my life such intellectual society as you get in Basle, to amuse you in the evenings. However, if you are all hypochondriacs, it is not a great benefit, I admit. It is, I think, women that you need, you young men of to-day. There is a difficulty, as I well know: as my friend Sulzer used to say, 'Where take women without stealing them?' Besides, one could steal at a pinch. I mean to say you ought to marry, or compose an opera; one would be as good, or as bad, as the other. All the same, I hold that marriage is the better.

"In the meanwhile, I could recommend you a palliative, but you always settle your *régime* in advance, so that one can say nothing to you. For example: our household here is so organised that we have a place such as was never offered me in the most difficult moments of my life, here for you: you should come and spend all the summer holidays;—but very prudently, you announced to us, at the beginning of winter, that you had resolved to pass the summer holidays on a very high and very solitary mountain in Switzerland! Does that not look like very careful guarding against a possible invitation? We could be useful to you in some directions: why do you despise that which is offered you in such good part? Gersdorff and all the society of Basle would be happy here: a thousand things are to be seen: I pass in review all my singers of the *Nibelungen;* the decorator decorates, the machinist machines; and then we are there, in flesh and blood.

"But one knows the eccentricities of friend Nietzsche!

"So I shall say no more about you, because it serves no purpose.

"Ah! *mon Dieu!* marry a rich woman! O, why should Gersdorff happen to be of the masculine sex! Marry, and then travel, and enrich yourself with those magnificent impressions which you desire so much! And then ... you will compose an opera which, surely, will be terribly difficult to execute. What Satan was it that made a pedagogue of you?

"Now, to end up: next year, in the summer, complete rehearsals (perhaps with orchestra) at Bayreuth. In 1876, the representations. Impossible earlier.

"I bathe every day, I could no longer endure my stomach. Bathe you too! And eat meat like me. "With all my heart,

"Your devoted,

"R. W."

Wagner had foreseen that his letter would be useless. He had not foreseen that it would be hurtful. Nietzsche repented that he had drawn forth these tender offers, which he could not accept. In writing, he had been weak; he was ashamed. Finally, the announcement and the approach of the Bayreuth rehearsals overwhelmed him. Should he go? Should he not go? If he did not go, how was he to excuse himself? Could he still hide his thoughts? Should he henceforth acknowledge all?

He had commenced a fourth "Unseasonable Thought," *We other Philologists;* he abandoned it, alleging, to explain this abandonment, weariness and the weight of his University duties. When he speaks thus, Nietzsche deceives either himself or us. Christmas came, and he went to spend ten days at Naumburg with his mother. He was at liberty and could work. But instead of writing, he composed and copied out his *Hymn to Friendship* for four voices. He spent Saint Sylvester's day in re-reading his youthful compositions: this examination interested him. "I have always seen admiringly," he wrote to Fräulein von Meysenbug, "how the invariability of character manifests itself in music. What a child expresses musically is in so clear a manner the language of his most essential nature that the man afterwards desires to revise nothing in it."

This musical debauch was a bad sign of his condition, a sign of weakness and of fear before his thoughts. Two letters, one from Gersdorff, the other from Cosima Wagner, came to disturb his solitary commemoration. His friends spoke to him of Bayreuth. The reminder plunged him in despair.

"Yesterday," he wrote to Fräulein von Meysenbug, "on the first day of the year, I saw the future with a real fear. It is terrible and dangerous to live—I should envy him who came by death in an honest manner. For the rest, I am resolved to live to an old age. I have my work. But it is not the satisfaction of living that will help me to grow old. You understand this resolution."

During January and February, 1875, Nietzsche did not work. He let depression get the better of him. "At very rare moments," he writes, "ten minutes every fortnight, I compose a *Hymn to Solitude.* I will show it in all its dreadful beauty."

In March, Gersdorff came to sojourn in Basle. Nietzsche, encouraged by his arrival, dictated some notes to him. He seemed to have escaped from his melancholy; then once more he was plunged into it by a fresh sorrow.

It had become his habit, a kindly habit and one conformable to his tastes, to live in common with his two colleagues, Overbeck and Romundt, who formed the intellectual society of which Wagner spoke with such esteem. Now, in February, 1875, Romundt announced to Overbeck and to Nietzsche that he was obliged to leave them to enter into Orders. Nietzsche experienced a feeling of stupefied indignation: for many months he had lived with this man, he called him his friend. Yet he had had no suspicion of the secret vocation now suddenly declared. Romundt had not been open with him. Subjugated by religious faith, he had lacked in simple good faith, and the duties of friendship of which Nietzsche had such an exalted ideal. Romundt's treachery reminded him of another treachery and made it easier for him to understand the news which was rumoured among Wagnerians: the master was about to compose a Christian Mystery—a *Parsifal.* Nothing was so displeasing to Friedrich Nietzsche as a return to Christianity: nothing seemed to him more weak or cowardly than such a capitulation to the problems of life. Some years before, he had known and admired the different projects on which Wagner conversed with his intimates: he then spoke of Luther, of the Great Frederick; he wished to glorify a German hero and repeat the happy experiment of *Die Meistersinger.* Why had he abandoned his projects? Why did he prefer Parsifal to Luther? and to the rude and singing life of the German Renaissance, the religiosity of the Graal? Friedrich Nietzsche then understood and measured the perils of the pessimism which accustoms souls to complaint, weakens and predisposes them to mystical consolations. He reproached himself for having taught Romundt a doctrine too cruel for his courage, and thus to have been the cause of his weakness.

"Ah! our Protestant atmosphere, good and pure as it is!" he wrote to Rohde; "I have never felt so strongly how well I am filled with the spirit of Luther. And the unlucky man turns his back on so many liberating geniuses! I ask myself if he is in his senses, and if it would not be better to treat him with cold water and douches; so incomprehensible is it to me, that such a spectre should rise up by me, and take possession of a man for eight years my comrade. And to crown all it is on me that the responsibility of this base conversion rests. God knows, no egoistic thought induces me to speak thus. But I believe too that I represent a sacred thing, and I should be bitterly ashamed if I merited the reproach of having the slightest connection with this Catholicism which I detest thoroughly."

He wished to bring back, to convince his friend, but no discussion was possible. Romundt did not answer and held to his resolve. He left on the fixed date. Nietzsche wrote to Gersdorff, and related the story of this departure.

"It was horribly sad: Romundt knew, repeated endlessly that henceforward he had lived the better and the happier part of his life. He wept a great deal and asked our forgiveness. He could not hide his misery. At the last moment I was seized with a veritable terror; the porters were shutting the carriage doors, and Romundt, wishing to continue speaking to us, wanted to let down the window, but it stuck; he redoubled his efforts, and while he tormented himself thus, hopelessly trying to make himself heard, the train went out slowly, and we were reduced to making signs to each other. The awful symbolism of the whole scene upset me terribly, and Overbeck as much as it did me (he confessed as much to me later): it was hardly endurable; I stayed in bed the next day with a bad headache that lasted thirty hours, and much vomiting of bile."

This day of illness marked the beginning of a very long attack. Nietzsche was obliged to leave Basle and to repose in the solitude of the mountains and woods. "I wander always alone," he writes, "clearing up many thoughts." What were these thoughts? We can ascertain them. "Send me a comforting message," he wrote to Rohde: "that your friendship may help me better to support this terrible affair. It is in my sentiment of friendship that I am hurt. I hate more than ever that insincere and hypocritical way of being a man of many friendships, and I will have to be more circumspect in the future."

Fräulein Nietzsche, who had passed the month of March at Bayreuth with the Wagners, came back to her brother, whose condition alarmed her. He seemed obsessed by the memory of Romundt. "That such a misadventure should occur between friends living under the same roof," he was constantly saying. "It is appalling." In reality he was thinking of the other friend, Richard Wagner, of the master he was losing. "What a peril I have run," he said to himself. "I admired, I was happy, I delivered myself over to and followed an illusion, but all illusions are connected, and accomplices. Wagnerism borders upon Christianity." Tirelessly he listened to his sister's accounts of the marvels of Bayreuth, of the activity, the enthusiasm, the joy of all. Walking one day with him in a public garden, she related for the tenth time this same story: she noticed that her brother was listening to her with a strange emotion. She interrogated him, plied him with questions, and then the secret which he had kept for a year escaped him in a long, eloquent plaint. He was suddenly silent. He remarked that a wayfarer was following and spying on him. He dragged his sister precipitately away, terrified by the idea that his words would be repeated at Bayreuth. A few days later, having recognised again the too curious wayfarer, he was able to learn his name: it was Ivan Turgenieff.

July, 1875, the month fixed for the rehearsals of the Tetralogy, approached, and these rehearsals were the sole preoccupation of Nietzsche's friends, the sole subject of their letters and their conversations. He continued to dissemble and dared not decide the question which was becoming urgent: Should he go to their rehearsals or not? His enervation increased day by day, bringing on the ordinary troubles; headaches, insomnia, sickness, internal cramp: finally his health served for an excuse. "As you are going to Bayreuth," he wrote to Gersdorff, "warn them that they will not see me. Wagner will be greatly provoked, I am not less."

About the beginning of July, when his friends were hurrying towards Bayreuth and the University of Basle had closed its doors, he retired to the little therapeutic station which his doctor had recommended, Steinabad, a spot lost in a valley of the Black Forest.

Friedrich Nietzsche had the faculty of occasionally rising above his own sorrows and his own joys. He knew how to enjoy the spectacle of his crises as though they were the intermingled voices of a symphony. Then he ceased to suffer, and contemplated with a sort of mystical rapture the tragic development of his existence. Such was his life during the few weeks of his cure at Steinabad. It brought him nevertheless no motive of happiness. His illness resisted remedies, and the doctors let him guess, as at the origin of all these attacks, an identical, indiscernible, and mysterious cause. He did not forget the nature of the illness that had killed his father at thirty-six years of age. He took the hint and felt the danger: but he even brought this menace into the spectacle of his life and considered it bravely.

Steinabad is near Bayreuth; Nietzsche was once more tempted. Would he go, or would he stay? This indecision was enough, he broke down utterly. Towards the end of July, a terrible attack which kept him two days in bed did away with these doubts. On the first of August he wrote to Rohde: "To-day, dear friend, if I am not mistaken, you are all meeting at Bayreuth. And I am not among you. In vain have I obstinately believed that I could all of a sudden emerge in your society and enjoy my friends. In vain; to-day, my cure being half completed, I say it with certainty...."

The attack lost its force; he was able to get up and walk in the woods. He had brought a *Don Quixote* with him: he read this book, "the bitterest of all," with its derision of every noble effort.

Still, he kept up his courage. He recalled without too poignant a sorrow his past that had been filled with joy. He faced without fear the menacing future; he thought of that grand work on Hellenism, an old, unabandoned dream; he thought of the interrupted succession of the "Thoughts out of Season;" and above all he delighted in conceiving the beautiful book he would write when he was sure of himself. "To this work," he thought, "I must sacrifice everything. For some years I have been writing a great deal, I have written too much; I have often made mistakes. Now I must keep silence and devote myself to many years' work; seven, eight years. Shall I live as long? In eight years I shall be forty. My father died four years earlier. Never mind, I must accept the risk and peril. The time of silence has returned for me. I have greatly slandered the modern men, yet I am one of them. I suffer with them, and like them, because of the excess and the disorder of my desires. As I shall have to be their master, I must first gain the mastery of myself and repress my trouble. That I may dominate my instincts, I must know them and judge them; I must restrict myself and analyse. I have criticised science, I have exalted inspiration, but I have not analysed the sources of inspiration; and to what unfathomable depths have I not followed it! My youth was my excuse, I needed intoxication. Now my youth is over. Rohde, Gersdorff, Overbeck, are at Bayreuth: I envy, yet pity them. They have passed the age of dreams, they ought not to be there. What task am I going to undertake? I will study natural sciences, mathematics, physics, chemistry, history, and political economy. I will accumulate an immense equipment for the knowledge of men. I will read ancient history books, novels, letters. The work will be hard, but I shall have Plato, Aristotle, Goethe, and Schopenhauer constantly by me; thanks to my well loved geniuses my pain will be less painful, my solitude less solitary."

Friedrich Nietzsche's thoughts were almost every day diverted by a letter from Bayreuth. He received and read it without bitterness. In a few notes written for himself alone, he fixed the memory of the joys he owed to Wagner. Then answering his friends: "I am with you in the spirit during three-quarters of my days," he told them; "I roam like a shadow around Bayreuth. Do not fear to excite my envy, tell me all the news, dear friends. During my walks I conduct entire pieces of music that I know by heart, and then I grumble and rage. Salute Wagner in my name, salute him deeply! Good-by, my well loved friends, this is for all of you. I love you with all my heart."

Friedrich Nietzsche came back to Basle somewhat the better for his cure. His sister joined him and wished to stay with him. He continued to lead the wholly meditative and almost happy existence of Steinabad, with his papers, his books, and his piano.

"*I dream*," he wrote (he underlines these words), "*I dream of an association of unrestricted men, who know no circumspection and wish to be called the 'destroyers'; they apply to everything the measure of their criticism, and sacrifice themselves to the truth. Everything that is suspect and false must be brought to light. We do not wish to construct prematurely, we do not know if we can construct, and whether it may not be better to construct nothing. There are cowardly and resigned pessimists; of these we do not wish to be.*"

He commenced the long studies which he had assigned himself. He examined firstly Dühring's book, *The Value of Life.* Dühring was a Positivist who led the combat against the disciples of Schopenhauer and Wagner. "All idealism deceives," he told them, "all life that seeks to escape beyond life vows itself to chimera." Friedrich Nietzsche had no objection to offer to these premises. "A sane life carries its worth in itself," said Dühring. "Asceticism is unhealthy and the sequel of an error." "No," answered Nietzsche. Asceticism is an instinct which the most noble, the strongest among men have felt: it is a fact, it must be taken into account if the value of life is to be appreciated. And even if a prodigious error be here indicated as being at work, then the possibility of such an error should be placed amongst the sombre features of being.

"The tragedy of life is not irreducible," said Dühring, "the sovereignty of egoism is only apparent; the altruistic instincts work in the human soul."

Egoism an appearance! exclaimed Nietzsche. Here Dühring falls into childishness. *Ich wollte er machte mir hier nichts vor!* God be praised if it were true! He talks nonsense, and if he seriously believes what he says, he is ripe for all the socialisms. Nietzsche finally held out as against Dühring for the tragic philosophy that Heraclitus and Schopenhauer had taught him. There is no possible evasion, all evasion is a lure and a cowardice. Dühring says it and he speaks truly; but he attenuates the task in presenting a sweetened image of that life in which we are set. It is either stupidity or falsehood: life is hard.

Friedrich Nietzsche was gay, or appeared so. In the evening (he did not work because of his eyes) his sister read Walter Scott's novels to him. He liked their simple narration. "The serene art, the andante," he writes; he also liked the heroic, naïve, and complicated adventures. "What fellows! what stomachs!" he exclaimed at the recitals of the interminable feasts; and Fräulein Nietzsche, seeing him so cheerful, was astonished to hear him a moment later play and develop at great length his *Hymn to Solitude.*

She was astonished not without reason: the gaiety of her brother was artificial; his sadness was real; he dissembled with her, and doubtless with himself.

He had begun to study Balfour Stewart's book on the conservation of energy: he stopped at the first pages. It was odious to him to work thus without the consolation of art, or the real joy of hoping. He thought he would be more interested in the Indian wisdom, and took up the English translation of the *Sutta Nipâta*. Only too well he understood its radical nihilism.

"When I am ill and in bed," he writes in December to Gersdorff, "I let myself be oppressed by the persuasion that life is without value, and all our ends illusory...." His crises were frequent: every fortnight he was disabled by the headaches, internal cramp, twitching of the eyes, which laid hold of him.

"I wander here and there, alone like a rhinoceros," Nietzsche had kept in mind this final phrase of a chapter of the *Sutta Nipâta,* and applied it to himself with melancholy humour. His best friends were then marrying. Nietzsche was ready to abuse marriage and women: one is rarely sincere when one speaks thus, and we know he was not.

"I have more and better friends than I deserve," he wrote in October, 1874, to Fräulein von Meysenbug; "what I now wish myself, I tell you in confidence, is a good wife, and as soon as possible. Then life will have given me all that I shall have asked of it. The rest is my affair."

Friedrich Nietzsche congratulated the fiancés, Gersdorff, Rohde, Overbeck, and rejoiced with them, but felt the difference of his own destiny.

"Be happy," he wrote to Gersdorff, "you who will no longer go wandering here and there, alone like a rhinoceros."

The year 1876 was about to begin, the representations of the Tetralogy were announced for the summer. Friedrich Nietzsche knew that his irresolution must then cease: "I was exhausted," he wrote later, "by the sadness of an inexorable presentiment—the presentiment that after this disillusion I should be condemned to mistrust myself more profoundly, to despise myself more profoundly, to live in a profounder solitude than before."

The impression of the Christmas and New Year festivals, always strong in him, aggravated his melancholy. He fell ill in December, only to get up again in March. He was still weak.

"I find it an effort to write, I shall be brief," he wrote to Gersdorff the 18th January, 1876; "I have never spent so sad and painful a Christmas or one of such dreadful foreboding. I have had to give up doubting. The malady which has attacked me is cerebral; my stomach, my eyes, give me all this suffering from another cause, whose centre is elsewhere. My father died at the age of thirty-six of inflammation of the brain. It is quite possible that things may go even quicker with me.... I am patient, but full of doubts as to what awaits me. I live almost entirely on milk. It has a good result; I sleep well. Milk and sleep are at present my best foods."

At the approach of spring, he wished to leave Basle: Gersdorff offered to go with him, and the two friends settled on the shores of the Lake of Geneva, at Chillon. They spent a bad fortnight there. Nietzsche's nerves were irritated by the least variation of the atmosphere, which was more or less humid and more or less charged with electricity, and he suffered from the "föhne," a soft wind which melts the snows in March. He let the softness and tepidity depress him, and could not restrain the heartrending expression of his doubts and his agonies. Gersdorff, obliged to return to Germany, went with an uneasy mind on his friend's account.

But Nietzsche felt better once he was left alone. Perhaps finer weather favoured him; perhaps he felt his distress less acutely when the compassionate Gersdorff was not near by, ever ready to lend an ear to his complaints. His humours became less bitter, and chance procured him a decisive relief, a liberating hour. Fräulein von Meysenbug had just published her *Memoirs of an Idealist.* Nietzsche had put these two volumes in his bag. Of this woman of fifty he was very fond, and every day he liked her more. She was always suffering and courageous, always fine and good. He did not put her on the level of Cosima Wagner. The superiority of her mind was not dazzling; but she was great-hearted, and Nietzsche infinitely esteemed this woman who was faithful to the real genius of women. Doubtless he began reading her book with moderate expectations: yet the work held him. It is one of the most beautiful records of the nineteenth century. Fräulein von Meysenbug had gone all through it: she had known all the worlds, all the heroes, all the hopes. Born in old Germany with its petty Courts—her father was Minister in one of them—as a child she had listened to the friends of Humboldt and Goethe; as a young girl, the humanitarian gospel touched her: detached from Christianity, she abandoned its observances. Then came 1848, and its dream; the Socialists, and their essays towards a more noble, a more brotherly life: she admired them, and wanted to work with them. Blamed by her people, she left them and went alone without asking help or advice. An idealist of action, not of dreams, she joined the communists of Hamburg; with them she instituted a sort of phalanstery, a rationalistic school in which the masters lived together. This school prospered under her direction; but, threatened by the police, she had to fly. Next she was in London among its proscripts of all the races, that mournful refuge, and tomb of the vanquished. Fräulein von Meysenbug earned her living by giving lessons: she knew Mazzini, Louis Blanc, Herzen: she was the friend and the consoler of these unhappy men. At the time of the second Empire, of Napoleon III., of Bismarck, and of the silence of the peoples—in Paris, with its brilliant culture— Fräulein von Meysenbug met Richard Wagner. She had long admired his music: she admired the man, listened to him, succumbed to his ascendancy, and, renouncing the religion of humanity, carried her fervour to the cult of art. But always she exercised and lavished her active goodness: Herzen died; he left two children, whom Fräulein von Meysenbug adopted, thus taking upon herself the anxiety of a double maternity. Friedrich Nietzsche had known these young girls and often admired the tenderness of their friend, her free and sane self-sacrifice: he had not known of what life of entire devotion this devotion was the flower.

He was encouraged by this book: Fräulein von Meysenbug reconciled him to life. Again he found his confidence and health. "My health," he wrote to Gersdorff, "is allied to my hopes. I am well when I hope."

He left his *pension* and went to spend some days in Geneva. There he discovered a friend, the musician Senger; he made the acquaintance of a few Frenchmen, exiled communards, and liked talking to them. He esteemed these fanatics with the square skulls, so prompt to self-sacrifice. It appears that he flirted with two "exquisite" Russians. Then he returned to Basle, and his first letter was sent to Fräulein von Meysenbug.

"BASLE, *Good Friday, April* 14, 1876.

"DEAR FRÄULEIN,—Four days or so back, finding myself alone on the shores of the Lake of Geneva, I spent a whole Sunday quite near you, from the earliest hour till the moon-bathed night. I have read you through and through, with a revived interest at every page, and I kept on repeating that never had I passed so blessed a Sunday. You have given me an impression of purity and love which will never leave me; and Nature, the day on which I read you, seemed to reflect this impression. You were before me as a superior form of my being, a very superior form; and which yet did not humiliate but encouraged me: thus you crossed my thoughts, and, measuring my life with yours, I am more easily able to feel what I lacked—so much! I thank you much more than I would do for a book.

"I was ill, I doubted my strength and my aims; I thought I should have to renounce everything, and my greatest fear was of the length of a life which can be but an atrocious burden if one renounces the highest aims. I am now saner and freer, and I can consider without torturing myself the duties I have to fulfil. How many times I have wished you near me to ask you some question which only a moral being higher than myself could answer! Your book gives me answers to such of these precise questions as touch me. I don't think I can ever be satisfied with my conduct, if I have not first your approbation. But it is possible that your book is a severer judge than you would be yourself. What should a man do, if, in comparing his life to yours, he does not wish to be taxed with unmanliness? I often ask myself this. He ought to do everything you have done and no more. But doubtless he could not; he lacks that sure guide, the instinct of a love that is always ready to give itself. One of the most elevated of moral themes *[einer der höchsten Motive]* that I have discovered, thanks to you, is maternal love without physical bonds between the mother and the child. It is one of the most magnificent manifestations of *Caritas*. Give me a little of that love, dear lady and dear friend, and think of me as one of those who need to be the son of such a mother. Ah! such a great need!

"We shall have lots of things to say to one another when we meet at Bayreuth. At present I again have hopes of being able to go, whereas, these two past months, I had put the very thought away from me. How I should like to be now the *saner* of us two, and capable of rendering you a service!

"Why can't I live near you?

"Adieu; I am and I remain, in all truth, yours,

"FRIEDRICH NIETZSCHE."

Fräulein von Meysenbug answered at once. "If my book had only been worth this joy, your letter to me, I would have been happy to have written it. If I can help you, I want to do so. Next winter, leave Basle, you must; look for a milder climate and a brighter one; how I feel, as you do, the annoyance of our separation. I sheltered this winter your young Basle pupil, Alfred Brenner, who is still ill; you shall bring him back to me. I will be able to find the two of you a health-giving home. Come, promise me." Nietzsche wrote immediately: "To-day I shall answer you in one word; thank you, I shall come."

Assured henceforth of sanctuary, Friedrich Nietzsche regained confidence and courage.

"I have recovered my good conscience," he wrote to Gersdorff a few days after his return; "I know that up to the present I have done all I could to enfranchise myself, and that in working thus, I have not worked for myself alone. I want to start off again on this road, and nothing more will stop me, neither memories, nor despairing presentiments. This is what I have discovered—the only thing that men respect and before which they bow, is a noble deed. Compromise, never! never! Profound success can only be assured by remaining faithful to oneself. I know already by experience what influence I exercise, and that if I became weaker or more sceptical, I should impoverish, besides my own, the hearts of many who develop with me."

He needed a pride of this sort to confront the imminent crisis. The disciples of the master gave him a dinner, and Nietzsche, who did not want to be present, had to excuse himself. He wrote an impassioned letter of which Wagner comprehended perhaps the hidden signification.

"Seven years ago, at Triebschen, I paid you my first visit. And every year, in this month of May, on this same day upon which we all celebrate the anniversary of your birth, I myself celebrate the anniversary of my spiritual birth. For since then, you live and work in me always like a drop of fresh blood that had as it were entered into my veins. This element that I owe to you urges me on, humiliates, encourages and stimulates me. It never allows me to rest, so much so that I should perhaps bear a grudge against you for this eternal disquietude if I did not know that it ever drives me on towards a freer and better state."

Wagner answered him at once in a few exuberant lines. He told of the toasts drunk to his glory and of his humorous responses, with so many puns, cock-and-bull stories and impenetrable allusions, that it is necessary to give up the attempt to translate. Nietzsche was moved by this letter. At the moment it arrived he was feeling very much the master of himself, very sure of his future. The history of his past years suddenly appeared as a grand adventure that was now for ever closed. He considered it with an indulgent regard, and, measuring the joys he owed to Wagner, he wished to express his gratitude. The other summer, at Steinabad, when in a similar state of mind, he had filled some pages of notes. He took them up again, in spite of a nervous affection of the eyes which prevented him from working without help, and undertook to draw from them the substance of a volume. Singular attempt! Disillusioned, he wrote an enthusiastic book, the most beautiful in Wagnerian literature. But a forewarned reader recognises almost from page to page the idea that Nietzsche expresses in masking it. He writes the eulogy of the poet; of the philosopher he does not speak; he denies, for him who can understand, the educative bearing of the work.

"For us," he writes, "Bayreuth signifies the consecration at the moment of battle.... The mysterious regard that tragedy turns towards us is not an enervating and paralysing charm, but its influence imposes repose. For beauty is not given to us for the very moment of battle; but for those moments of calm which precede and interrupt it, for those fugitive moments in which, reanimating the past, anticipating the future, we penetrate all the symbols; for those moments when, with the impression of a slight weariness, a refreshing dream descends upon us. The day and the strife are about to begin, the sacred shadows fade away, and art is once more far from us; but its consolation is still shed upon man, as a morning dew...."

There exists a radical opposition between these thoughts and those that inspired *The Birth of Tragedy.* Art is no longer a reason for living, but a preparation for life, a necessary repose. Three menacing lines end Nietzsche's little book: "Wagner is not the prophet of the future as we might fain believe, but the interpreter and the glorifier of a past." Nietzsche had not been able to keep back these admissions. Brief and disguised as they were, he had hoped that they might not be heard, and his hope, it seems, was justified. Wagner wrote as soon as the pamphlet had appeared:

"FRIEND!—Your book is prodigious!

"Where did you learn to know me so well? Come quickly, and stay here during rehearsals until the representations.

"Yours,

"R. W.

"July 12th."

The rehearsals began in the middle of July, and Nietzsche, who did not wish to miss one of them, went, in spite of the precarious state of his health, with an impatience that astonished his sister. Two days later she received a letter: "I almost regret ever having come; up till now, everything is wretched.... On Monday I went to the rehearsal; it displeased me, I was obliged to go out."

What was happening? Fräulein Nietzsche waited with great uneasiness. She was slightly reassured by a second letter:

"MY DEAR GOOD SISTER,—At present things are better...." But the last sentence read strangely: "I must live very much to myself, and decline all invitations, even Wagner's. He finds that I make myself scarce." Almost immediately came the last letter: "I hope to leave: it is too senseless to stay here. I await with terror every one of these long musical evenings. Yet I stay. I can stand it no longer. I shall not be here even for the first performance; I will go no matter where—but I want to leave; here everything is unbearable."

What had occurred? Had the mere sight of the world driven him away so soon? Nietzsche had led a very hard existence, during the past two years, "the friend of enigmas and problems." He had forgotten men: he suffered on encountering them again. A Titan, Wagner, held them captive, protected them against every enigma and too disquieting "problem"; and in this shadow they seemed satisfied. They never reflected, but repeated passionately the formulas that had been given them. Some Hegelians had come: Wagner offered himself to them as a second incarnation of their master. All the Schopenhauerians were there; they had been told that Wagner had translated into music the system of Schopenhauer. A few young people were calling themselves "idealists," "pure Germans": "My art," declared Wagner, "signifies the victory of German idealism over Gallic sensualism." All, Hegelians, Schopenhauerians, pure Germans, agreed in the pride of triumph: they had *succeeded*. Succeeded! Nietzsche heard this extraordinary word in silence. What man, he pondered, what race ever did succeed? Not even the Greek, which was bruised in its most beautiful flights. What effort had not been in vain? So, taking his eyes off the comedy, Nietzsche examined Wagner: was this dispenser of joys in the end great enough to become uneasy in the hour of victory? No; Wagner was happy, because he had succeeded; and the satisfaction of such a man was more shocking and sadder still than that of the crowd.

But happiness, however low it be, is still happiness. An exquisite intoxication had seized the little town of Bayreuth. Nietzsche had felt and shared this intoxication; he kept the remorse and envy of it. He listened to a rehearsal: the entrance into the sacred theatre, the emotion of the public, the presence of Wagner, the darkness, the marvellous sounds, touched him. How sensible he had remained to the Wagnerian infection. He got up in haste and went out; it is the explanation of his letter: "*Yesterday evening, I went to a rehearsal; it displeased me; I was obliged to go out.*"

A new element aggravated his trouble. He was informed definitely of the significance of the forthcoming work, *Parsifal*. Richard Wagner was about to declare himself a Christian. Thus, in eighteen months, Nietzsche observed two conversions: Romundt was weak and perhaps the victim of chance; but Nietzsche knew that with Wagner everything was grave, and answered to the necessities of the century. Neo-Christianity did not yet exist: Nietzsche felt it all through *Parsifal*. He perceived the danger run by the modern man, so uncertain of himself, and tempted by this Christian faith, which is so firm a thing, which calls, which promises and can give peace. If he did not redouble his efforts to discover in himself a new "possibility of life," it was certain that he would fall back into a Christianity, cowardly like his inspiration. Then Nietzsche saw these men, whose happiness he had instinctively despised, menaced by a final collapse, and led gently, and as if by the hand, towards this collapse by the master, by the impostor who had subjugated them. Not one of them knew whither this powerful hand might not soon lead them, scarcely one of them was a Christian, but they were all on the eve of becoming Christians. How far away was that May day of 1872 in which Richard Wagner conducted, in this same Bayreuth, Schiller and Beethoven's ode to liberty and joy!

Friedrich Nietzsche saw clearly for them all: the spectacle of these unconscious lives made him feel desperate, as the sight of the world in the Middle Ages had made those mystics desperate, who had always before their eyes the accusing and bleeding image of the Christ. He would have liked to have torn these people from their torpor, to have warned them by a word, prevented them with a cry. "I ought to," he thought, "as I alone understand what is happening...." But who would have listened to him? He held his peace, he dissembled his dreadful impressions, and wished to observe without weakness or desertion the tragic solemnities.

But he could not. Soon he weakened and had to fly. "*I should be insane to stay here. I await with terror each of these long musical evenings, and yet I stay. I can bear no more.... I shall go, no matter where, but I will go: here everything is torture to me....*"

The heights which separate Bohemia from Franconia rise some miles from Bayreuth, and the village of Klingenbrunn, where Nietzsche retired, is situated in the forests which cover them. The crisis was brief and less severe than he had dreaded. Now that he had perceived in a clearer manner the dangers of the Wagnerian art, he saw the remedy more plainly. "Religiosity," he wrote, "when it is not upheld by a clear thought, rouses disgust." He renewed his Steinabad meditations and re-affirmed the resolutions then made. He would make a clean sweep of the past; resist the seductions of metaphysics; deprive himself of art; reserve judgment; like Descartes, begin by doubting. Then, if some new security could be discovered, he would raise the new grandeur on immovable foundations.

He wandered up and down the silent forests; their severe peace was a discipline: "If we do not give firm and serene horizons to our souls like those of the woods and mountains," he wrote, "then our inner life will lose all serenity. It will be broken up like that of the men of towns; it will not know happiness and will not be able to give it." Then, all of a sudden he released the cry of his sick soul: "I shall give back to men," said he, "the serenity which is the condition of all culture. And the simplicity. *Serenity, Simplicity, Greatness!*"

Nietzsche, once more master of himself, returned to Bayreuth without delay: he wished to complete his experience. The excitement of the crowd was even greater than on the day of his departure. The old Emperor William was present, on his way to the grand manœuvres. He had paid Wagner the compliment of being present on two evenings. From all Bavaria and Franconia, citizens and peasants had hurried hither to salute their Emperor, and there was almost a famine in the little invaded town.

The performances began; Nietzsche heard them all. He listened in silence to the observations of the faithful and measured the abyss which he had so long skirted. He continued to see his friends: Fräulein von Meysenbug, Miss Zimmern, Gabriel Monod, E. Schuré, Alfred Brenner, who did not fail to notice in him a reserve and a silence singular at times. Often he went off alone, during the intervals or in the afternoons, with a pleasant and charming spectator, Madame O——, who was slightly Parisian, slightly Russian. He liked the delicate and surprising conversation of women, and he excused this one for being a Wagnerian.

M. Schuré, who met Nietzsche at these festivals, gives a description of him which merits repetition. "As I talked to him I was struck by the superiority of his mind and the strangeness of his physiognomy. A large forehead; short hair brushed up off his forehead; the projecting cheekbones of the Slav. The strong drooping moustache, the sharp cut of the face, would have given him the air of a cavalry officer, had it not been for an indescribable something in his address that was at the same time timid and haughty. The musical voice, the slow speech, denoted the organism of the artist; the prudent and meditative bearing was a philosopher's. Nothing was more deceiving than the apparent calm of his expression. The fixed glance betrayed the melancholy labour of his thought. It was the glance of a fanatic, of a keen observer, and of a visionary. This double character added a disturbed and disturbing element, the more so because it always seemed riveted upon one point. In his effusive moments this look was moistened with the softness of a dream, but very soon it became hostile again.... During the general rehearsals, and the first three performances of the Tetralogy, Nietzsche appeared to be sad and dejected...."

Each evening was a triumph, and each of them added to Nietzsche's distress. The *Rhinegold,* the *Valkyrie*—these old pieces recalled his youth, his enthusiasms for Wagner, whom he did not know, whom he did not dare hope to know. *Siegfried:* souvenirs of Triebschen; Wagner was completing this score when Nietzsche entered into his intimacy.

Siegfried was Nietzsche's favourite among the Wagnerian heroes. He found himself again in this young man, who had never known fear. "We are the knights of the spirit," he had then written in his notes, "we understand the song of the birds and follow them." No doubt he was almost happy when he heard *Siegfried;* it was the only one of Wagner's dramas which he could listen to without remorse. Lastly, *The Twilight of the Gods.* Siegfried has mixed in the crowd of men; they deceive him; one evening he naïvely relates his life; a traitor strikes him from behind and kills him. The giants are annihilated, the dwarfs vanquished, the heroes powerless; the gods abdicate; the gold is given back to the depths of the Rhine, whose surging waters cover over the world, and as they await death, men contemplate the universal disaster.

It was the end. The curtain fell slowly, the symphony was extinguished in the night, and the spectators rose suddenly, with one accord, and gave vent to a loud burst of cheering. Then the curtain rose once more and Richard Wagner appeared, alone, dressed in a redingote and cloth trousers, holding his little figure erect. With a sign he called for silence; every murmur ceased.

"We have shown you what we wished to show you," he cried, "and what we can show you when all wills are directed to one object; if on your side you support us, then you will have an art."

He retired, then returned; again and again he was recalled. Nietzsche watched his master standing in the limelight, and he alone in the hall did not applaud.

"There he is," he thought, "*my ally*... the Homer who has been fertilised by Plato...."

The curtain fell for the last time, and Nietzsche, silent, lost in the crowd, followed his tide like a wreck.

CHAPTER V

CRISIS AND CONVALESCENCE

Friedrich Nietzsche returned to Basle. His eyesight was feeble and painful, so that he had to accept the help which two friends offered him: one of them was a young student named Köselitz, whom he had jokingly called *Peter Gast, Peter the Guest*—the surname stuck to him; the other was that Paul Rée, the Jew, with the acute mind, whom he had known for two years. Thanks to their devotion he was able to re-read the notes written at Klingenbrunn; he hoped to find matter in them for the second "Unseasonable Thought." Paul Rée was then publishing his *Psychological Observations,* reflections inspired by the English and French masters, Stuart Mill and La Rochefoucauld. Friedrich Nietzsche heard this little work read, and appreciated it. He admired this prudent style of conducting thought; he enjoyed it on the morrow of the emphatic ceremonies of Bayreuth, as though it were a repose; and he resolved to study at the school of Rée and of his masters. Nevertheless he always felt the immense void which his renouncement of Richard Wagner left in him.

"At this moment," he wrote, the 20th September, 1876, "I have every leisure to think of the past—farthest and nearest—for my oculist makes me sit idle for long periods in a darkened room. Autumn, after such a summer, is for me, and no doubt not only for me, more *autumn* than any other. After the great event comes an attack of blacker melancholy, and to escape it one cannot fly too quickly towards Italy or towards work, or towards both."

He had obtained the leave for which he had asked, and the sole gladness which he had in life was the certainty that he would be free for some months from all professional duties.

He left Switzerland at the end of October. Alfred Brenner and Paul Rée accompanied him. The three Germans went down towards Genoa, and thence took a steamer to Naples, where Fräulein von Meysenbug was expecting them.

"I found Nietzsche," she writes, "disappointed sufficiently, because the journey and the arrival in Naples, in the middle of this noisy, clamorous, importunate people, had been very disagreeable to him. In the evening, however, I asked the visitors to take a drive to Pausilippe. It was such an evening as one sees only down here; sky, earth, and sea floated in a glory of indescribable colours, which filled the soul as an enchanting music, a harmony from which every discordant note was gone. I observed how Nietzsche's face lit up in joyous and almost childlike astonishment, as though he were dominated by a profound emotion; finally he gave vent to enthusiastic exclamations, which I welcomed as a happy augury for the efficacy of his visit."

Fräulein von Meysenbug had hired a villa—it was an old pension—on that slope which glides rapidly towards the sea, carrying its olives, its lemons, its cypresses, and its vines with it down to the waves. "On the first floor," she writes, "there were rooms with terraces for the gentlemen; on the second, rooms for myself and my maid, with a big sitting-room for our common use."

She installed her guests in this retreat which she had selected for them; but they had to wait a while before they could enjoy the retired life for which they were in search. A too illustrious neighbour was stopping hard by—none other than Richard Wagner, who, accompanied by all his people, was resting at Sorrento after the immense effort and triumph of Bayreuth.

He showed no signs of fatigue. His days were spent in walking, his nights in conversation. With Fräulein von Meysenbug and his friends he held a sort of court.

We wonder if Friedrich Nietzsche had expected thus to find his master before him again? He could not avoid taking part in the walks, and in the evening parties: but he displayed a slight reserve. Whilst Richard Wagner talked of his future projects and of his coming work, and of the religious ideas which he wished to express, Nietzsche preferred to isolate himself with Paul Rée and to talk of Chamfort and of Stendhal. Richard Wagner observed these conversations. Now, he disliked Jews, and Rée displeased him. "Be careful," said he to Nietzsche, "that man will do you no good." Nietzsche did not modify his attitude. He spoke little, or, if he did mix in conversation, displayed a forced liveliness and a gaiety which were not altogether natural. Fräulein von Meysenbug was more than once surprised:

"But I never suspected," she writes, "that any change had come over his sentiments, and I abandoned myself with a whole heart to the delights which came to complete those of Bayreuth. The joy I experienced in living in a like intimacy led me to quote one day, as we sat together at table, a thought from Goethe of which I was very fond: 'Happy he who, without hatred, withdraws from the world, presses a friend to his breast, and thus enjoys that something which men know not nor suspect, that which crosses the labyrinth of the heart at night.' The Wagners did not know this quotation, and were so enchanted with it that I had to repeat it to them. Alas! I did not guess that the demons who also cross the labyrinth of the heart at night and intimately contemplate the divine mystery of sympathy between noble minds, had already begun their work of sowing discord and division."

Towards the end of November, Richard Wagner having left Sorrento, Fräulein von Meysenbug and her friends were able to regulate their lives with a view to study. They arranged the employment of their time: up to noon, work and solitude; at noon, breakfast; after breakfast, a walk and conversation; in the evening, work and solitude; at night, after dinner, reading. Paul Rée, the only healthy member in this society of invalid intellectuals, read aloud. Nietzsche and Fräulein von Meysenbug were short-sighted; Brenner's lungs were affected. Who were their authors? Jacob Burckhardt, whose course of lectures on Greek culture they were studying (a student of Basle had lent his notes); a little of Michelet; Herodotus; Thucydides. A question posed, a doubt expressed, sometimes interrupted Paul Rée's readings; and it was almost always Friedrich Nietzsche who concluded the short debate.

"Nietzsche was indeed the soul of sweetness and kindliness!" writes Fräulein von Meysenbug in her charming account. "How well his good and amiable nature counterbalanced his destructive intelligence! How well he knew how to be gay, and to laugh with a good heart at the jokes which often came to disturb the serious atmosphere of our little circle. When we were together in the evening, Nietzsche comfortably installed in an arm-chair in the shade of a screen; Dr. Rée, our obliging reader, seated at the table on which the lamp was placed; young Brenner, near the chimney-piece opposite me, helping me to peel oranges for dinner; I often said, laughing: 'We represent truly an ideal family; here are we four people, who scarcely knew each other before, who are not united by any tie of relationship, who have no memories in common, and we now live together in absolute concord, in the most complete personal liberty, and in a perfect content of mind and heart.' So plans were soon sketched for the renewal and enlargement of this happy experience...."

Would it be impossible to come back each year to this Italian coast, to call one's friends thither, and thus to found a spiritual refuge, free of every school, of every Church? On the morrow of 1848 Fräulein von Meysenbug had inspired at Hamburg a sort of Socialist phalanstery, which became the subject of one of the finest chapters of her book, and remained to her as one of the greatest memories of her life. Friedrich Nietzsche in no wise abandoned his ancient dream of a lay cloister. Thus the memories of the old lady agreed with the hopes of her young companion. Paul Rée and Alfred Brenner did not refuse their co-operation, and the four friends gave the project their serious consideration.

"Already we are in quest of an appropriate locality," writes Fräulein von Meysenbug, "for it was at Sorrento, in the heart of this delicious scenery, and not in the close air of a town, that our project was to take shape. We had discovered near the shore various spacious grottoes enlarged by the hand of man, veritable rock halls, in which a sort of pulpit is actually to be seen, which seems to be especially put there for a lecturer. It is here that, during the hot days of summer, we thought of giving our lessons. We had besides conceived the plan of the school rather on the Greek model than according to modern ideas, and the teaching was chiefly to be a mutual instruction in the Peripatetic manner...."

Nietzsche wrote to his sister: "My idea, the school of the educators, or, if you like, *modern cloister, ideal colony, free university,* is always floating in the air. What will befall it, who can tell? Already we have, in imagination, named you directress and administrative head of our establishment for forty persons."

At the beginning of spring Brenner and Rée left Sorrento. Fräulein von Meysenbug and Nietzsche, now alone together, read to one another, but only a little, for reading tried the eyes of both. They preferred to talk. Nietzsche was never tired of listening to his companion's recitals. She told him of the lofty days of 1848. This he liked and, above all, he liked that she should talk to him of Mazzini.

He did not forget the chance by which he had had the Italian hero as carriage companion in April, 1871, as they were crossing the Alps. *No compromise: live resolutely in the whole, the good, and the beautiful....* Mazzini had repeated this maxim of Goethe's to him, and Nietzsche associated it with his recollection of the man. Fräulein von Meysenbug had known Mazzini in London. She had admired his authority in command, his exactitude in obedience, his readiness to serve every servant of the cause, whether he were called Cavour or Garibaldi. He had paid the price of this humility; for, forgotten in the hour of victory, the exile's ban had been maintained against him alone. Nevertheless, he had wished to end his days in his well-loved Liguria, and he had come there to die, hiding his name and race. The doctor who took care of him was astonished—he had taken him for an Englishman—when he heard him speak in so pure an Italian. "Look you," replied the dying man, "no one has ever loved Italy so much as I loved her." Friedrich Nietzsche listened to these stories.

"The man I venerate most," said he to Fräulein von Meysenbug, "is Mazzini."

Could Fräulein von Meysenbug have guessed that her young companion, this young, tender, and enthusiastic German, had just declared war within himself on those instincts of tenderness and enthusiasm which obstructed the clarity of his views?—that Nietzsche, the continuator of Schopenhauer, the friend of Wagner, was now choosing La Rochefoucauld, Chamfort, Stendhal for masters? Could she have guessed that this friend who dreamed with her of setting up a lay cloister was training himself, during his long walks, to face the melancholy of a life of revolt and of solitude? He formulated the rules of such a life:

You must neither love nor hate the people.

You must in no way occupy yourself with politics.

You must be neither rich nor poor.

You must avoid the path of those who are illustrious and powerful.

You must take a wife from outside your people.

You must leave to your friends the care of bringing up your children.

You must accept none of the ceremonies of the Church.

Fräulein von Meysenbug knew at last. One day Nietzsche handed to her a pile of MSS. "Read," said he; "here are some impressions which came to me down there, under that tree; I have never sat down in its shade without plucking a thought." Fräulein von Meysenbug read, and discovered an unsuspected Nietzsche, a critic and a denier. "Do not publish that," she said. "Wait, reflect!" Nietzsche's only answer was a smile. She insisted; the conversation grew animated; they made peace in reading Thucydides.

At the beginning of May, Nietzsche, incommoded by the heat, wished to leave. Fräulein von Meysenbug wanted him to postpone his departure in order that he might master his first fatigue before he began the trying voyage. He would not listen to her.

"Nietzsche is really going to-morrow," she wrote to Rée; "you know that when he is thus determined upon something he carries it out, even though the sky sends the most serious warnings to turn him from it. In that he is no longer a Greek, as he is not attentive to oracles. Just as, in the most frightful weather, he starts out on an excursion, so now he goes, tired to death, in defiance of the raging wind which is lashing up the sea, and will certainly make him ill, for he is determined to make the voyage from Naples to Genoa by sea."

"Yes, he has gone," she wrote in another letter. "The charm of Sorrento in flower could not keep him; he must go, but it is horribly painful to me to let him travel thus; he is unpractical and so bad at extricating himself from a difficulty. Luckily the sea is a little calmer to-day.... Alas, there is so much to regret! Eight days ago we had sketched plans for his near and distant future. Was his brusque resolution dictated by a feverish desire to fly from his malady, which he suddenly fancied had some connection with our spring temperature, which is truly a little abnormal? But how could he have been any better elsewhere this miserable spring? I think that at the last moment it occurred to him that his departure was nevertheless precipitate. But it was too late.... This melancholy multiplication of departures has quite upset me...."

Friedrich Nietzsche went to take a cure at the waters of Rosenlaui. He experienced very little benefit from it, and his immediate future preoccupied his thoughts. In September he had to resume his professorial duties. It was his daily bread, and a daily discipline from which he feared to be freed. But he also knew the horrible ennui of it. He had been given reason to hope that the authorities at Basle would consent to grant him, in consideration of his services and of his illness, a definite discharge with a sufficient pension. Fräulein von Meysenbug advised him to retire; his sister, on the contrary, advised him to retain his office, and Nietzsche chose to listen to his sister. But the nearer came the date of his return, the more lively grew his revolt.

"It is a thing which I know, which I feel," he then wrote to a woman who was helping him in his work, the mother of one of his pupils, Marie Baumgarten, "that I have in store a loftier destiny. I can make use of Philology, but I am more than a Philologist. 'I misrepresent myself.' Such was the persistent theme of my last ten years. Now that a year of retired life has made everything so visible and so clear (I cannot express how rich I feel and how much of a creator of joy, *in spite* of every affliction, as soon as I am left alone with myself), now, I tell you with complete confidence that I am not returning to Basle to stay there. How will it come about? I do not know, but my liberty (Ah! how modest my material necessities are; little matters to me), my liberty, I shall conquer it for myself."

His sister came to join him at Basle and lived with him. At first his pleasure was great, but he soon recognised that he could not talk with this girl who was altogether a Wagnerian and quite devoted to the ideas of Bayreuth. Paul Rée was the only man whose company he liked; but Paul Rée was detained in North Germany by considerations of health, and could not, as Nietzsche had hoped, come to Basle.

"I hope that I shall soon learn," he wrote to him, "that the evil demons of sickness are leaving you in peace. All that I wish for you in the New Year is that you remain as you are, and that you remain for *me* as you have been.... Let me tell you that friendship has never been so sweet to me as in this last year, thanks to you.... When I hear of your work, my mouth waters, for I desire to be with you so much. We have been made to understand each other aright; we always come together, I think, like good neighbours, to whom the idea occurs, at the same moment, that they should pay each other a visit, and who meet on the confines of their lands.... When shall we have a good conversation upon human affairs, a personal, not an epistolary conversation?"

In December he wrote to Rée: "Ten times a day I wish to be near you." Nevertheless he finished his book, or, to be more accurate, he did not finish it, for he preserved the attractive freedom of his notes. It was thus that they came to him, one after another, without any connection; and it pleased him that they should thus remain. His deplorable health prevented him from putting a weft across them, from imposing an order upon them. And what did it matter? He recalled those French writers whose loyalty he loved: Pascal, Larochefoucauld, Vauvenargues, Montaigne. He wished to leave, after their example, some disorder and some discontinuity in his thoughts. He wished to write a simple book which should call the most urgent enthusiasts back to prudence. Round Wagner and Bayreuth, "beautiful souls" were innumerable. Friedrich Nietzsche, who had just missed being one of these, wished, by talking in the manner of old Socrates, to make them feel the absurdity of their faith. *Human, All Too Human,* was the title which he had chosen. Right at the end of his conscious life, he recounted the object of his book.

"A torch in my hand," he writes, "and the light not smoky,[5] I have cast a lively light upon this subterranean world of the Ideal. It is war, but war without powder and without smoke, without war-like attitudes, without pathos, without dislocated limbs— all that would still be 'idealism.' Error after error, I took them and placed them on the ice, and the ideal was not even refuted—it froze. Here, for example, freezes 'the Genius'; in this other corner freezes 'the Saint'; beneath a thick stopper of frozen ice 'the Hero'; and, lastly, it is 'the Faith' which freezes, she who is named 'Conviction'; and then here is 'Pity,' which notably grows cold—in fact, nearly everywhere freezes 'the thing in itself.'"

Certainly this work is paradoxical. No one is so ardent as Friedrich Nietzsche, no one has such a belief in his work, in his mission, in the sublime ends of life; and yet he labours to scoff at them. He reverses every thesis that he has hitherto upheld. *Pereat Veritas, fiat vita!*—he had once written. Now he writes, *Pereat vita, fiat Veritas!* Above poetry he places science; above Æschylus, that same Socrates whom he had at other times denounced. No doubt it is only a pretence, and he knows it. The ideas which he expresses are not really his own. He arms himself with irony for a combat which will be short: for he is not an ironist. He wants to find, and is convinced that he

---

[5] Lit. torchlike.

will find, an unknown lyricism which shall inspire his great works. *Human, All Too Human,* is the sign of a time of crisis and of passage, but what a surprising crisis, what a difficult passage! "The book is there," wrote Nietzsche, "to the great astonishment of the prostrate invalid."

On January 3, 1879, he received the poem *Parsifal,* which Richard Wagner sent him. He read it, and could better measure the always increasing distance which separated him from his old master. He wrote to the Baron von Seydlitz:

"Impression from the first reading: more Liszt than Wagner; the spirit of the counter-reformation; for me who am too accustomed to the Greek and human atmosphere, all this belongs to a too limited Christianity; the psychology is fantastic; there is no flesh and far too much blood (the Last Supper especially has far too much blood about it for me); I do not like hysterical chambermaids. The style seems like a translation from a foreign language. But the situations and their developments—are they not in a vein of the greatest poetry? Never did a musician propose a higher task to his music."

Friedrich Nietzsche, in this letter, did not speak all his thoughts. Certain features of it *(no flesh and far too much blood)* let us divine, as already active and vehement within him, that repugnance which he was to express ten years later. Nevertheless he loved this incomparable master, and for the first time he was obliged to put clearly to himself the problem of the rupture. He had received the poem *Parsifal;* should he reply, and, if so, in what terms? or should he take the more frank and simple course of leaving it unanswered?

His doubts and vexations increased. It is not easy to gauge his condition at this time. He scarcely confided in his sister. His letters to Paul Rée, which would no doubt enlighten us, are not printed.

Since Christmas, 1877, Friedrich Nietzsche had more leisure, his professional work having been reduced by some hours. He took advantage of this to leave Basle every week and wander alone in the neighbouring regions. He did not go to the high mountains; he had little taste for these "monsters" and preferred the Jura, the Black Forest, whose wooded heights reminded him of the places of his childhood.

What were his thoughts? We may conjecture that he was occupied solely with Wagner and his book. One month, two months had passed, and he had not acknowledged the receipt of *Parsifal. Human, All Too Human* was printed, and the publisher was waiting. But how should he forewarn the master, how prepare him for this surprising document? His disciples had accustomed him to the most obsequious homage, the most profound intellectual deference. Nietzsche knew that his independent work would scandalise the dovecot of Bayreuth. When the moment for his pronouncement came he took fright. He was as much concerned for the public as for Wagner himself. He was ashamed of the philosophy which he was giving forth as his own. He had written these pages, and he regretted nothing; he had followed, as he had the right to follow, the vital logic which ruled his mind. But he also knew that this same logic would bring him back one day towards a new lyricism, and it would have suited him to disguise somewhat the interlude of his years of crisis. He then conceived a singular idea: he would not sign his book; he would publish it in an enigmatical manner, anonymously; Richard Wagner alone would know the mystery and know that *Human, All Too Human* was the work of his friend, of his disciple, who at the bottom of his soul remained still faithful. He wrote out a long draft of a letter which is preserved to us:

"I send you this book: *Human, All Too Human;* and at the same time I tell you, you and your noble companion, in complete confidence, my secret; it suits me that it should be also yours. The book is mine....

"I find myself in the condition of mind of an officer who has carried a redoubt. Though wounded he is upon the heights and waves his standard. More joy, far more joy than sorrow, though the neighbouring spectacle be terrible.

"I have told you that I know no one who is really in agreement with me in thought. And yet I fancy that I have thought, not as an individual, but as the representative of a group; the most singular sentiment of solitude and of society....

"... The swiftest herald who does not know precisely if the cavalry is coming behind him, or even if it exists."

The publisher rejected the proposal and Nietzsche had to abandon it. At last his mind was made up. Europe was about to celebrate, in May, 1878, the hundredth anniversary of Voltaire's death. Friedrich Nietzsche decided that he would publish his book at this time, and he would dedicate it to the memory of the great pamphleteer.

"In Norway those periods during which the sun remains all day beneath the horizon are called *times of obscurity,*" he wrote in 1879; "during that time the temperature goes down slowly and incessantly. What a marvellous symbol for all thinkers for whom the sun of man's future has been obscured for a time!" Nietzsche knew his *time of obscurity.* Erwin Rohde disapproved of his book, Richard Wagner made no reply; but Nietzsche knew how he was being judged in the master's circle. "The caricaturist of Bayreuth," said they, "is either an ingrate or a madman." An unknown donor (Gersdorff, was it not?) sent from Paris a box in which Friedrich and Lisbeth Nietzsche found a bust of Voltaire and a short note: *The soul of Monsieur Voltaire presents his compliments to Monsieur Friedrich Nietzsche.* Lisbeth Nietzsche could not tolerate the idea that her brother, pure German at heart, should range himself under the banner of a Frenchman, and of such a Frenchman! She wept.

No doubt some of his friends passed a different judgment. "Your book," said Jacob Burckhardt, "enlarges the independence of the mind." "Only one book," wrote Paul Rée, "has suggested as many thoughts to me as has yours—the conversations of Goethe and Eckermann." Peter Gast remained faithful, Overbeck and his wife were sure friends. Nietzsche did not feel his defeat the less for it "*Human, All Too Human*" had no success. Richard Wagner, it was said, was amused by the smallness of the sales.

He chaffed the publisher: "Ah, ah! now you see Nietzsche is read only when he defends our cause; otherwise, no."

In August, 1878, *Human, All Too Human* was judged and condemned in the *Journal* of Bayreuth. "Every German professor," wrote the anonymous author, in whom Nietzsche recognised, or believed that he recognised, Richard Wagner, "has to write once in his life a book to consecrate his fame. But as it is not given to all the world to find a truth, one contents oneself, to obtain the desired effect, with proving the radical nonsense of the views of a predecessor, and the effect is so much the greater when the predecessor who is put to shame was the more considerable man."

This low style of judgment grieved Friedrich Nietzsche. He now proposed to explain, in a tone of serenity and respect, his attitude in respect to his old masters, Schopenhauer and Wagner. Only it seemed to him that the time for courtesies had gone by, and, after reconsidering his Sorrento notes, he undertook to write a sequel to the thoughts of *Human, All Too Human.*

His sister had left him; in September he was leading a painful and miserable life, a few features of which we can apprehend. He was avoided, for his agitated condition gave alarm. Often, on coming out of the University, he would meet Jacob Burckhardt. The wise historian would slip off by a clever manœuvre; he esteemed his colleague, but dreaded him. In vain Nietzsche sought to gather new disciples around him. "I am hunting for men," he wrote, "like a veritable corsair, not to sell them into slavery, but to carry them off with me to liberty." This unsociable liberty which he proposed failed to seduce the young men. A student, Herr Schaffler, has recorded his recollections: "I attended Nietzsche's lectures," says he; "I knew him very slightly. Once, at the end of a lecture, he chanced to be near me, and we walked out side by side. There were light clouds passing over the sky. 'The beautiful clouds,' he said to me, 'how rapid they are!' 'They resemble the clouds of Paul Veronese,' I answered. Suddenly his hand seized my arm. 'Listen,' said he; 'the holidays are coming; I am leaving soon, come with me, and we shall go together to see the clouds at Venice.' ... I was surprised, I stammered out some hesitating words; then I saw Nietzsche turn from me, his face icy and rigid as death. He moved away without saying a word, leaving me alone."

The break with Wagner was his great and lasting sorrow. "Such a farewell," he wrote, "when one parts because agreement is impossible between one's manner of feeling and one's manner of judging, puts us back in contact with that other person, and we throw ourselves with all our strength against that wall which nature has set up between us and him." In February, 1879, Lisbeth Nietzsche wrote to Cosima Wagner: had her brother advised her to make the overture? Did he know of it? Did he approve of it? We cannot say. Cosima answered with an imperial and sweet firmness. "Do not speak to me of *Human, All Too Human,*" she wrote. "The only thing that I care to remember in writing to you is this, that your brother once wrote for me some of the most beautiful pages that I know.... I bear no malice against him: he has been broken by suffering. He has lost the mastery of himself, and this explains his felony." She added, with more spirit than sense, "To say that his present writings are not definitive, that they represent the stages of a mind that seeks itself, is, I think, curious. It is almost as if Beethoven had said: 'See me in my third manner!' Moreover, one recognises as one reads that the author is not convinced by his work; it is merely sophism without impulse, and one is moved to pity."

Miscellaneous Opinions and Apophthegms, which formed the sequel to *Human, All Too Human,* appeared in 1879. But the offence which this second volume might have given was attenuated and, as it were, warded off, by reason of the pity which Nietzsche now inspired in those who had formerly known him. His state of health grew worse. His head, his stomach, his eyes, tormented him without intermission. The doctors began to be disquieted by symptoms which they could not ascertain, by an invalid whom they could not cure. It appeared to them that his eyesight, and perhaps his reason, were threatened. He divined their alarms. Peter Gast waited at Venice, called to him from there; but Nietzsche was forced to abandon the project of a voyage; he had to shut himself up in his room at Basle behind closed shutters and drawn curtains.

What was to become of him? Rohde, Gersdorff, touched by the wreck of this man of whom they had hoped so much, wrote to Overbeck: "They say that Nietzsche is lost, advise us." "Alas," replied Overbeck, "his condition is desperate." Even Richard Wagner remembered and was touched. "Can I forget him," he wrote to Overbeck, "my friend who separated from me with such violence? I clearly see that it would not have been right to demand conventional considerations from a soul torn by such passions. One must be silent and have pity. But I am in absolute ignorance of his life, and of his sufferings; this afflicts me. Would it be indiscreet if I asked you to write me news of my friend?"

Apparently Nietzsche did not know of this letter. He had written, a few months earlier, among other notes: "Gratitude is a bourgeois virtue; it cannot be applied to a man like Wagner." His happiness would have been great, had he been able to read the identical thought, written by his master, "It would not have been right to demand conventional considerations from a Nietzsche."

Overbeck and his wife attended the invalid. They wrote to his sister that she ought to be at his side. She came at once and scarcely recognised the stooping, devastated man, aged in one year by ten years, who thanked her for coming with a gesture of his hand.

Friedrich Nietzsche gave up his professorship; he sent in his resignation, which was accepted. In recompense for his services he was to receive a pension of three thousand francs.

Lisbeth took him away. He thought himself a lost man, and expressed his last wishes. "Make me a promise, Lisbeth; let my friends only accompany my corpse; let none who are merely indifferent or curious be present. I shall no longer be able to defend myself, and you must do it. Let no priest, let no one come and speak insincere words over my coffin. See that I am buried like a loyal pagan, with no lies told."

He longed for the most desert and silent places, for the most complete solitude; she brought him to the valleys of the Upper Engadine. At that time very few people went up there. Nietzsche discovered this remote Switzerland and derived an unexpected comfort from the light and pure quality of the air, and the kindly light of the meadows, which soothed his worn-out eyes. He liked the scattered lakes, which recalled a Finland, the villages with their singing names, the fine peasant race, which proclaimed the presence of Italy beyond the glaciers. "This nature is familiar to me," he wrote to Rée; "it does not astonish me, there is an understanding between us." With a convalescent's surprise he began to live again. He wrote scarcely any letters; he wrote for himself, and it is in his work that we must seek the information which his correspondence formerly gave us. This is how he narrates his ascent towards the Engadine.

"*Et in Arcadia ego.*—Above the hills which take the shape of waves, across the austere pines and the old fir-trees, I have turned my gaze upon a little lake whose water is green and milky. Around me were rocks of every contour, a soil painted in discordant colours with grasses and flowers. Before me a flock moved, now scattering, now closing up its ranks; some cows, grouped afar-off, below a forest of pines, stood out in relief under the evening light; others, nearer, more sombre; and everything calm in the peace of the approaching twilight. My watch registered half-past five. The monarch of the herd was walking in the foam-white brook; he stepped out slowly, now stemming the fierce tide, now giving way to it: no doubt he found a kind of ferocious delight in so doing. Two human beings, brown skinned, of Bergamesque origin, were the shepherds of this flock: the young girl dressed almost like a boy. To the right, above a large belt of forest, edges of rocks, fields of snow; to the left, two enormous prongs of ice, far over me, in a veil of clear mist. Everything grand, calm, luminous. This beauty, thus suddenly perceived, thrilled, so as to bring into the soul a mute adoration of this moment of revelation. Into this world of pure light and sharp outline (exempt from disquiet and desire, expectation and regret), one was tempted to introduce Grecian heroes—involuntarily, as though it were the most natural thing. One had to feel in the manner of Poussin and his pupils; in a thoroughly heroic and idyllic manner. And it is thus that certain men have lived, thus that they have felt life, lastingly, within and without themselves; and I recognise among them one of the greatest of all men, one who discovered a style of heroic and idyllic philosopher: Epicurus."

Friedrich Nietzsche stayed in the Engadine, poorly lodged, sparingly fed, till September came; but he was satisfied, though deprived of friends, with his music and books. His sufferings were not intolerable: he could work and had soon filled six copybooks with pencil notes of his calmer thoughts, which, though always sceptical, were not bitter, but seemed, as it were, tempered by the unexpected indulgence. He had no illusions concerning this respite which he had received. It was a respite and no more, and he did not hope. Nevertheless he rejoiced that, before his breakdown, he had the opportunity of saying what happiness had been procured him by the simple contemplation of things, of human nature, of the mountains and the sky; he hastened to harvest this last felicity. At the beginning of September, 1879, he sent his completed work to Peter Gast.

"My dear, dear friend," he wrote, "when you receive these lines my manuscript will be in your hands. Perhaps you will feel a little of the pleasure which I have myself when I think of my work that is now completed. I am at the end of my thirty-fifth year, 'the middle of life,' they used to say some thousand years ago: it is the age at which Dante had his vision, as he tells us in the first verses of his poem. I am now in this middle of life, and on all sides so hard pressed by death, that at any hour it may take me; my life is such that I must foresee a *rapid* death, in spasms.... So I feel like a very old man, and the more because I *have done* the work of my life. I have poured out a good drop of oil, I know it, it will be accounted to me. I have experienced my manner of life to the full; many will experience it after me. My continual, my bitter sufferings have not altered my humour up to the present. On the contrary, it seems to me that I feel gayer, more kindly, than ever I was: whence comes this influence which fortifies me and ameliorates my condition? Not from men, for all but a few are provoked against me,[6] and do not grudge the trouble of letting me know it. Dear friend, read this last manuscript from end to end, and see if any trace of suffering or of depression is there disclosed. I *think not,* and this very conviction assures me that there must be some hidden strength in my thoughts, and not that lassitude, that powerlessness, which those who do not approve of me would like to find in them."

At this instant of his life Nietzsche made ready to die. How? It is not too hazardous to guess. He was waiting for that "rapid end in spasms," which had swept off his father in madness, and a pious sentiment brought him back to the domestic hearth. Released from the obligations which kept him at Basle, free to choose his retreat, he resisted the call of Peter Gast from Venice. It was no time for learning to know and to love a new beauty. "No," said he, "in spite of Overbeck, in spite of my sister, who press me to rejoin you, I shall not go. In certain circumstances, as I think, it is fitting that one should be closer to one's mother, one's hearth, one's souvenirs of childhood...."

It was to Naumburg, therefore, that he proceeded. He wished to lead there a life of entire peace, and to distract himself from thought by manual labour. In a tower of the old ramparts he hired a great room. Below the old wall there extended an unused piece of land, and this he took on lease and cultivated. "I have ten fruit trees," he wrote, "and roses, lilacs, carnations, strawberries, goose-berry bushes, and green gooseberries. At the beginning of next year I shall have ten rows of vegetables growing."

---

[6] This is an evangelical reminiscence, thinks Peter Gast. Scriptural suggestions are frequent in the language and thought of Nietzsche.

But the invalid was soon obliged to abandon these plans. The winter was rigorous. Friedrich Nietzsche could not withstand either the glare of the snow which dazzled his eyes, or the humid air which depressed and shattered his nerves. In a few weeks he had lost the benefit derived from his visit to the Engadine.

The Traveller and his Shadow, the proofs of which Peter Gast had corrected, was published. Apparently it was better understood than the preceding collections had been. Rohde wrote Nietzsche a letter which pleased him. Certainly he did not express unqualified admiration. "This clear but never emotional view of humanity," said he, "pains him who loves you and who hears the friend in every word." But, on the whole, he admired.

"What you give to your readers," he wrote, "you can scarcely surmise, for you live in your own mind. But a voice like yours is one which we never hear, either in life or in books. And, as I read you, I continue to experience what I experienced at your side in the time of our comradeship: I feel myself raised into a higher order of things, and spiritually ennobled. The conclusion of your book penetrates the soul. You can and you should, after these discordant harmonies, give us yet softer, yet diviner strains.... Farewell, my dear friend, you are always he who gives, I am always he who receives...."

Nietzsche was happy. "Thanks, dear friend," he wrote on the 28th of December, 1879; "your old affection sealed anew—it is the most precious gift which these Christmas days have brought me." But his answer was brief, and the last two lines of his letter give the reason: "My condition has again become terrible, my tortures are atrocious; *sustineo, abstineo;* and I am astonished at it myself."

This very strong language contains no exaggeration. His mother and sister, who saw him suffer, bear witness to the awful days through which he passed. He accepted suffering as a test, as a spiritual exercise. He compared his destiny to that of men who were great in sorrow—Leopardi, for instance. But Leopardi was not brave, for, in his sickness, he defamed life, and—Nietzsche discovered this hard truth—an invalid has not the right to be a pessimist. Or the Christ. But even Christ weakened upon the cross. "Father, Father!" He cried out, "why hast Thou forsaken Me?" Friedrich Nietzsche had no God, no father, no faith, no friends. Every prop he had taken from himself, and yet he did not bend. To complain, even in a passing manner, would be to avow defeat. He refused to make the avowal. Suffering did not overwhelm him; on the contrary, it instructed him, and animated his thought.

"The enormous tension of the intellect, bent on the mastery of pain," he writes, "shows everything in a new light: and the unspeakable charm of every new light is often powerful enough to overcome all the allurements of suicide, and to make the continuance of life appear as most desirable to the sufferer. Scornfully he reviews the warm and comfortable dream-world, wherein the healthy man moves unthinkingly; scornfully he reviews the noblest and dearest of the illusions in which he formerly indulged; this contempt is his joy, it is the counterpoise which enables him to hold his own against physical pain, a counterpoise the necessity of which he now feels.... Our pride revolts as it never did before: joyfully does it defend life against such a tyrant as pain, that tyrant that would force us to testify against life. To stand for life in the face of this tyrant is a task of infinite fascination."[7]

Friedrich Nietzsche supposed that his end was close at hand. On the 14th of January, wishing to give a last indication of his thought to some friend, he wrote Fräulein von Meysenbug a letter which is a farewell and a spiritual testament. What an effort it must have cost him!

"Although to write is one of the fruits which is most strongly forbidden me, still I want you to have one more letter from me, you whom I love and venerate like a beloved sister—it will be the last! For the awful and almost incessant martyrdom of my life gives me a thirst for death, and, according to certain signs, I am now near enough to that access of fever, which shall save me, to be permitted to hope. I have suffered so much, I have renounced so many things that there is no ascetic, of any time, to whose life I have not the right to compare my life in this last year. Nevertheless I have acquired a great deal. My soul has gained in purity, in sweetness, and I no longer need religion or art for that. (You will remark that I have some pride; that is because in my state of entire abandonment I have been able finally to discover my intimate sources of consolation.) I think that I have done the work of my life as a man may to whom no time is left. But I know that for many men I have poured out a drop of good oil, that many men will be guided by me towards a higher, a more serene, and lucid life. I give you this supplementary information: when my *humanity* shall have ceased to be, men will say so. No sorrow has been or will be able to induce me to give false evidence on life, as I know it.

"To whom should I say all this if not to you? I think—but it is immodest to say so—that our characters resemble each other. For instance: both of us are brave, and neither distress nor contempt has been able to turn us from the path which we recognised as the right path. And both of us have known, in us, around us, many a truth, the dazzling splendour of which few of our contemporaries have perceived—we hope for humanity and, silently, offer ourselves in sacrifice for it, do we not?

"Have you good news of the Wagners? For three years I have heard nothing of them. They, too, have forsaken me. I knew for long that Wagner would separate from me as soon as he should have recognised the difference of our efforts. I have been told that he writes against me. Let him: all means must be used to bring the truth to light! I think of him with a lasting gratitude, for I owe him some of the strongest incitements towards spiritual liberty. Madame Wagner, as you know, is the most sympathetic woman whom I have met. But our relations are ended, and assuredly I am not the man to resume them. It is too late.

"Receive, dear friend, who are a sister to me, the salutation of a young old man to whom life has not been cruel, although it has come about that he desires to die."

---

[7] *The Dawn of Day,* cxiv. This book, published in June, 1881, gives very reliable autobiographical indications on the period here studied.

He lived, nevertheless. Paul Rée came to see him, read to him, and succeeded in distracting his thoughts. The weather, which had tried him so severely, grew warmer, and the snow, which had dimmed his eyesight, melted. Peter Gast, living as in the previous year at Venice, steadily wrote and called to him. In the middle of February he felt, with surprise, a reawakening of strength; his desires, his curiosities returned to him, and he set out at once.

He stayed for a month on the shores of Lake Garda, at Riva, and the improvement in his letters gave his relatives some hope. On the 13th of March he was at Venice: from that day the end of this crisis and his convalescence must be dated.

He had not yet loved Italy. What parts of it did he know? The Lakes: but their somewhat oppressive tepidity was ill-suited to him, and he did not relish their over-soft harmonies. Naples and its Gulf: but he was repelled by the Neapolitan crowd; the splendour of the spectacle had no doubt conquered, but it had scarcely charmed him. No intimate union had been established between this dazzling scenery and his spiritual passions. But from the first moment he yielded to the fascination of Venice. In Venice he found, at a glance, without effort, what his Greek masters—Homer, Theognis, Thucydides—had formerly given him: the sensation of a lucid intellect, which lived without dreams or scruples. Against dreams, against scruples, against the prestige of a romantic art, he had been fighting for four years. The beauty of Venice was his deliverance. He remembered his agonies and smiled at himself. Had he not flattered himself in supposing that he was the most wretched of men? What man who suffered has not had this thought, this childish conceit?

"When a first dawn of assuagement, of recovery, supervenes," he wrote, "then we ungratefully humiliate the pride which formerly made us bear our sorrow, we deal with ourselves like naïve simpletons—as if something unique had happened to us! Again we look around at men and at nature, with desire; the tempered lights of life recomfort us; again health plays its magical tricks with us. We contemplate the spectacle as if we were transformed, benevolent and still fatigued. In this condition one cannot hear music without weeping."

Peter Gast attended him with touching kindness. He accompanied him in his walks, read to him, played him his favourite music. At this period Friedrich Nietzsche liked Chopin above all musicians; he discovered a daring, a freedom of passion in his rhapsodies, which is seldom the gift of German art. Doubtless we must think of Chopin in reading those last words, "In this condition one cannot hear music without weeping."

Peter Gast also played the part of secretary, for Nietzsche had recovered his ardour for work. Day by day he dictated his thoughts. He chose, immediately, the title for a new collection (he gave up the idea quickly), L'Ombra di Venezia. Indeed, did he not owe to the presence of Venice this richness, this force, this subtlety of his mind? He essayed new researches. Was it true, as he had written, that a cold calculation of interest determines the actions of men? that a mean desire for safety, for ease, for happiness, had created that excessive beauty to which Venice stands witness? Venice is unique; nevertheless, she exists and must be explained. A spiritual portent must explain the physical marvel. What, then, are the hidden springs which determine our acts? Life, Schopenhauer used to say, is a pure *Will to Live;* every being desires to persevere in being. We may go further, thinks Friedrich Nietzsche, and say that life aspires ever to extend and surpass itself. Its desire is, not conservation, but growth; a principle of conquest and of exaltation must be linked to its essence. How is this principle to be formulated? Nietzsche did not yet know; but the idea was with him, and importunate. He felt that he was on the eve of a discovery, on the threshold of an unknown world; and he wrote, or dictated, to his friend:

"Actions are never what they appear to be. We have had such difficulty in learning that external things are not what they appear to us. Well, it is the same with the internal world! Deeds are in reality 'something other'—more we cannot say of them, and all deeds are essentially unknown."

In July he tried the waters of Marienbad. He lived in a little inn, situated opposite the wood, where he walked all the length of the day.

"I am absorbed, and excavate zealously in my moral mines," he wrote to Peter Gast, "and it seems to me that I have become an altogether subterranean being—it seems to me, at this moment, that I have found a passage, an opening; a hundred times I shall be thus persuaded and then deceived."

In September he was at Naumburg; he seemed to be in a joyful and talkative humour; his sister Lisbeth recognised on his face that expression of cheerful sweetness which denotes good mental work, a plenitude and an afflux of thoughts. On the 8th of October, fearing the fogs, he descended towards Italy. He stopped at Stresa, on the shore of the Lake Maggiore. But the climate did not agree with his nerves, and unsettled his meditations. It was with terror that he recognised once more that the tyranny of external influences held him at its mercy. He took fright; could he, if he lived always in a state of suffering, express those innumerable ideas, philosophical and lyrical, which pressed on him? To acquire health was, he thought, his first duty. He left Stresa and travelled towards Sorrento.

Genoa was on his road, and there he stopped. The place charmed him at first sight. Its people were vigorous, frugal, and gay; the temperature, in November, almost that of summer. In Genoa was combined the double energy of mountain and of sea. Nietzsche liked those robust palaces that stood athwart the little streets. Such monuments had been raised by Corsair merchants to their own glory, by men whose instincts were fettered by no scruples. And his visionary spirit evoked them, for he stood in need of those Italians of a former time who were so lucid, so grasping, and who had in them so little of the Christian; who lied to others, but were frank towards themselves, without sophistry. He needed them in order to repress that romantic reverie which was not to be extinguished in him. He desired, like Rousseau, a return to nature. But Rousseau's Europe was one thing, and Nietzsche's another. Rousseau's offended against the sentiments of piety, against human sympathy, against goodness; Nietzsche's was a sluggish Europe under the domination of the herd, and it offended against other sentiments; very different, too, was the oppressed nature which he exalted and in which he sought the cure and the refreshment of his soul.

He wished to make a stay at Genoa. After some trouble he found a perfect home: a garret, with a very good bed, at the top of a staircase of a hundred and four steps, in a house which looked out on a path so steep and stiff that no one passed that way, and that grass grew between the paving stones—Salita delle Battistine, 8.

He arranged his life in a manner as simple as his domicile, and thus realised one of his many dreams. Often he used to say to his mother: "How do the common people live? I would like to live like them." His mother would laugh. "They eat potatoes and greasy meat; they drink bad coffee and alcohol...." Nietzsche sighed: "Oh, those Germans!" In his Genoese house, with its poor inmates, customs were different. His neighbours lived soberly. He imitated them and ate sparely; his thought was quicker and livelier. He bought a spirit lamp, and, under his land-lady's teaching, learnt how to prepare his own risotto, and fry his own artichokes. He was popular in the big house. When he suffered from headaches, he had many visitors, full of concern for him. "I need nothing," he would say, simply: "*Sono contento.*"

In the evening, in order to rest his eyes, he would lie stretched out on his bed, without light in the room. "It is poverty," opined the neighbours; "the German professor is too poor to burn candles." He was offered some: he was grateful, smiled, and explained the circumstances. They called him *Il Santo, il piccolo Santo.* He knew it, and it amused him. "I think," he wrote, "that many among us, with their abstemious, regular habits, their kindliness and their clear sense, would, were they transported into the semi-barbarism of the sixth to the tenth centuries, be revered like Saints." He conceived and drew up a rule of life:

"An independence which offends no one; a mollified, veiled pride, a pride which does not discharge itself upon others because it does not envy their honours or their pleasures, and is able to stand the test of mockery. A light sleep, a free and peaceful bearing, no alcohol, no illustrious or princely friendships, neither women nor newspapers, no honours, no society—except with superior minds; in default of them, the simple people (one cannot dispense with them; to see them is to contemplate a sane and powerful vegetation); the dishes which are most easily prepared, and, if possible, prepared by oneself, and which do not bring us into contact with the greedy and lip-smacking rabble."

For Friedrich Nietzsche health was a fragile possession, and the more precious in that it must be incessantly conquered, lost, and reconquered. Every favourable day made him feel that surprise which constitutes the happiness of convalescents.

On jumping from his bed, he equipped himself, stuffed into his pouch a bundle of notes, a book, some fruit and bread; and then started out on the road. "As soon as the sun is risen," he wrote, "I go to a solitary rock near the waves and lie out on it beneath my umbrella, motionless as a lizard, with nothing before me but the sea and the pure sky." There he would remain for a long time, till the very last hours of the twilight. For these hours were kindly to those weak eyes of his, that were so often deprived of light and so often blinded by it—those menaced eyes, the least of whose joys was a delight.

"Here is the sea," he wrote, "here we may forget the town. Though its bells are still ringing the Angelus—that sad and foolish, yet sweet sound at the parting of day and night—only another minute! Now all is hushed! There lies the broad ocean, pale and glittering, but it cannot speak. The sky is glistening in its eternal mute evening glory, in red, yellow, green hues; it cannot speak either. The small cliffs and crags, projecting into the sea—as though trying to find the most lonely spot—not any of them can speak. This eternal muteness which suddenly overcomes us is beautiful and awful; it makes the heart swell...."[8]

How often has he celebrated this hour, when, as he says, the humblest fisherman "rows with golden oars." Then he collected the fruits of the day; he wrote the thoughts which had come to him, clothed in the form and the music of their words. He continued the researches which he had begun at Venice. What is human energy? What is the drift of its desires? How are the disorders of its history, the quagmire of its manners, to be explained? He now knows the answer, and it is this, that the same cruel and ambitious force thrusts man against man, and the ascetic against himself. Nietzsche had to analyse and to define this force in order to direct it; this was the problem which he set himself, and he was confident that he would one day resolve it. Willingly he compared himself to the great navigators, to that Captain Cook who for three months navigated the coral-reefs, fathom-line in hand. In this year 1881, his hero was the Genoese, Christopher Columbus, who, when no land had yet appeared, recognised on the waves meadow grasses which had been carried into the open sea by some unknown river, the waters of which were milky and still free from salt.

"Whither do we wish to go?" he wrote. "Do we long to cross the sea? Whither does this powerful desire urge us which we value above all our other passions? Why this mad flight towards that place where every sun has hitherto *sunk* and *perished?* Will they, perhaps, one day, relate of us that we also steered westward, hoping to reach an unknown India, but that it was our fate to suffer shipwreck on the Infinite? Or else, my brothers, or else?"

Nietzsche liked this lyrical page; he placed it at the end of his book as a final hymn. "What other book," he wrote, "concludes with an Or Else?"

By the end of January he had finished his work. But he was not able to re-copy his manuscript; his hand was too nervous, his eyesight too weak. He sent it on to Peter Gast. On the 13th of March the copy was ready, and Nietzsche announced it to the publisher.

---

[8] *The Dawn of Day,* p. 301. This passage is taken from Miss Johanna Volz's translation. London: T. Fisher Unwin.

"Here is the manuscript, from which I find it hard to part.... Now, hurry, hurry, hurry! I shall leave Genoa as soon as the book is out, and till then I shall live on cinders. Be quick, hurry up the printer! Can't he give you a written promise that by the end of April, at the latest, I shall have my book in hand, ready, complete? ... My dear Herr Schmeitzner, let us all, for this once, do our best. The contents of my book are so important! It is a matter involving our honour that it be faulty in nothing, that it come into the world worthy and stainless. I conjure you, do that for me; no advertising. I could tell you a great deal more about it, but you will be able to understand it all by yourself when you have read my book."

The publisher read the manuscript, but understood it ill; he displayed no enthusiasm. In April, Nietzsche, still at Genoa, was still waiting for his proofs. He had hoped to surprise his friends by despatching an unexpected piece of work, and had said nothing to anyone, Peter Gast excepted. At last he renounced the pleasure of having a secret. "Good news!" he wrote to his sister. "A new book, a big book, a decisive book! I cannot think of it without a lively emotion...." In May, he rejoined Peter Gast in a village of Venetia, Recoaro, at the foot of the Alps. His impatience grew every day. The delays of his publisher prevented him from clearing up the new thoughts which already pressed hard on him.

The Dawn of Day—this was the title which he finally selected—appeared at the most unfavourable time of the year, in July.

CHAPTER VI

THE LABOUR OF ZARATHUSTRA

I

The Conception of the Eternal Return

Friedrich Nietzsche regarded *The Dawn of Day* as the exercise of a convalescent who amuses himself with desires and ideas, and finds in each a malicious or a delightful pleasure. It had been a game which must have an end. I must now choose from among these half-perceived ideas, he thought, I must lay hold of one, express it in its full force, and close my years of retreat and hesitation. "In times of peace," he had written, "the man of warlike instinct turns against himself." Hardly done with his combats, he sought a new occasion for battle.

He had remained, up to mid-July, in Venetia, on the lower slopes of the Italian Alps. He had to seek a cooler refuge. He had not forgotten those high Alpine valleys which had given him, two years earlier, in his ill-health a respite and a rapid joy. He went up towards them and installed himself in a rustic fashion in the Engadine, at Sils-Maria. He had, for one franc a day, a room in a peasant house; a neighbouring inn furnished him with his meals. Passers by were rare, and Nietzsche, when he found himself in talkative humour, used to visit the curé or the schoolmaster. These good people always remembered this very singular German professor who was so learned, so modest, and so good.

He was then reflecting on the problems of naturalistic philosophy. Spencer's system had just come into vogue. Friedrich Nietzsche despised this cosmogony which affected to supplant Christianity and yet remained in submission to it. Spencer ignored Providence, yet believed in progress. He preached the reality of a concert between the movements of things and the aspirations of humanity. He preserved the Christian harmonies in a God-less universe. Friedrich Nietzsche had been a pupil at more virile schools; he heard Empedocles, Heraclitus, Spinoza, Goethe, thinkers who with a calm regard could study Nature without seeking in her some assent to their longings. He remained obedient to these masters, and he felt growing and ripening in him a great and a new idea.

We can divine from his letters the emotion with which he was seized. He needed to be alone, and energetically defended his solitude. Paul Rée, who admired *The Dawn,* wished to go to him and tell him so. Friedrich Nietzsche learnt this and was in despair.

"MY GOOD LISBETH," he wrote to his sister, "I cannot make up my mind to telegraph to Rée not to come. Nevertheless, I must consider him an enemy who comes to interrupt my summer's work, my work in the Engadine, that is to say my duty itself, my 'one thing necessary.' A man here, in the middle of all these thoughts which gush out from all sides within me—it would be a terrible thing; and if I cannot defend my solitude better, I leave Europe for many years, I swear it! I have no more time to lose."

Fräulein Nietzsche forewarned Paul Rée, who abandoned his project.

At length he found it, the idea, the presentiment of which had agitated him with such violence. One day, when he was going across the wood of Sils-Maria as far as Silvaplana, he sat down not far from Surlei at the foot of a pyramidal rock; at this moment and in this place he conceived the Eternal Return. He thought: Time, whose duration is infinite, must bring back, from period to period, an identical disposition of things. This is necessary; therefore it is necessary that all things return. In a number of days that is unforeseeable, immense, yet limited, a man like to me in everything, myself in fact, seated in the shade of this rock, will again find in this very place this very idea. And this very idea will be rediscovered by this man not once only, but an infinite number of times, for this movement which brings things back is infinite. Therefore we must throw all hope aside and think resolutely: no celestial world will receive men, no better future will console them. We are the shadows of a blind and monotonous nature, the prisoners of every moment. But beware! this redoubtable idea which forbids hope ennobles and exalts every minute of our lives; the moment is no longer a passing thing, if it come back eternally; the least thing is an eternal monument endowed with infinite value, and, if the word "divine" has any sense, divine. "Let everything return ceaselessly," he wrote, "it is the extreme *rapprochement* of a world of becoming with a world of being: summit of meditation."[9]

The emotion of the discovery was so strong that he wept, and remained for a long time bathed in tears. So his effort had not been in vain. Without weakening before reality, without withdrawing from pessimism, but, on the contrary, leading the pessimistic idea to its final consequences, Nietzsche had discovered this doctrine of the Return, which, by conferring eternity on the most fugitive things, restores in each of them the lyrical power, the religious value necessary to the soul. In a few lines he formulated the idea, and dated it: "the beginning of August, 1881, at Sils-Maria, 6,500 feet above the sea and far more than that above all human things!"

He lived for some weeks in a condition of rapture and of anguish: no doubt the mystics knew similar emotions, and their vocabulary suits his case. He experienced a divine pride; but simultaneously recoiled in fear and trembling, like those prophets of Israel before God receiving from Him the function of their mission. The unhappy man, who had been so wounded by life, faced with an indescribable horror the perpetuity of the Return. It was an insupportable expectation, a torment; but he loved this torment, and he forced this idea of the Eternal Return on himself as an ascetic does martyrdom. "Lux mea crux," he wrote in his notes, "crux mea lux! Light my

---

[9] This formula is given in the *Wille zur Macht*, paragraph 286.

cross, cross my light!" His agitation, which time did not appease, became extreme. He grew alarmed, for he was not unaware of the danger which lay over his life.

"On my horizon thoughts rise, and what thoughts!" he wrote to Peter Gast on the 14th of August. "I did not suspect anything of this kind. I say no more of it, I wish to maintain a resolute calm. Alas, my friend, presentiments sometimes cross my mind. It seems to me that I am leading a very dangerous life, for my machine is one of those which may GO SMASH! The intensity of my sentiments makes me shudder and laugh —twice already I have had to stay in my room, and for a ridiculous reason; my eyes were inflamed, why? Because while I walked I had cried too much; not sentimental tears, but tears of joy; and I sang and said idiotic things, being full of a new idea which I must proffer to men...."

Then he conceived a new task. All that he had hitherto done was but an awkward experiment or research; the time was come when he should erect the structure of his work. Of what work? He hesitated: his gifts as an artist, as a critic, as a philosopher, seduced him in various directions. Should he put his doctrine in the form of a system? No, it was a symbol and must be surrounded with poetry and rhythm. Could he not renew that forgotten form which was created by the thinkers of the most ancient Greece? Lucretius had handed down the model. Friedrich Nietzsche welcomed this idea; it would please him to translate his conception of nature into poetic language, into musical and measured prose. He sought, and his desire for a rhythmical language, for a living and, as it were, palpable form, suggested a new thought to him: could he not introduce at the centre of his work a human and prophetic figure, a hero? A name occurred to him; Zarathustra, the Persian apostle, the mystagogue of fire. A title, a subtitle, four lines rapidly written, announced the poem:

MIDDAY AND ETERNITY

Sign of a New Life

"Zarathustra, born on the borders of Lake Urumiyah, left his country when thirty years old, went towards the province of Aria, and in ten years of solitude composed the Zend-Avesta."

Henceforward his walks and meditations were no longer solitary. Friedrich Nietzsche never ceased to hear and gather the words of Zarathustra. In three distiches of a soft and almost tender seduction he tells how this companion entered into his life:

Sils-Maria

I sat there waiting—waiting for nothing, Enjoying, beyond good and evil, now The light, now the shade; there was only The day, the lake, the noon, time without end. Then, my friend, suddenly one became two—And Zarathustra passed by me.

In September the weather suddenly became cold and snowy. Friedrich Nietzsche had to leave the Engadine.

The intemperate weather had tried him; he lost his exaltation, and a long period of depression set in. He constantly thought of the Eternal Return, but now, having lost courage, he only felt a horror of it. "I have lived again through the days at Basle," he wrote to Peter Gast. "Over my shoulder death looks at me." His complaints are brief; a word is enough to let us divine the abysses. Thrice, during these weeks of September and October, he was tempted to suicide. "Whence came this temptation? It was not that he wished to avoid suffering; he was brave. Did he then wish to prevent the ruin of his intellect? This second hypothesis is perhaps the true one.

He stopped at Genoa. The damp winds and the lowering skies of the capricious autumn continued to try him. He bore impatiently with the absence of light. A melancholy of another kind complicated his trouble: *The Dawn of Day* had had no success. The critics had ignored the work, his friends had read it with difficulty; Jacob Burckhardt had expressed a polite but prudent judgment. "Certain parts of your book," he wrote, "I read like an old man, with a feeling of vertigo." Erwin Rohde, the dearest, the most esteemed, had not acknowledged the receipt of the book. Friedrich Nietzsche wrote to him from Genoa on October 21st:

"DEAR OLD FRIEND,—No doubt some embarrassment delays you. I pray you, in all sincerity, not to write! There will be no change in our mutual sentiments; I cannot bear to think that in sending a book to a friend I exercise upon him a sort of pressure. What matters a book! What I have still to do matters more—or why should I live? The moment is bitter, I suffer much. Cordially your "F. N."

Erwin Rohde did not answer even this letter. How explain the want of success of *The Dawn?* Doubtless it is a very old story, the constant, the universal, the irremediable misadventure of the unrecognised genius because he is a genius, a novelty, a surprise, and a scandal. Nevertheless we may, perhaps, grasp some definite reasons. Nietzsche, since he had withdrawn from the Wagnerian circle, had no more friends; and a group of friends is the most indispensable intermediary between a great mind which is trying its skill and the mass of the public. He is alone before unknown readers, who are disconcerted by his incessant variations. He hopes that the lively form of his work will capture and conquer them. But even the form is unfavourable. No book has so difficult an address as a collection of aphorisms and brief thoughts. The reader must give all his attention to every page and decipher an enigma; lassitude comes quickly. Besides, it is probable that a German public, with little feeling for the art of prose, unskilful in grasping its features, accustomed to slow and sustained effort, was ill-prepared to understand this unforeseen work.

November was fine; Friedrich Nietzsche recovered his spirits. "I lift myself above my disasters," he wrote He wandered over the mountains of the Genoese coast, he returned to the rocks on which had come to him the prose of *The Dawn*. Such was the mildness of the weather that he could bathe in the sea. "I feel so rich, so proud," he wrote to Peter Gast, "altogether *principe Doria*. I miss only you, dear friend, you and your music!"

Since the representations of the *Nibelungen* at Bayreuth—that is, for five years—Friedrich Nietzsche had deprived himself of music. *Cave musicam!* he wrote. He feared that if he abandoned himself to the delight in sound he would be recaptured by the magic of Wagnerian art. But he was finally delivered from these fears. His friend Peter Gast had played him, in June, at Recoaro, songs and choruses which he had amused himself in composing on the epigrams of Goethe. Paul Rée had said one day, "No modern musician would be capable of putting to music such slight verses." Peter Gast had taken up the challenge and won, thought Nietzsche, who was ravished by the vivacity of the rhythm. "Persevere," he advised his friend; "work against Wagner the musician, as I work against Wagner the philosopher. Let us try, Rée, you and I, to free Germany. If you succeed in finding a music suited to the universe of Goethe (it does not exist), you will have done a great thing." This thought reappears in each of his letters. His friend is at Venice, he is at Genoa, and he hopes that this winter Italy will inspire in them both, the two uprooted Germans, a new metaphysic and a new music.

He took advantage of his improved health to go to the theatre. He listened to the *Semiramis* of Rossini, and four times to the *Juliette* of Bellini. One evening he was curious to hear a French work, the author being unknown to him:

"Hurrah! dear friend," he wrote to Peter Gast, "another happy discovery, an opera of Georges Bizet (who is he, then?), *Carmen*. It is like a story of Mérimée's, clever, powerful, sometimes touching. A true French talent which Wagner has not misguided, a frank disciple of Berlioz.... I almost think that *Carmen* is the best opera which exists. As long as we live it will remain in all the repertoires of Europe."

The discovery of *Carmen* was the event of his winter. Many times he spoke of it, many times he returned to it; when he heard this frank and impassioned music, he felt better armed against the romantic seductions which were always powerful in his soul. "*Carmen* delivers me," he was to write.

Friedrich Nietzsche again found the happiness which he had enjoyed in the preceding year; a like happiness, but sustained by a graver kind of emotion: the full midday of his thought rose after the dawn. Towards the end of December he passed a crisis and surmounted it. A sort of poem in prose commemorated this crisis. We will translate it here. It is the consequence of his meditations, of those examinations of conscience which he used to write down, as a young man, each Saint Sylvester's Day:

"*For the New Year.*—I still live, I still think: I must still live, for I must still think. *Sum, ergo cogito: cogito, ergo sum.* This is the day upon which every one is permitted to express his desire and his dearest thought: I, too, shall then express the inner wish which I form to-day, and say what thought I take to heart, this year, before all other—what thought I have chosen as the reason, guarantee, and sweetness of my life to come! I wish to try each day to see in all things necessity as a beauty—thus shall I be one of those who make things beautiful. *Amor fati,* let that be henceforward my love! I do not wish to go to battle against the hideous. I do not wish to accuse, I do not even wish to accuse the accusers. *To avert my gaze,* let that be my sole negation. In a word, I wish to be, in every circumstance, a Yea-Sayer!"

The thirty days of January passed without a cloud appearing in the sky. He was to dedicate to this fine month, as a sign of gratitude, the fourth book of the *Gay Science,* which he entitled *Sanctus Januarius;* an admirable book rich in critical thought, in intimate refinements, and from the first to the last line dominated by a sacred emotion—*Amor fati.*

In February Paul Rée, passing through Genoa, stayed some days with his friend, who showed him his favourite walks and brought him to those rocky creeks "where in some six hundred years, some thousand years," he wrote gaily to Peter Gast, "they will raise a statue to the author of *The Dawn"* Then Paul Rée went on to Rome, where Fräulein von Meysenbug was waiting for him. He had a curiosity to penetrate into the Wagnerian world there, which was greatly excited in expectation of *Parsifal;* it was in July, at Bayreuth, that the Christian mystery was to be presented. Friedrich Nietzsche did not wish to accompany Paul Rée, and the approaching performance of the *Parsifal* only made his ardour for work the more active. Had he not—he, too—a great work which he must ripen? Had he not to write his anti-Christian mystery, his poem of the Eternal Return? It was his constant thought. It procured him a happiness, thanks to which he could recall with less torturing regret the master of by-gone days. Richard Wagner seemed very far and very near; very far as regards his ideas, but what are ideas worth to a poet? Very near in sentiments, desires, lyrical emotion; and were not these the essential things? All disaccord between poets is only a question of shades, for they inhabit the same universe, they work with a like heart to give a significance and a supreme value to the movements of the human soul. Reading this page which Nietzsche then wrote, it is easier to understand the condition of his mind:

"*Stellar Friendship.*—We were friends, and we have become strangers to each other. Ah, yes; but it is well so, and we wish to hide nothing, to disguise nothing from one another; we have nothing to be ashamed of. We are two ships, each with a bourne and a way. By chance we have crossed paths; we have made holiday together—and then our two good ships have so tranquilly reposed in the one port and under the same sun, that it seemed as though they had both attained their bourne. But the all-powerful force of our mission has driven us afresh towards divers seas and suns—and perhaps we shall not meet, or recognise one another again: the divers seas and suns will have transformed us! We had to become strangers; a reason the more why we should mutually respect ourselves! No doubt there exists a far off, invisible and prodigious cycle which gives a common law to our little divagations: let us uplift ourselves to this thought! But our life is too short, our vision too feeble; we must content ourselves with this sublime possibility. And if we must be enemies upon earth, in spite of all we believe in our stellar friendship."

What form did the poetical exposition of the Eternal Return then take in his soul? We do not know. Nietzsche did not care to talk about his work; he liked to complete it before making announcements. However, he wished that his friends should know the new movement in which his thought was engaged. He addressed to Fräulein von Meysenbug a letter in which Wagner was treated without deference, then he added a mysterious enough promise: "If I am not illusioned as to my future, it is by my work that what is best in the work of Wagner will be continued—and here, perhaps, is the comical side to the adventure."

At the beginning of spring Friedrich Nietzsche, following out a caprice, made a bargain with the captain of an Italian sailing vessel bound for Messina and crossed the Mediterranean. The passage was a terrible one, and he was sick to death. But his stay was at first happy: he wrote verses, a pleasure which he had not known for several years. They are impromptus and epigrams, perhaps inspired by those Goethean sallies which Peter Gast had put to music. Nietzsche then sought for a corner of nature and of humanity favourable to the production of his great work: Sicily, "Curb of the world where Happiness has her habitation," as old Homer teaches, struck him as an ideal refuge, and, suddenly forgetting that he could not bear the heat, he decided to stay in Messina for the whole summer. Some days of sirocco, towards the end of April, prostrated him, and he prepared for departure. It was in these circumstances that he received a message from Fräulein von Meysenbug, who urged him very keenly to stop at Rome. Rome was a natural stage on his journey, and he accepted. Why was Fräulein von Meysenbug thus insistent? We know. This excellent woman had never been resigned to the unhappiness of the friend whose destiny she had vainly sought to sweeten. She knew the delicacy, the tenderness of his heart, and often wished to find him a companion; had he not written to her, "I tell you in confidence, what I need is a good woman"? In the spring of this year she thought that she had found her.[10]

This accounted for her letter. It was Fräulein von Meysenbug's habit to do good, and her taste; but perhaps she sometimes forgot that goodness is a difficult art in which the results of defeat are cruel.

The girl whom Fräulein von Meysenbug had met was called Lou Salomé. She was scarcely twenty years old; she was a Russian and admirable as regards her intelligence

[10] This intimate history has never been known except to a few people, who are now, for the most part, out of our ken. Two women survive: one, Frau Förster-Nietzsche, has published some accounts which one would wish were more lucid and tranquil; the other, Miss Salomé, has written a book on Friedrich Nietzsche in which some facts are indicated and some letters cited; she has refused to enter into polemics on a subject which, as she considers, concerns herself alone. Oral traditions are numerous and contradictory. Some, rife in Roman society, where the adventure took place, are less favourable to Miss Salomé; she appears as a sort of Marie Bashkirtseff, an intellectual adventuress who was somewhat too enterprising. Others, rife in Germany among Miss Salomé's friends, are very different. We have heard all these traditions. The first have influenced the account which we have given in the *Cahiers de la quinzaine,* the second volume of the tenth series, pp. 24 *et seq.;* the second, which we learned later, we now prefer. But all hope of certainty must be adjourned.

and intellectual ardour; her beauty was not perfect, but the more exquisite for its imperfections, and she was fascinating in the extreme. Sometimes it happens that there arises, in Paris, in Florence, in Rome, some excited young lady, a native of Philadelphia, of Bucharest, or of Kief, who comes with a barbarous impatience to be initiated into culture and to conquer a hearth in our old capital. The lady in question was of rare quality assuredly; her mother followed her across Europe, carrying the cloaks and the shawls.

Fräulein von Meysenbug conceived an affection for her. She gave her Nietzsche's works; Lou Salomé read them and seemed to understand. She talked to her at great length of this extraordinary man who had sacrificed friendship with Wagner for the maintenance of his liberty: He is a very rugged philosopher, she said, but he is the most sensitive, the most affectionate friend, and, for those who know him, the thought of his solitary life is a source of sadness. Miss Salomé displayed a great deal of enthusiasm and longing; she declared that she felt vowed to a spiritual share in such a life, and that she wished to make Nietzsche's acquaintance. In concert with Paul Rée, who, it seems, had known her for a longer time, and also appreciated her, Fräulein von Meysenbug wrote to Friedrich Nietzsche.

He arrived, he heard the praises of Miss Lou sung; she was a woman of elevated feeling, shrewd and brave; intransigent in research and in affirmation; a heroine in the manner of her childhood; it was the promise of a great life. He agreed to see her. One morning, at St. Peter's, she was presented to him and conquered him at once. He had forgotten, during his long months of meditation, the pleasure of being listened to and of talking. "The young Russian" (it is thus that he calls her in his letters) listened deliciously. She spoke little, but her calm look, her assured and gentle movements, her least words, left no doubt as to the quickness of her mind and to the presence of a soul. Very quickly, perhaps at first sight, Nietzsche liked her. "There's a soul," he said to Fräulein von Meysenbug, "which has made a little body for itself with a breath."[11] Miss Salomé did not let herself be thus enticed. Nevertheless, she felt the singular quality of the man who talked to her; she had long conversations with him, and the violence of his thought troubled her even in her sleep. The adventure—it was in fact a drama—commenced at once.

A few days after this first interview, Miss Salomé and her mother left Rome. The two philosophers, Nietzsche and Rée, went with her, both of them enthusiasts for the young girl. Nietzsche said to Rée:

"There's an admirable woman, marry her." "No," answered Rée; "I am a pessimist, and the idea of propagating human life is odious to me. Marry her yourself; she is the companion that you want...." Nietzsche dismissed this idea. Perhaps he said to his friend, as he had said to his sister: "I marry! Never, I would have to be a bar somewhere or other." Miss Salomé's mother examined these two men who were so attentive to her child; Friedrich Nietzsche perplexed her; she preferred Paul Rée.

---

[11] "Da ist eine Seele welche sich mit einen Hauch eine Körperchen geschaffen hat."

The two friends and the two philosophers stopped at Lucerne. Friedrich Nietzsche wished to show his new friend that house at Triebschen where he had known Richard Wagner. Who was not then thinking of the master? He brought her as far as the poplars whose high foliage enclosed the gardens. He recounted to her the unforgettable days, the gaieties, the magnificent angers of the great man. Seated by the border of the lake, he talked in a low, contained voice, and turned his face a little away, for it was troubled by the memory of those joys of which he had deprived himself. Suddenly he grew silent, and the young girl, observing him, saw that he wept.

He confessed all his life to her; his childhood, the pastor's house, the mysterious grandeur of the father who had been so quickly taken away; the pious years, the first doubts, and the horror of this world without a God in which one must resolve to live; the discovery of Schopenhauer and of Wagner, the religious feeling which they had inspired in him and which had consoled him for the loss of his faith.

"Yes," said he (Miss Salomé reports these words), "my adventures began in this manner. They are not ended. Where will they lead me? Whither shall I adventure again? Should I not come back to the faith? to some new belief?"

He added gravely: "In any case a return to the past is more likely than immobility."

Friedrich Nietzsche had not yet avowed his love; but he felt its force and no longer resisted. Only he feared to declare himself. He begged Paul Rée to speak in his name, and withdrew.

On the 8th of May, settled for some days in Basle, he saw the Overbecks and confided in them with a strange exaltation. A woman has come into his life; it is a happiness for him; it will benefit his thought, which will henceforward be livelier, richer in its shades and emotion. Assuredly he would prefer not to marry Miss Lou, he disdains all fleshly ties; but perhaps he ought to give her his name for her protection against scandalmongers, and from this spiritual union would be born a spiritual son: the prophet Zarathustra. He is poor; this is a vexation, an obstacle. But could he not sell all his future work in a lump to some publisher for a considerable sum? He thought of doing so. These out-bursts did not fail to trouble the Overbecks, who augured ill of a liaison so bizarre and of an enthusiasm so ready.

Friedrich Nietzsche at last received Lou Salomé's reply: she did not wish to marry. An unhappy love affair, which had just crossed her life, left her, she said, without strength to conceive and nourish a new affection. She therefore refused Nietzsche's offer. But she was able to sweeten the terms of this refusal: the only thing of which she could dispose, her friendship, her spiritual affection, she offered.

Friedrich Nietzsche returned at once to Lucerne. He saw Lou Salomé and pressed her to give a more favourable reply; but the young girl repeated her refusal and her offer. She was to be present in July at the Bayreuth festivals, from which Nietzsche wished to abstain. She promised to rejoin him when they were over and to stay for some weeks at his side. She would then listen to his teaching, she would confront the last thought of the master with that of the liberated disciple. Nietzsche had finally to accept these conditions, these limits which the young girl placed on their friendship. He advised her to read one of his books, *Schopenhauer as Educator*. He was always glad to acknowledge this work of his youth, this hymn to the bravery of a thinker and to voluntary solitude. "Read it," he said to her, "and you will be ready to hear me."

Friedrich Nietzsche left Basle and re-entered Germany, desirous of becoming reconciled to his country. He was, as we know, accustomed to such absorbing and unexpected desires. A Swiss, whom he had met at Messina, had praised the beauty of Grunewald, near Berlin; he wished to settle there, and wrote to Peter Gast, to whom, six weeks earlier, he had suggested as a summer residence Messina.

He went to visit this Grunewald, which pleased him well enough; but he saw, on the same occasion, Berlin and a few Berliners, who displeased him extremely. He perceived that his last books had not been read, and that his thought was ignored. He was only known as the friend of Paul Rée, and no doubt his disciple. This he did not like. He went without delay to spend some weeks in Naumburg, where he dictated the manuscript of his coming book, *La Gaya Scienza*[12]. To his own people, it seems, to his mother and to his sister, he spoke discreetly of the new friend. His gaiety amazed them: they did not discern its cause. They did not know that their strange Friedrich had in his heart a sentiment, a hope of happiness, which Lou Salomé had been far from discouraging.

The representation of *Parsifal* was fixed for the 27th July. Friedrich Nietzsche went to stay in a village of the Thuringian forests, Tautenburg, not far from Bayreuth, where all his friends were to foregather: the Overbecks, the Seydlitzs, Gersdorff, Fräulein von Meysenbug, Lou Salomé, Lisbeth Nietzsche. He alone was absent from the rendezvous. At this moment a word from the master would perhaps have sufficed to bring him back; perhaps he waited for and hoped for this word. Fräulein von Meysenbug wished to make an attempt at reconciliation: she dared to name Nietzsche in Wagner's presence. Wagner told her to be silent and went out of the room banging the door.

So Friedrich Nietzsche, who no doubt never knew of this overture, remained in those forests in which he had spent such hard days in 1876. How miserable he had then been and now how rich he was! He had repressed his doubts; a great thought animated his mind, a great affection his heart. Lou Salomé had just dedicated to him, as a sign of spiritual sympathy, a beautiful poem.

TO SORROW.

Wer kann dich fliehn, den du ergriffen hast,
Wenn du die ernsten Bliche auf ihn richtest?

---

[12] The *y* in the word *Gaya* does not seem to be Italian. We follow Nietzsche's orthography.

Ich will nicht flüchten, wenn du mich erfasst,
Ich glaube nimmer, dass du nur vernichtest!

Ich weiss, durch jedes Erden—Dasein muss du gehn,
Und nichts bleibt unberührt von dir auf Erden:
Das Leben ohne dich—es wäre schön,
Und doch—auch, du bist werth, gelebt zu werden.[13]

Peter Gast, having read these verses, thought they were Nietzsche's, who rejoiced over his error.

"No," he wrote to him, "this poetry is not by my hand. It is one of the things which exercise upon me a tyrannical power, I have never been able to read it without tears; it has the accent of a voice which I might have waited for, expected since my childhood. My friend Lou, of whom you have not yet heard, has written it. Lou is the daughter of a Russian general, she is twenty years old; her mind is as piercing as an eagle's vision, she has the courage of a lion, and yet she is a very feminine child, who, perhaps, will hardly live...."

He re-read his manuscript for the last time and sent it to the printer. He hesitated a little at the moment of publishing this new collection of aphorisms. His friends, as he knew, would find fault with these too numerous volumes, these too brief essays, these scarcely formed sketches. He listened to them, heard what they had to say, answered them with an apparent good will. No doubt his modesty was feigned; he could not bring himself to believe that his essays, short though they were, his sketches, which were so weak in form, were not worth being read.

He thought much of the Bayreuth festivals, but he dissembled or only half avowed his regrets. "I am well content that I cannot go," he wrote to Lou Salomé. "And, nevertheless, if I could be at your side, in good humour to talk; if I could say in your ear this, that, well, I could endure the music of the *Parsifal* (otherwise I could not)."

Parsifal triumphed. Nietzsche mockingly welcomed the news. "Long live Cagliostro!" he wrote to Peter Gast. "The old enchanter has again had a prodigious success; the old gentlemen sobbed."

The "young Russian" came to rejoin him as soon as the festivals were over; Lisbeth Nietzsche accompanied her. The two ladies installed themselves in the hotel where Friedrich Nietzsche awaited them; then he undertook to initiate his friend.

She had heard the Christian mystery at Bayreuth, the history of human sorrow traversed like an ordeal and consoled at last by beatitude. Friedrich Nietzsche taught her a more tragic mystery: sorrow is our life and our destiny itself; let us not hope to

---

[13] "Who that hath once been seized by thee can fly, if he hath felt thy grave look turned on him? I shall not save myself, if thou takest me, I shall never believe thou dost naught but destroy. Yea, thou must visit all that liveth upon earth, nothing upon earth can evade thy grip: life without thee—it were beautiful, yet—thou too art worthy to be lived."

traverse it; let us accept it more entirely than the Christians ever did! Let us espouse it; let us love it with an active love; let us be, like it, ardent and pitiless; hard to others as to ourselves; cruel, let us accept it; brutal, let us accept it. To lessen it is to be cowardly; and let us meditate on the symbol of the Eternal Return to practise our courage. "Unforgettable for me are those hours in which he revealed to me his thoughts," wrote Miss Salomé. "He confided them to me, as though they were a mystery unspeakably hard to tell; he only spoke of them in a low voice, with every appearance of the most profound horror. And truly life had been for him such bitter suffering that he suffered from the Eternal Return as from an atrocious certainty." That Miss Salomé listened to these confessions with great intelligence and real emotion, the pages which she afterwards wrote assure us.

She conceived a brief hymn which she dedicated to Friedrich Nietzsche:

"As friend loves friend,
So love I thee, life surprising!
Do I weep or joy in thee,
Givest thou me joy or suffering,
I love thee with thy joy and pain.
And if thou must destroy me,
I shall suffer, leaving thee.
As the friend who teareth himself from the arms of the friend,
I caress thee with my whole strength:
Hast thou no other joy for me?
So be it, I have still—thy suffering."

Friedrich Nietzsche, delighted with the gift, wished to reply to it by another gift. For eight years he had forbidden himself musical composition, which enervated and exhausted him. He undertook to compose a sorrowful dithyramb on the verses of Miss Salomé. This work was too moving and caused him great pain: neuralgia, crises of doubt, barrenness and satiety. He had to take to his bed. Even from his room he addressed short notes to Lou Salomé. "In bed, terrible attack. *I scorn life.*"

But these weeks at Tautenburg had their secret history of which we know little. Lou Salomé, writes Fräulein Nietzsche, was never the sincere friend of her brother; he roused her curiosity, but her passion, her enthusiasm, were only feigned, and she was often wearied by his terrible agitation. She wrote to Paul Rée, from whom Fräulein Nietzsche was surprised to receive a very singular message: "Your brother," he said, "tires our friend; shorten, if it be possible, the meeting."

We are inclined to think that Fräulein Nietzsche was jealous of this initiation which she had not received, jealous, too, of this young Slav, whose charm was tinged with mystery, and that we must take what she has to say with caution.

No doubt, Nietzsche alarmed Lou Salomé by the violence of his passions and by the loftiness of his demands. She had not foreseen, in offering to be his friend, the crises of a friendship ruder than a stormy love. He demanded an absolute assent to each of his thoughts. The young girl refused such assent: may the intellect, like the heart, be given? Nietzsche could not brook her proud reserve, and reproached her, as though it were a fault, for the independence which she wished to preserve. A letter to Peter Gast gives us a glimpse into these disputes.

"Lou remains another week with me," he wrote, on the 20th of August, from Tautenburg. "She is *the most intelligent of all women.* Every five days a little tragical scene arises between us. All that I have written to you about her is absurd, and not less absurd, no doubt, than what I now write to you."

This somewhat cautious and reticent phrasing does not suggest that the heart had escaped its captivity. Lou Salomé left Tautenburg; Friedrich Nietzsche continued to write letters to her, many of which are known to us. He confided his work and projects to Lou Salomé: he wished to go to Paris or Vienna to study the physical sciences and deepen his theory of the Eternal Return; for it was not enough that it should be fascinating and beautiful, Nietzsche wished that it should be true. Thus we saw him, and always will see him, hampered by his critical spirit when he pursues a lyrical inspiration; hampered by his lyrical genius when he pursues a critical analysis. He related to her the happy success of the *Hymn to Life* which her verses had inspired, and which he was submitting to the judgment of his musical friends. An orchestral conductor gave him hope of a hearing: ready for hope as he was, he communicated the news. "By this little path," he writes, "we can reach posterity *together*—all other paths remaining open." On September 16th he wrote from Leipsic to Peter Gast. "Latest news: on the 2nd of October Lou comes here; two months later we leave for Paris; and we shall stay there, perhaps for years. Such are my projects."

His mother and sister blamed him; he knew it, and their hostility did not displease him: "All the virtues of Naumburg are against me," he wrote, "it is well that it is so ..."

Two months later, the friendship was broken. Perhaps we may perceive what had happened. Lou Salomé came to find Nietzsche at Leipsic, as she had promised; but Paul Rée accompanied her. No doubt she wished Nietzsche to understand once and for all the nature of a friendship which was always open to him: free, not slavish; sympathy, not intellectual devotion. Had she well weighed the difficulties of such an enterprise, the dangers of such an attempt? These two men were in love with her. What was her attitude between them? May she not have yielded, when she tried to keep them both by her, to some instinct, perhaps an unconscious one, of intellectual curiosity, of conquest and feminine domination? Who can say, who will ever know?

Friedrich Nietzsche became melancholy and suspicious. One day he imagined that his companions, talking together under their breath, were laughing at him. A piece of gossip reached him, and upset his mind. The story, puerile though it be, must be told. Rée, Nietzsche, and Lou Salomé had been photographed together. Lou Salomé and

Rée had said to Nietzsche: "Get into this child's cart: we will hold the shafts; it will be a symbol of our union." Nietzsche had answered: "I refuse; Miss Lou will be in the cart; we will hold the shafts, Paul Rée and I." This Miss Lou did. And she (according to the story repeated to him) sent the photograph to numerous friends, as a symbol of her supremacy.

A more cruel thought soon began to torture Friedrich Nietzsche: Lou and Rée are in agreement against me, he thought; their agreement condemns them, they love one another and are deceiving me. Then all became poor and vile around him. A miserable strife terminated the spiritual adventure of which he had dreamed. He lost his strange and seductive disciple; he lost the best and most intelligent friend of his last eight years. Finally, affected and impaired by these humiliating conditions, he himself did a wrong to friendship and denounced Rée to Lou.

"He has a marvellous mind," he said, "but it is feeble and aimless. His education is the cause of the trouble: every man should have been brought up in some sort for a soldier. And every woman, in some sort, for a soldier's wife."

Nietzsche had neither the experience nor the necessary resolution to decide an infinitely painful situation. His sister, who detested Miss Salomé, encouraged his suspicions and his rancours. She intervened in a brutal manner, and, it seems, without authorisation, wrote the young girl a letter which determined the rupture. Miss Salomé was angry. We have the rough draft of the last letter which Friedrich Nietzsche addressed to her; it throws little light on the detail of these difficulties.

"But, Lou, what letters yours are! A little angry schoolgirl writes in this way. What have I got to do with these bickerings? Understand me: I wish you to rise in my opinion; not to sink again.

"I only reproach you for this: you ought to have sooner given an account of what I expected from you. At Lucerne I gave you my essay on Schopenhauer—I told you that my views were essentially there, and that I believed that they would also be yours. Then you should have read and said: No (in such matters I hate all *superficiality*). You would have spared me much! Your poem, 'Sorrow,' written by you, is a profound counter-truth.

"I believe that no one thinks more good things of you than I do, or more bad. Do not defend yourself: I have already defended you, to myself and to others, better than you could do it. Creatures like you are only bearable to others when they have a *lofty object.*

"How poor you are in veneration, in gratitude, in piety, in courtesy, in admiration, in delicacy—I do not speak of higher things. How would you answer if I asked you: Are you brave? Are you incapable of treason?

"Do you not then feel that when a man like myself approaches you, he needs to constrain himself very greatly? You have had to do with one of the most for-bearing and benevolent of men possible: but against petty egoism and little weaknesses, my argument, know it well, is *disgust*. No one is so easily conquered by disgust as I. I have not deceived myself again on any point whatsoever; I saw in you that holy egoism which forces us to serve what is highest in us. I do not know by what sorcery's aid you have exchanged it for its contrary, the egoism of the cat, which only desires life.

"Farewell, dear Lou, I shall not see you again. Protect your soul from like deeds, and succeed better with others in regard to things that, so far as I am concerned, are irreparable.

"I have not read your letter to the end, but I have read too much of it. Your,

"F. N."

Friedrich Nietzsche left Leipsic.

II

Thus Spake Zarathustra

His departure was prompt, like a flight. He passed through Basle and stopped with his friends the Overbecks, who listened to his plaint. He had awakened from his last dream; everyone had betrayed him: Lou, Rée, feeble and perfidious; Lisbeth, his sister, who had acted grossly. Of what betrayal did he complain, and of what act? He did not say, and continued his bitter complaints. The Overbecks wished him to stay with them for some days. He escaped them; he wished to work, and surmount alone the sadness of having been deceived, the humiliation of having deceived himself. Perhaps he also wished to put to profit that condition of paroxysm and the lyrical *sursum* whither his despair had carried him. He left. "To-day," said he to his friends, "I enter into a complete solitude."

He left, and stopped in the first instance at Genoa. "Cold, sick. I suffer," he wrote briefly to Peter Gast. He left this town, where he was importuned perhaps by memories of a happier time, and moved away along the coast. At the time of which we speak, Nervi, Santa Margherita, Rapallo, Zoagli, were places unknown to the tourist, market towns inhabited by fishermen who, each evening, drew in their barques to the recesses of the coves and sang as they mended their nets. Friedrich Nietzsche discovered these magnificent spots, and chose, to humiliate his misery there, the most magnificent of them, Rapallo. He relates, in simple language, the circumstances of his sojourn:

"I spent my winter, 1882 to 1883, in the charming and quiet bay of Rapallo that is hollowed out by the Mediterranean not far from Genoa, between the promontory of Portofino and Chiavari. My health was not of the best; the winter was cold, rainy; a little inn,[14] situated at the very edge of the sea, so near it that the noise of the waves prevented me sleeping at night, offered me a shelter very unsatisfactory from all points

---

[14] Albergo la Poata (information given by M Lanzky).

of view. Nevertheless—and it is an instance of my maxim that all that is decisive comes 'nevertheless '—it was during this winter and in this discomfort that my noble Zarathustra was born. In the morning I would climb towards the south by the magnificent mountain road, towards Zoagli, among the pines and dominating the immense sea; in the evening (according as my health permitted it) I would go round the bay of Santa Margherita as far as Portofino.... On these two roads came to me all the first part of Zarathustra (*fiel mir ein*); and more, Zarathustra himself, as type; more exactly he fell upon me (*überfiel mich*)...."

In ten weeks he conceived and completed his poem. It is a new work and, if one affects to follow the genesis of his thought, a surprising one. No doubt, he meditated a lyrical work, a sacred book. But the essential doctrine of this work was to be given by the idea of the Eternal Return. Now, in the first part of Zarathustra, the idea of the Eternal Return does not appear. Nietzsche follows a different and opposing idea, the idea of the Superman, the symbol of a real progress which modifies things, the promise of a possible escape beyond chance and fatality.

Zarathustra announces the Superman, he is the prophet of good tidings. He has discovered in his solitude a promise of happiness, he bears this promise; his strength is sweet and benevolent, he predicts a great future as the reward of a great work. Friedrich Nietzsche, in other times, will put a more bitter speech into his mouth. If one reads this first part, and takes care not to confound it with those which immediately follow, one will feel the sanctity, the frequent suavity of the accent.

Why this abandonment of the Eternal Return? Nietzsche does not write a word which throws light upon this mystery. Miss Lou Salomé tells us that at Leipsic, during his short studies, he had realised the impossibility of founding his hypothesis in reason. But this did not diminish the lyrical value of which he knew how to take advantage a year later; and this cannot explain, in any case, the appearance of a contrary idea. What are we to think? Perhaps his stoicism was vanquished by the betrayal of his two friends. "*In spite of all*," he wrote on December 3rd to Peter Gast, "I would not like to live these latter months over again." We know that he never ceased to experience in himself the efficacy of his thoughts. Incapable of enduring the cruel symbol, he did not think that he could sincerely offer it to men, and he invented a new symbol, Uebermensch, the Superman. "I do not desire a recommencement," he writes in his notes (*ich will das leben nicht wieder*). "How was I able to endure the idea? In creating, in fixing my view on the Superman, who says *yea* to life, I have myself tried to say *Yea*—alas!"

To the cry of his youth: *Ist Veredlung möglich?* (Is the ennobling of man possible?) Friedrich Nietzsche desires to reply, and to reply *Yes*. He wishes to believe in the Superman, and succeeds in doing so. He can grasp this hope; it suits the design of his work. What does he propose to himself? Among all the inclinations which urge him, this one is strong: to answer the *Parsifal*, to oppose work to work. Richard Wagner desired to depict humanity drawn from its languor by the Eucharistie mystery, the troubled blood of men renovated by the ever poured out blood of Christ.

Friedrich Nietzsche wishes to depict humanity saved from languor by the glorification of its own essence, by the virtues of a chosen and willing few which purify and renew its blood. Is this all his desire? Surely not. *Thus Spake Zarathustra* is more than an answer to the *Parsifal*. The origins of Nietzsche's thoughts are always grave and distant. What is his last wish? He desires to guide and direct the activity of men; he wishes to create their morals, assign to the humble their tasks, to the strong their duties and their commandments, and to raise them all towards a sublime destiny. As a child, as a youth, as a young man, he had this aspiration; at thirty-eight years of age, at this instant of crisis and of decision, he finds it again and desires to act. The Eternal Return no longer satisfies him: he cannot consent to live imprisoned in a blind nature. The idea of the Superman on the contrary captivates him: it is a principle of action, a hope of salvation.

What is the import of this idea? Is it a reality or a symbol? It is impossible to say. Nietzsche's mind is rapid and always oscillating. The vehemence of the inspiration which carries him along leaves him neither leisure nor strength to define. He hardly succeeds in understanding the ideas which agitate him, and interprets them himself in divers ways. At times, the Superman appears to him as a very serious reality. But more often, it seems, he neglects or disdains all literal belief, and his idea is no more than a lyrical phantasy with which he trifles for the sake of animating base humanity. It is an illusion, a useful and beneficent illusion, he would say, were he still a Wagnerian, dared he to re-adopt the vocabulary of his thirtieth year. Then he had liked to repeat the maxim from Schiller: *Dare to dream and to lie*. We may believe that the Superman is chiefly the dream and falsehood of a lyrical poet. Every species has its limits which it cannot transgress. Nietzsche knows this and writes it.

It was a painful labour. Friedrich Nietzsche, ill-disposed to conceive a hope, had frequent revolts against the task which he imposed on himself. Every morning on awakening from a sleep which chloral had rendered sweet, he rediscovered life with frightful bitterness. Conquered by melancholy and rancour, he wrote pages which he had at once to re-read attentively, to correct or erase. He dreaded these bad hours in which anger, seizing him like a vertigo, obscured his best thoughts. Then he would evoke his hero, Zarathustra, always noble, always serene, and seek from him some encouragement. Many a passage of his poem is the expression of this agony. Zarathustra speaks to him:

"Yea: I know thy danger. But by my love and hope, I conjure thee: reject not thy love and thy hope.

"The noble one is always in danger of becoming an insolent, a sneering one and a destroyer. Alas, I have known noble ones who lost their highest hope. Then they slandered all high hopes.

"By my love and my hope I conjure thee; do not cast
away the hero in thy soul! believe in the holiness of thy
highest hope."

The struggle was always perceptible; nevertheless Friedrich Nietzsche advanced his work. Every day he had to learn wisdom anew, and to moderate, crush, or deceive his desires. He succeeded in this rude exercise and managed to bring back his soul into a calm and fecund condition. He completed a poem which was but the opening of a vaster poem. Zarathustra, returning towards the mountains, abandons the world of men. Twice again, before he dictates the tables of his law, he is to descend to it. But what he says suffices to give us a glimpse of the essential forms of a humanity obedient to its élite. It consists of three castes: at the bottom, the popular caste, allowed to retain its humble beliefs; above, the caste of the chiefs, the organisers and warriors; above the chiefs themselves, the sacred caste, the poets who create the illusions and dictate the values. One recalls that essay by Richard Wagner on art, religion, and politics, formerly so much admired by Nietzsche: in it a similar hierarchy was proposed.

In its ensemble the work is serene. It is Friedrich Nietzsche's finest victory. He has repressed his melancholy; he exalts force, not brutality; expansion, not aggression. In the last days of February, 1882, he wrote these final pages, which are perhaps the most beautiful and the most religious ever inspired by naturalistic thought.

"My brethren, remain faithful to the earth, with all the force of your love! Let your great love and your knowledge be in accord with the meaning of the earth. I pray you and conjure you.

"Let not your virtue fly far from terrestrial things, and beat its wings against the eternal walls! Alas! there is always so much virtue gone astray!

"Like myself, bring back towards the earth the virtue which goes astray—yea, towards the flesh and towards life; that it may give a meaning to the earth, a human meaning...."

Whilst he completed the composition of this hymn on the Genoese coast, Richard Wagner died in Venice. Nietzsche learnt the news with a grave emotion, and recognised a sort of providential accord in the coincidence of events. The poet of *Siegfried* was dead; so be it! humanity would not be for a moment deprived of poetry, since Zarathustra had already spoken.

For more than six years he had given no sign of life to Cosima Wagner; now he had to tell her that he had forgotten nothing of past days and that he shared her sorrows. "You will approve of me in this, I am sure" he wrote to Fräulein von Meysenbug.[15]

---

[15] An unpublished letter, communicated by M. Romain Rolland.

On the 14th of February he wrote to Schmeitzner, the publisher:

"To-day I have some news for you: I have just taken a decisive step—I mean, one profitable to you. It concerns a little work, scarcely 100 pages long, entitled: *Thus Spake Zarathustra,* a book for all and none. It is a poem or it is a Fifth Gospel, or something which has no name; by far the most serious, and also the most happy, of my productions and one that is open to all."

He wrote to Peter Gast and to Fräulein von Meysenbug: "This year," said he, "no society. I shall go straight from Genoa to Sils!" Thus did Zarathustra, who left the great city and returned to the mountains. But Friedrich Nietzsche is not Zarathustra; he is feeble, solitude exalts and frightens him. Some weeks passed. Schmeitzner, the publisher, was slow: Nietzsche grew impatient and modified his projects for the summer; he wished to hear the sound of human speech. His sister, at Rome with Fräulein von Meysenbug, guessed that he was accessible and weary, and seized this opportunity of a reconciliation. He did not defend himself and promised to come.

Here he was at Rome. His old friend immediately introduced him into a brilliant society. Lenbach was there, and also that Countess Dönhoff, to-day Princess von Buelow, an amiable woman and a great musician. Friedrich Nietzsche felt with vexation how different he was from these happy talkers, how he belonged to another world, how they misunderstood him. A curious, a singular man, they think; a very eccentric man. A great mind? No one ventured to pass this rash judgment. And Friedrich Nietzsche, so proud when he was alone, was astonished, disturbed, and humiliated. It seemed that he had not the strength to despise these people who did not hearken to him; he was disquieted and began to fear for his well-beloved son, Zarathustra.

"They will run through my book," he wrote to Gast, "and it will be a subject of conversation. That inspires me with disgust. Who is serious enough to hear me? If I had the authority of old Wagner, my affairs would be in a better way. But at present *no one* can save me from being delivered over to 'literary people.' To the devil!"

Other vexations affected him: he had taken to chloral, during the winter, in order to combat his insomnia. He deprived himself of it and recovered, not without difficulty, his normal sleep. Schmeitzner, the publisher, did not hurry to print *Thus Spake Zarathustra;* what was the cause of the delay? Nietzsche enquired and was told: Five hundred thousand copies of a collection of hymns had first to be printed for the Sunday-schools. Nietzsche waited some weeks, received nothing, asked again; another story: the collection of hymns was published, but a big lot of anti-Semitic pamphlets had to be printed and thrown upon the world. June came: *Zarathustra* had not yet appeared. Friedrich Nietzsche lost his temper and suffered for his hero, who was thwarted by the two platitudes, Pietism and anti-Semitism.

He was discouraged and ceased to write; he left his luggage at the station with the books and manuscripts which he had brought: one hundred and four kilos of paper.

Everything in Rome harassed him: the nasty people, a mob of illegitimates; the priests, whom he could not tolerate; the churches, "caverns with unsavoury odours." His hatred of Catholicism is instinctive and has far-off origins; always when he approaches it, he shudders. It is not the philosopher who judges and reproves; it is the son of the pastor, who has remained a Lutheran: who cannot endure the other Church, full of incense and idols.

The desire came to him to leave this town. He heard the beauty of Aquila praised. Friedrich von Hohenstaufen, the Emperor of the Arabs and the Jews, the enemy of the popes, resided there; Friedrich Nietzsche wished to reside there, too. Still, the room which he occupied was a fine and well-situated one, Piazza Barberini, at the very top of a house. There one could forget the town: the murmur of water falling from a triton's horn stilled the noise of humanity and sheltered his melancholy. There it was that, one evening, he was to improvise the most poignant expression of his despair and solitude:

"I am light; alas if I were night! But this is my solitude, to be always surrounded by light.

"Alas that I am not shadow and gloom! How I would drink from the breasts of light!

"... But I live in my own light, I drink the flames which escape from me!"

Thus Spake Zarathustra, a Book for All and None, at last appeared during the first days of June.

"I am very much on the move," wrote Nietzsche. "I am in agreeable society, but as soon as I am alone I feel moved as I have never been." He soon knew the fate of his book. His friends spoke to him very little of it; the newspapers, the reviews, did not mention it; no one was interested in this Zarathustra, the strange prophet who in a biblical tone taught unbelief. "How bitter it is!" said Lisbeth Nietzsche and Fräulein von Meysenbug; these two women, Christians at heart that they were, took offence. "And I," wrote Nietzsche to Peter Gast, "I who find my book so gentle!"

The heat dispersed this Roman society. Friedrich Nietzsche knew not where to go. He had hoped for such different days! He had been persuaded that he would move lettered Europe, that he would at last attract readers to himself, or (more precisely perhaps) that he would attract, not towards his feeble self, but towards Zarathustra, who was so strong, disciples or even servitors. "For this summer," he wrote in May to Peter Gast, "I have a project: to choose, in some forest, some castle formerly fitted up by the Benedictines for their meditations, and to fill it with companions, chosen men ... I must go on a quest for new friends." About the 20th June, thunderstruck by the loss of his hopes, he went up towards his favourite retreat, the Engadine.

Lisbeth Nietzsche, who was returning to Germany, accompanied him. Never had she seen him more brilliant or more gay, she said, than during these few hours of travel. He improvised epigrams, *bouts-rimes,* the words of which his sister suggested; he laughed like a child, and, in fear of troublesome people who would have disturbed his delight, he called and tipped the guard at every station.

Friedrich Nietzsche had not seen the Engadine since that summer of 1881 in which he had conceived the Eternal Return and the words of Zarathustra. In the clutch of these memories and of the sudden solitude, carried away by a prodigious movement of inspiration, he wrote in ten days the second part of his work.

It was bitter. Friedrich Nietzsche could no longer repress the rancours, the menace of which he had felt last winter; he could no longer unite force to sweetness; "I am not a hunter of flies," Zarathustra used to say, and he disdained his adversaries. He had spoken as a benefactor, and he had not been heard. Nietzsche put into his mouth another speech: "Zarathustra the judge," he wrote in his short notes; "the manifestation of justice in its most grandiose form; of justice which fashions, which constructs, and which, as a consequence, must annihilate."

Zarathustra the judge has only insults and lamentations upon his lips. He sings this nocturnal chant which Nietzsche, at Rome, had one evening improvised for himself alone:

"I am light; alas if I were night! But this is my solitude, to be always surrounded by light."

This is no longer the hero whom Friedrich Nietzsche had created so superior to all humanity; it is a man in despair, it is Nietzsche, in short, too weak to express anything beyond his anger and his plaints.

"Verily, my friends, I walk among men as among the fragments and members of man.

"To see men broken and scattered as though they lay over a butcher's shambles, this is to my eye the most frightful thing.

"And when my eye fleeth from the present to the past, it ever findeth the same: fragments, members, and frightful catastrophes—but no men!

"The present and the past upon the earth—alas, my friends, these are to *me* the most unbearable things; and I could not live were I not a visionary of what must come.

"A visionary, a creator, the future itself and a bridge unto the future—alas! in some sort also, a cripple upon this bridge: Zarathustra is all this.... I walk among men, the fragments of the future: of the future which I contemplate in my visions."

Friedrich Nietzsche derided the moral commandments which had upheld ancient humanity: he wished to abolish them and to establish his own. Shall we know it at length, this new law? He delays in telling it to us. "The qualities of the Superman become more and more visible," he writes in his notes. He would wish that it were so; but can he, absorbed as he is in discontent and bitterness, enunciate, define a form of virtue, a new good, a new evil, as he had promised? He tries. He is the prey of a bitter and violent mood, and the virtue which he exalts is naked force undisguised, that savage ardour which moral prescriptions have always wished to attenuate, vary, or overcome. He yields to the attraction which it exercises upon him.

"With delight I regard the miracles which the ardent sun brings to birth, says Zarathustra. They are tigers, palm-trees, rattlesnakes.... Verily, there is a future even for evil, and the hottest noon has not yet been discovered for man.... One day there will come to the world the greatest dragons.... Thy soul is so far from what is great that thou wouldst find the Superman awful in his goodness."

There is emphasis upon this page. The words are noisy rather than strong. Perhaps Nietzsche disguises in this way an embarrassment of thought: he does not insist upon this gospel of evil, and prefers to adjourn the difficult moment in which his prophet will announce his law. Zarathustra must first complete his duties as judge, the annihilator of the weak. He must strike: with what weapon? Here Nietzsche again takes up the idea of the Eternal Return which he had withdrawn from his first section. He modifies the sense and the application of it. It is no longer an exercise of spiritual life, a process of internal edification; it is a hammer, as he says, an instrument of moral terrorism, a symbol which disperses dreams.

Zarathustra assembles his disciples and wishes to communicate to them the doctrine, but his voice falters; he is silent. Suddenly he is moved by pity, and the prophet himself suffers as he evokes the terrible idea. He hesitates at the moment that he is about to destroy these illusions of a better future, these expectations of another life and of a spiritual beatitude which veil from men the misery of their state. He grows anxious. A hunchback, who divines this, interpolates with a sneer: "Why doth Zarathustra speak unto his disciples otherwise than he speaketh unto himself?" Zarathustra feels his fault and seeks a new solitude. The second part is thus completed.

On the 24th June of this year, 1882, Nietzsche was installed at Sils; before the 10th of July he wrote to his sister:

"I beg you instantly to see Schmeitzner and engage him orally or by writing, as you think best, to give the second part of *Zarathustra* to the printer as soon as the manuscript is delivered. This second part exists to-day: try to imagine it, the vehemence of such a creation; you will scarcely be able to exaggerate it. There is the danger. In Heaven's name, arrange things with Schmeitzner; I am too irritable myself."

Schmeitzner promised and kept his word; in August the proofs arrived. Nietzsche had not strength enough to correct them and left the work to Peter Gast and his sister. The terrible things which he had said, the more terrible things which he had yet to say, bruised him.

Other vexations were added to the melancholy of his thought. An awkward step on his sister's part awoke again the dissensions of the previous summer. In the spring, during their reconcilement, he had said to her, aware of her quarrelsome nature: "Promise me never to go back on the stories of Lou Salomé and of Paul Rée." For three months she had kept her peace, then she broke her word and spoke. What did she say? We do not know; we are again in the obscurity of this obscure history. "Lisbeth," he wrote to Madame Overbeck, "absolutely wants to avenge herself on the young Russian." No doubt she reported to him some fact, some observation of which he was ignorant. A sickening irritation laid hold of him. He wrote to Paul Rée, and this is the letter, a sketch of which has been found. (Was it sent as we read it? It is not certain.)

"Too late, almost a year too late, I learn of the part which you took in the events of last summer, and my soul has never been so overwhelmed with disgust as it is at present, to think that an insidious individual of your kind, a liar and a knave, had been able to call himself my friend for years. It is a crime, in my opinion, and not only a crime against me, but above all against friendship, against this very empty word, friendship.

"Fie, sir! So you are the calumniator of my character, and Miss Salomé has only been the mouthpiece, the very unsatisfactory mouthpiece, of the judgment which you passed on me; so it is you who, in my absence, naturally, spoke of me as though I were a vulgar and low egoist, always ready to plunder others; so it is you who have accused me of having, so far as concerned Miss Salomé, pursued the most filthy designs under a mask of idealism; so it is you who dare to say of me that I was mad and did not know what I wanted? Now, of a surety, I understand better the whole of this business which has made men whom I venerated and many whom I esteemed, as my nearest and dearest, strangers to me.... And I thought you my friend; and nothing, perhaps, for seven years has done more harm to my prospects than the trouble that I took to defend you.

"It seems then that I am not very well advanced in the art of knowing men. That furnishes you no doubt with matter for mockery. What a fool you have made of me! Bravo! As regards men of your stamp, rather than understand them, I had rather they mocked me.

"I would have great pleasure in giving you a lesson in practical morals with a pair of pistols; I would succeed perhaps, under the most favourable circumstances, in interrupting once and for all your works on morals: one needs clean hands for that, Dr. Paul Rée, not dirty ones!"

This letter cannot be considered sufficient to condemn Paul Rée. Friedrich Nietzsche wrote it in a moment of anger upon information given by his sister, who was often more impassioned than accurate. It is a precious witness to his impression; to the ill-known data of the cause, it is a mediocre witness. What was the conduct of Paul Rée? What were the rights and wrongs? In April, 1883, six months after the difficulties of Leipsic, he had offered Nietzsche the dedication of a work on the origins of the moral conscience, a work altogether inspired by Nietzschean ideas. Nietzsche had refused this public compliment: "I no longer want," he wrote to Peter Gast, "to be confounded with any one." A letter written by George Brandes in 1888 shows us Paul Rée living in Berlin with Miss Salomé, as "brother and sister," according to both their accounts. There is no doubt that Rée helped Miss Salomé, towards 1883, to write her book on Friedrich Nietzsche: a very intelligent and a very noble book. We incline to believe that between these two men there was only the misfortune of a common love which the same woman inspired in them.

Friedrich Nietzsche wrote long and febrile letters. He complained of being alone at forty years, betrayed by his friends. Franz Overbeck grew anxious and went up to Sils-Maria to distract him from the solitude which wounded and consumed him. His sister, a prudent lady, and bourgeois in her tastes, advised him in answer to his complaints: "You are alone, it is true," said she to him; "have you not sought solitude? Get an appointment in some University: when you have a title and pupils, you will be recognised and people will cease to ignore your books." Nietzsche listened indulgently, but did listen, and wrote to the Rector of Leipsic, who, without hesitation, dissuaded him from making any overtures, no German University being in a position to allow an atheist, a declared anti-Christian, among its teachers. "This reply has given me courage!" wrote Nietzsche to Peter Gast; to his sister he sent a strong letter whose thrusts she felt.

"It is necessary that I be misunderstood, better still, I go to meet calumny and contempt. My 'near ones' will be the first against me: last summer I understood that, and I was magnificently conscious that I was at last on my road. When it comes to me to think, 'I can no longer endure solitude,' then I experience an unspeakable *humiliation before myself*—I feel myself in revolt against what there is of highest in me...."

In September he directed his steps towards Naumburg, where it was his intention to stay some weeks. His mother and sister inspired in him a mixed feeling, which baffles analysis. He liked his own people because they were his own, and because he was tender, faithful, infinitely sensible to memories. But every one of his ideas, every one of his desires, drew him from them, and his mind despised them. Nevertheless the old house of Naumburg was the only place in the world where there was, so long as he stayed there for a short time only, some sweetness of life for him.

Mother and daughter were quarrelling. Lisbeth loved a certain Förster, an agitator, an idealogue of Germanist and anti-Semitic views, who was organising a colonial enterprise in Paraguay. She wished to marry him and to follow him; her despairing mother wished to retain her. Madame Nietzsche welcomed her son as a saviour and related to him the mad projects which Lisbeth was forming. He was overwhelmed; he knew the person and his ideas, he despised the low and dull passions which the propaganda excited, and suspected him of having spoken maliciously of his work. That Lisbeth, the companion of his childhood, should follow this man was more than he could allow. He called her, spoke violently to her. She answered him bravely. There was little that was delicate or subtle in this woman's composition, but she had energy. Friedrich Nietzsche, so weak in the depth of his soul, valued in her the quality which he lacked. He might sermonise, scold, but he could not get his way.

The late autumn came, and Naumburg was covered with fogs. Nietzsche left and went to Genoa. These quarrels had lessened his self-respect.

"Things go badly with me, very badly," he wrote in October to Fräulein von Meysenbug; "my visit in Germany is the cause. I can live only at the seaside. Every other climate depresses me, destroys my nerves and eyes, makes me melancholy, puts me into a black humour—that awful tare; I have had to combat it in my life more than the hydras and other celebrated monsters. In trivial ennui is hidden the most dangerous enemy; great calamity adds to one's stature...."

Towards mid-November he left Genoa, and, circling the western coast, began the quest for a winter residence. He passed by San Remo, Mentone, Monaco, and stopped at Nice, which enchanted him. There he found that keen air and that plenitude of light, that multitude of bright days which he needed: "Light, light, light," he wrote'; "I have regained my equilibrium."

The cosmopolitan city displeased him, and at first he rented a room in a house of the old Italian city, not Nice, but Nizza, as he always wrote. For neighbours he had quite simple people, workmen, masons, employés, who all spoke Italian. It was in similar conditions that in 1881 he had enjoyed at Genoa a certain happiness.

He chased away his vain thoughts and made an energetic effort to complete *Zarathustra*. But then arose the greatest of his misfortunes: the difficulty of his work was extreme, perhaps insurmountable. To complete *Zarathustra*—what did that imply? The work was immense: it had to be a poem which would make the poems of Wagner forgotten; a gospel which should make the Gospel forgotten. From 1875 to 1881, during six years, Friedrich Nietzsche had examined all the moral systems and shown the illusion which is at their foundation; he had defined his idea of the Universe: it was a blind mechanism, a wheel which turned eternally and without object. Yet he wished to be a prophet, an enunciator of virtues and of purposes: "I am he who dictates the values for a thousand years," he said in those notes in which his pride bursts forth. "To imprint his hand on the centuries, as on soft wax, write on the will of millennia as upon brass, harder than brass, more noble than brass, there," Zarathustra was to say, "is the beatitude of the Creator."

What laws, what tables, did Nietzsche wish to dictate? What values would he choose to honour or depreciate? and what right had he to choose, to build up an order of beauty, an order of virtue, in nature, where a mechanical order reigns? He had the right of the poet, no doubt, whose genius, the creator of illusions, imposes upon the imagination of man this love or that hatred, this good or that evil. Thus Nietzsche would answer us, but he did not fail to recognise the difficulty. On the last pages of the second part of his poem he avowed it.

"This, this is my danger," says Zarathustra, "that my glance throweth itself to the summit, whereas my hand would fain grasp and rest upon—the void."

He wished to bring his task to a head. He had felt, this very summer, as something very close and urgent, the tragic menace that hung over his life. He was in haste to complete a work which he could at last present as the expression of his final desires, as his final thought. He had intended to complete his poem in three parts; three were written and almost nothing was said. The drama was not sketched. Zarathustra had to be shown at close quarters with men, announcing the Eternal Return, humiliating the feeble, strengthening the strong, destroying the ancient ways of humanity; Zarathustra as lawgiver dictating his Tables, dying at last of pity and of joy as he contemplates his work. Let us follow his notes:—

"Zarathustra reaches at the same moment the most extreme distress and his greatest happiness. At the most terrible moment of the contrast, he is broken.

"The most tragical history with a divine dénouement.

"Zarathustra becomes gradually more grand. His doctrine develops with his grandeur.

"The Eternal Return shines like a sun setting on the last catastrophe."

"In the last section great synthesis of him who creates, who loves, who destroys."

In the month of August, Nietzsche had indicated a dénouement. His condition of mind was then very bad, and his work suffered in consequence. He now took up the draft again, and tried to make the best of it.

It was a drama which he had the ambition to write. He places his action in an antique frame, in a city devastated by the pest. The inhabitants wish to commence a new era. They seek a lawgiver; they call Zarathustra, who descends among them, followed by his disciples.

"Go," said he to them, "announce the Eternal Return."

The disciples are afraid and avow it.

"We can endure thy doctrine," they say, "but can this multitude?"

"We must make an experiment with truth!" answers Zarathustra. "And if the truth should destroy humanity, so be it!"

The disciples hesitate again. He commands: "I have put in your hands the hammer which must strike men; strike!"

But they fear the people and abandon their master. Then Zarathustra speaks alone. The crowd as it hears him is terrified, loses its temper and its wits.

"A man kills himself: another goes mad. A divine pride of the poet animates him: everything *must* be brought to light. And at the moment that he announces the Eternal Return and the Superman together, he yields to pity.

"Everyone disowns him. 'We must,' they say, 'stifle this doctrine and kill Zarathustra.'

"'There is now no soul on the earth who loves me,' he murmurs; 'how shall I be able to love life?'

"He dies of sadness on discovering the suffering which is his work.

"'*Through love I have caused the greatest sorrow;* now I yield to the sorrow which I have caused.'

"All go, and Zarathustra, left alone, touches his serpent with his hand: 'Who counsels wisdom to me?'—The serpent bites him. The eagle tears the serpent to bits, the lion throws itself upon the eagle. As soon as Zarathustra sees the combat of the animals, he dies.

"Fifth Act: The Lauds.

"The league of the faithful who sacrifice themselves upon the tomb of Zarathustra. They had fled: now, seeing him dead, they become the inheritors of his soul and rise to his height.

"Funeral ceremony: 'It is we who have killed him.'—The Lauds.

"The great Noon. Midday and eternity."

Friedrich Nietzsche abandoned this plan, which yet gives glimpses of great beauty. Did he dislike displaying the humiliation of his hero? Probably, and we shall note his search for a triumphant dénouement. But it is chiefly to be noted that he has dashed against a fundamental difficulty, the nature of which he perhaps does not plainly conceive: the two symbols on which he bases his poem, the Eternal Return and the Superman, in conjunction create a misunderstanding which renders the completion of the work impossible. The Eternal Return is a bitter truth which suppresses all hope. The Superman is a hope, an illusion. From one to the other there is no passage, the contradiction is complete. If Zarathustra teaches the Eternal Return, he will fail to excite in men's souls an impassioned belief in superhumanity. And if he teaches the Superman, how can he propagate the moral terrorism of the Eternal Return? Nevertheless, Friedrich Nietzsche assigns him these two tasks; the breathless disorder of his thoughts drives him to this absurdity.

Does he clearly perceive the problem? We do not know. These real difficulties against which he breaks are never avowed. But if he perceives them ill, at least he feels the inconvenience and seeks by instinct some way of escape.

He writes a second sketch which is certainly skilful: the same scene, the same fever-stricken city, the same supplication to Zarathustra, who comes among a decimated people. But he comes as a benefactor and is careful about announcing the terrible doctrine. First, he gives his laws and has them accepted. Then, and only then, will he announce the Eternal Return. What are these laws which he has given? Friedrich Nietzsche indicates them. Here is one of the very rare pages, in which we discern the order which he has dreamed.

"*(a)* The day divided afresh: physical exercises for all the ages of life. Competition as a principle.

. . . . . .

"*(b)* The new nobility and its education. Unity. Obtained by selection. For the foundation of each family, a festival.

"*(c)* The *experiments.* (With the *wicked, punishments.*) Charity in a new form, based on a concern for the generations to come. The wicked respectable so far as they are destroyers, for destruction is necessary. And also as a source of strength.

"To let oneself be taught by the wicked, not to deny them competition. To utilise the degenerate.—Punishment justifiable when the criminal is utilised for experimental purposes (for a new aliment). Punishment is thus made holy.

"*(d)* To save woman by keeping her woman.

"*(e)* The *slaves* (a hive). The humble and their virtues. To teach the enduring of repose. Multiplication of machines. Transformation of the machines into beauty.

"'For you faith and servitude!'

"The times of *solitude.* Division of the times and days. Food. Simplicity. A feature of union between the poor and the rich.

"Solitude necessary from time to time, that the being may examine himself and concentrate.

. . . . . .

"The *ordinance of festivals,* founded on a system of the Universe: festival of cosmic relations, festival of the earth, festival of friendship, of the great Noon."

Zarathustra explains his laws, he makes them loved by all; he repeats his sermons nine times, and finally announces the Eternal Return. He speaks to the people; his words have the accent of a prayer.

The great question:

"The laws have already been given. Everything is ready for the production of the Superman—grand and awful moment! Zarathustra reveals his doctrine of the Eternal Return—which may now be endured; he himself, for the first time, endures it.

"*Decisive moment:* Zarathustra interrogates all this multitude assembled for the festival.

"'Do you wish,' he says, 'the return of it all?' All reply: Yes!

"He dies of joy.

"Zarathustra dying holds the earth locked in his arms. And although no one said a word, they all knew that Zarathustra was dead."

It is a fine issue: Nietzsche was soon to find it too easy, too fine a one. This Platonic aristocracy, rather quickly established, left him in doubt. It corresponded exactly to his desires; did it correspond to his thoughts? Nietzsche, ready in the destruction of all the ancient moralities, did not find that he had the right of proposing another so soon? *All answered: Yes!* Was that conceivable? Human societies would always draw after them an imperfect mass which would have to be constrained by force or by laws. Friedrich Nietzsche knew it: "I am a seer," he wrote in his notes; "but my conscience casts an inexorable light upon my vision, and I am myself the doubter." He gave up this last plan. Never was he to recount the active life and the death of Zarathustra.

No document admits us to the secret of his sadness. No letter, no word presents us with the expression of it, We may, surely, take this very silence as the avowal of his distress and humiliation. Friedrich Nietzsche had always wished to write a classical work, a history, system, or poem, worthy of the old Greeks whom he had chosen for masters. And never had he been able to give a form to this ambition.

At the end of this year 1883 he had made an all but despairing attempt; the abundance, the importance of his notes let us measure the vastness of a work which was entirely vain. He could neither found his moral ideal nor compose his tragic poem; at the same moment he fails in his two works and sees his dream vanish. What is he? An unhappy soul, capable of short efforts, of lyrical songs and cries.

The year 1884 opened sadly. Some chance fine weather in January reanimated him. Suddenly he improvised: no city, no people, no laws; a disorder of complaints, appeals, and moral fragments which seem to be the debris left over from the ruin of his great work. It is the third part of Zarathustra. The prophet, like Friedrich Nietzsche, lives alone and retired upon his mountain. He speaks to himself, deceives himself, forgets that he is alone; he threatens, he exhorts a humanity which neither fears nor hearkens to him. He preaches to it the contempt of customary virtues, the cult of courage, love of strength and of the nascent generations. But he does not go down to it, and no one hears his predication. He is sad, he desires to die. Then, Life, who surprises his desire, comes to him and raises his courage.

"O Zarathustra!" says the goddess, "do not crack thy whip so terribly. Thou knowest, noise murdereth thought. And even now I have very tender thoughts. Hear me, thou art not faithful enough unto me, thou lovest me not nearly as much as thou sayst, I know, for thou thinkest of leaving me...."

Zarathustra listens to the reproach, smiles and hesitates. "True," he says at last, "but thou also knowest. ..." They gaze at each other, and he tells her something in her ear, among all her confused, stupid yellow tresses. "What though I die?" he says; "nothing can separate, nothing can reconcile, for every moment has its return, every moment is eternal."

"What," answers the goddess, "that thou knowest, Zarathustra? That no one knoweth."

Their eyes meet. They look at the green meadow over which the cool of evening was spreading; they weep, then, in silence, they listen, they understand the eleven sayings of the old bell which strikes midnight in the mountain.

One! Oh man! Lose not sight!

Two! What saith the deep midnight?

Three! I lay in sleep, in sleep;

Four! From deep dream, I woke to light.

Five! The world is deep,

Six! And deeper than ever day thought it might.

Seven! Deep is its woe—

Eight! And deeper than woe—delight.

Nine! Saith woe: Pass, go!

Ten! Eternity's sought by all delight—*Eleven!* Eternity deep by all delight.[16]

Twelve!

. . . . . .

Then Zarathustra rises: he has recovered his security, his sweetness, and his strength. He takes up his staff and sings as he goes down towards men. A similar versicle completes the seven strophes of his hymn:

> "Never yet have I found the woman by whom I would like
> to have children, if it be not the woman whom I love: for I
> love thee, oh Eternity!

> "For I love thee, oh Eternity!"

At the opening of the poem Zarathustra entered the great town—the Multi-coloured Cow he names it—and began his apostolate. At the end of the third part Zarathustra descends to the great town to recommence his apostolate there. Friedrich Nietzsche, a vanquished warrior, after two years of labour, has quailed. In 1872 he sent to Fräulein von Meysenbug the interrupted series of his lectures on the future of Universities: "It gives one a terrible thirst," he said to her, "and, in the long run, nothing to drink." The same words apply to his poem.

III

Heinrich von Stein

In April, 1884, the third and fourth sections (of *Zarathustra*) were published simultaneously. For the moment Nietzsche seems to have been happy.

"Everything comes in its own good time," he wrote to Peter Gast on March 5th. "I am forty and I find myself at the very point I proposed, when twenty, to reach at this age. It has been a fine, a long, and a formidable passage."

"To you," he wrote to Rohde, "who are *homo litteratus,* I need not hesitate to avow that in my opinion I have with this *Zarathustra* brought the German language to its pitch of perfection. After Luther and Goethe a third step remained to be taken—and consider, my old and dear comrade, were ever strength, subtlety, and beauty of

---

[16] Translation published by T. Fisher Unwin.

sound so linked in our language? My style is a dance; I trifle with symmetries of all sorts, and I play on these symmetries even in my selection of vowels."

This joy lasted only for a little while. Without fresh work to hand Nietzsche's ardour had no purpose and turned to ennui. Should he arrange his system methodically, draw up a "philosophy of the future"? He considers this, but finds that he is weary of thought and of writing. What he needs is rest and the refreshment of music; but the music which he could love does not exist. Italian music is flabby, German music preachy, and his taste is for the live and the lyrical; for something grave and delicate; something rhythmical, scornful, and passionate. *Carmen* pleases him well enough, and yet to *Carmen* he prefers the compositions of his disciple, Peter Gast. "I need your music," he wrote to Gast.

Peter Gast was at this time in Venice, where Nietzsche wished to join him. But Venice was damp, and he dared not leave Nice before mid-April. Clearly an invalid's exigencies are becoming each year more and more urgent. A gloomy day lowers his spirits, a week without the sun prostrates him.

On the 26th of April he arrived in Venice. Peter Gast found rooms for him not far from the Rialto, with windows that opened on the Grand Canal. He had not been in Venice for four years, and it was with a child's pleasure that he remade the acquaintance of the loved city. He stayed in the labyrinth of Venice; Venice—whose spirit is compounded of the magic of sun and water, the gracefulness of a gay and tactful people, and glimpses of unexpected gardens with flowers and mosses springing among the stones. "One hundred profound solitudes," he notes, "compose Venice— hence her magic. A symbol for the men of the future." For four or five hours every day he walked the little streets as he had walked the hills, sometimes isolating himself, sometimes moving with the Italian crowd.

He was endlessly reflecting upon the difficulties of his task. What should he write next? He had thought of annotating some verses of his poem by means of a series of pamphlets, but then no one had read the words of Zarathustra. Those friends to whom they had been sent preserved a melancholy silence which constantly astonished him. A young author, Heinrich von Stein, was almost alone in sending him a word of warm congratulation. Nietzsche therefore gave up the idea, feeling that it would be ridiculous to comment upon a Bible which the public ignored.

Very seriously he considered a "philosophy of the future." His intention was to give up, or at least to defer, further work on his poem; he would confine himself to long study—"five, six years of meditation and of silence, maybe"—and formulate his system in a precise and definite manner. Various projects were in his mind when, towards the middle of June, he left Venice for Switzerland. He wished first to read certain books on historical and natural science in the libraries of Basle, but his stay in that town was brief, for he found the heavy heat oppressive and his friends there failed to please him. Either they had not read *Thus Spake Zarathustra* or they had read it very badly. "I might have been among cows," he wrote to Peter Gast, and returned to the Engadine.

On the 20th of August Heinrich von Stein wrote that he was coming.

Stein was at this time a very young man, scarcely twenty-six years of age. But there was no German writer of whom greater things were expected than of him. In 1878 he had published a little volume called *The Ideals of Materialism, Lyrical Philosophy.* Friedrich Nietzsche made the acquaintance of the author, in whose essay he recognised a research analogous to his own. He thought that he had found a kindred spirit, a comrade in his task; but this hope deceived him. Fräulein von Meysenbug had prided herself on bringing Heinrich von Stein under Wagner's influence. It was her defect to be always more benevolent than far-sighted. Thanks to her good offices, Wagner's house was opened to Stein as it had been opened ten years earlier to Nietzsche, and there Stein lived in spite of Nietzsche's warning, "You admire Wagner, and it is right that you should do so—provided your admiration does not last long." Wagner talked, and Stein, who could neither free himself from the master's influence nor oppose it, listened. His intellectual quest, which had hitherto been unquiet but fruitful, now came to an end. He closed his notebooks; he was conquered by a man too great for him, sucked in and sucked dry.

The works which he published—he died at thirty—are temperate and acute, but they lack one quality, precisely that which gives a high value to his first essays— audacity, daring, the charm of a nascent thought, ill-expressed but intense.

Nietzsche continued to interest himself in Stein, and superintended the young man's work and his friendships. "Heinrich von Stein," he wrote in July to Madame Overbeck, "is at present the adorer of Miss Salomé. My successor in that employment as in much else." The danger that Stein ran caused him a great deal of uneasiness. Stein, however, read and appreciated his books, as Nietzsche rejoiced to know.

He was strangely moved on receiving the letter, for Stein had seemed to understand *Thus Spake Zarathustra,* and it might be that a longing for liberty was the explanation of his visit. Stein would make up to him for all the friends that he had lost; and what a revenge, moreover, if he should conquer this disciple of Wagner's, this philosopher from Bayreuth! He hastily sent a welcome, signed "The Solitary of Sils-Maria."

There is a possible interpretation of Stein's movements which never occurred to Nietzsche.

It must be remembered that Stein was the intimate and faithful friend of Cosima Wagner; and certainly he did not now come to Nietzsche without first consulting this shrewd woman and receiving her approbation. Moreover, Nietzsche himself had not yet attacked, but had merely withdrawn from Wagner. In July, 1882, he had seemed favourable to a reconciliation. Fräulein von Meysenbug's endeavours, whether he had authorised them or no, caused him to consider the possibility; and in February, 1883, after Wagner's death, he wrote to Cosima Wagner. He had so far been able to avoid saying anything irreparable, and all his later work, even the very end of *Zarathustra,* with its very vague lyricism, did not close the door on the hope of an understanding. This was Stein's own impression, and he wrote to Nietzsche:

"How I long for you to come this summer to Bayreuth and hear *Parsifal*. When I think of that work I imagine a poem of pure beauty, a spiritual adventure that is purely human, the development of a youth who becomes a man. I can find in *Parsifal* no pseudo-Christianity of any sort and fewer tendencies than in any other of Wagner's works. If I write to you—in a spirit at once audacious and timid—it is not because I am a Wagnerian, but because I wish for *Parsifal* such a hearer as you, and for such a hearer as you I wish *Parsifal*."

Cosima Wagner's judgments were sound, and she knew Nietzsche's worth. She now carried the heavy burden of Wagner's fame; she had a tradition to prolong, a heritage to maintain. By recalling Nietzsche to her side she would aid an extraordinary man, a rare soul that was wasting itself in solitary effort, and she would aid herself at the same time—or so she may have thought. One does not like to say in so many words that she chose Heinrich von Stein as emissary and conciliator. But one may be certain that she knew of, and did not disapprove, the young man's attempt.

If there was such a thing as a Wagnerian equal to the enterprise, it was Heinrich von Stein. He was the most open-minded of the disciples. For him that mysticism of doubtful quality which *Parsifal* propagated was not the last word in religion. He included Schiller, Goethe, and Wagner in one tradition as the creators of myths and the educators of their age and race. For him the theatre of Bayreuth was not an apotheosis, but a promise, an instrument for the future, the symbol of a lyrical tradition.

Stein was anxious to acquit himself well of his mission, but he spoke little. It was Nietzsche himself, the man, to whom he appealed, who spoke, and who saw that he was heard. We may perhaps picture the interview and Nietzsche's words:

"You admire Wagner? Who does not? As well as you and better than you have I known, revered, and hearkened to him. I learnt from him not the style of his art, but the style of his life—his valour and enterprise. I am aware that I have been accused of ingratitude, which is a word I ill understand. I have continued my work. In the best sense of the word, I am his disciple. You frequent Bayreuth, which is very agreeable for you, too agreeable. Wagner offers you for your delight all the legends, all the beliefs of the past—German, Celtic, pagan, and Christian. You should leave him for the same reason that I left him, because this delight is destructive to the spirit which seeks truth. Mark you, I say no word against art or religion. I believe that their day will be again. Not one of the old values will be abandoned. They will re-appear, transfigured no doubt, and more powerful and more intense, in a world thoroughly illuminated to its depths by science. We shall rediscover all the things that we loved in our childhood and in our adolescence, all that has upheld and exalted our fathers—a poetry, a goodness, the most sublime virtues, the humblest, too, each in its glory and its dignity. But we must accept the darkness, we must renounce and search. ... The possibilities are unheard of, but alone I am weak. Help me, therefore; stay or come back here, six thousand feet above Bayreuth!"[17]

Stein listened. His diary reveals the growing vividness of his impressions:

"24 viii. '84. Sils-Maria. Evening with Nietzsche.

"27. His freedom of intellect, the imagery of his speech, a great impression. Snow and winter winds. Headaches. At night I watch him suffer.

"29. He has not slept, but has all the ardour of a young man. A sunny and magnificent day!"

After three days, the too-youthful emissary left, greatly moved by what had passed, and promising to rejoin Nietzsche at Nice, as the latter, at least, understood. Nietzsche felt that he had greatly carried the day. "Such an encounter as ours must have an early and far-reaching importance," he wrote to Stein a few days after his departure. "Believe me, you now belong to that little band whose fate, for good or ill, is linked to mine." Stein answered that the days at Sils-Maria were to him a great memory, a grave and solemn moment of his life; and then, rather prudently, went on to speak of the binding conditions imposed on him by his works and his profession. What he did *not* say was, "Yes, I am yours."

Was Nietzsche's mind open enough to perceive the reservation? One cannot tell. He was making marvellous plans, and dreamt anew of an "ideal cloister." To Fräulein von Meysenbug he made the naïve proposal that she should come to Nice and spend the winter near him.

Chance permits us to discover the depths of his soul. He had gone down to Basle in September, and there Overbeck visited him at his hotel, and found him in bed, suffering from a sick headache, very low in himself, and at the same time exceedingly talkative. His excited speech troubled Overbeck, who was initiated into the mystery of the "Eternal Return." "One day we shall be here together again in this very place; I again, as I now am, sick; you again, as now you are, amazed at my words." He spoke in a low and trembling voice, and his face was troubled—this is the Nietzsche that Lou Salomé has described. Overbeck listened gently, but avoided argument of any sort, and left with evil forebodings. Not until the tragic meeting in Turin in January, 1889, was he again to see his friend.

Nietzsche merely passed through Basle. His sister, whom he had not seen since the quarrel of the previous autumn, gave him a rendezvous at Zürich. It was to announce her marriage, which had taken place in secret some months before. She was now no longer Fräulein Nietzsche but Madame Förster, ready to leave for Paraguay with the colonists who were under the charge of her husband. Recrimination would therefore have been a waste of time. The step had been taken; Nietzsche did not

---

[17] Phrase in a passage from *Ecce Homo*.

discuss it, and did his best to be pleasant once again to the sister who was lost to him. "My brother," wrote Madame Förster, "seems to be in a very satisfactory condition. He is bright and charming; we have been together for six weeks, talking, laughing over everything."

She has left us a record of these days which she supposes—or pretends to suppose—were happy. Nietzsche came upon the works of one Freiligrath, a mediocre and popular poet. On the cover of the volume was inscribed *Thirty—eighth Edition.* With comical solemnity he exclaimed, "Here, then, we have at last a true German poet. The Germans buy his verse!" He decided to be a good German for the day, and bought a copy. He read and was hugely diverted—

> "Wüstenkönig ist der Löwe;
> Will er sein Gebiet durchfliegen."
> (King of deserts is the lion:
> Will he traverse his dominion.)

He declaimed the pompous hemistiches. The Zürich hotel resounded with his childish laughter as he amused himself improvising verses on every subject in the manner of a Freiligrath.

"Hullo!" said an old general to the brother and sister. "What is amusing you two? It makes one jealous to hear you. One wants to laugh like you."

It is unlikely that Nietzsche had much cause for laughter. One wonders whether he could contemplate those thirty-eight editions of Freiligrath without bitterness. During his stay in Zürich he went to the library to look through the files of the newspapers and reviews for his name. It would have meant a good deal to him to have read a capable criticism of his work, to have seen his thought reflected in another's; but no voice ever answered his labours.

"The sky is beautiful, worthy of Nice, and this has lasted for days," he wrote to Peter Gast on September 30th. "My sister is with me, and it is very agreeable for us to be doing each other good when for so long we had been doing harm only. My head is full of the most extravagant lyrics that ever haunted a poet's skull. I have had a letter from Stein. This year has brought me many good things, and one of the most precious of its gifts has been Stein, a new and a sincere friend.

"In short, let us be full of hope; or we may better express it by saying with old Keller—

> "'Trinkt, O Augen, was die Wimper hält
> Von dem goldnen Ueberfluss der Welt! '"

Brother and sister left Zürich, the one bound for Naumburg, the other for Nice. On the way Nietzsche stopped at Mentone. Hardly had he settled down there than he wrote: "This is a magnificent place. I have already discovered eight walks. I hope that no one will join me. I need absolute quiet."

It is possible that the project which he had formed at the beginning of the summer, when he spoke of six years of meditation and of silence, was again in his mind. But he lacked the force of will which long and silent meditation demands. He was, however, deeply moved by the hope of a friend and by the loss of a sister, and his lyric impatience broke the bonds. Yielding to instinct he composed poems off-hand— songs, short stanzas, epigrams. Practically all the poems which are to be found in his later works—the light verse, the biting distich, inserted in the second edition of the *Gaya Scienza,* the grandiose Dionysian chants—were finished or conceived during these few weeks. And once more he began to think of the still incomplete *Thus Spake Zarathustra.* "A fourth, a fifth, a sixth part are inevitable," he writes. "Whatever happens I must bring my son Zarathustra to his noble end. Alive, he leaves me no peace."

At the end of October Nietzsche left Mentone. The sight of so many invalids disturbed him, and he set out for Nice.

There an unexpected companion, Paul Lanzky by name, soon joined him. Lanzky was an "intellectual," by birth a German and by taste a Florentine, who lived a wandering life. Chance had put the works of Nietzsche into his hands; and he had understood them. Applying to Schmeitzner, the publisher, for the author's address, he was told—" Herr Friedrich Nietzsche lives a very lonely life in Italy. Write to Poste Restante, Genoa." The philosopher replied promptly and graciously, "Come to Nice this winter and we will talk!" So Nietzsche was not so unsociable and solitary after all! This correspondence took place during the autumn of 1883, but Lanzky was not free at the moment, and begged to be excused. In October, 1884, he reached the rendezvous. Meanwhile he had had the opportunity of acquainting himself with the two last sections of *Zarathustra,* and had published very intelligent summaries of them in a Leipsic magazine and in the *Rivista Europea* of Florence.

On the very morning of his arrival in Nice there was a knock at his door. A gentle-looking man entered the room and came towards him smiling. "Also Sie sind gekommen!" said Nietzsche. "So here you are!" He took him by the arm, and examined curiously this student of his works. "Let's see what you are made of!"

Nietzsche's eyes were fixed upon him; those eyes which had once been beautiful, and were, at moments, still beautiful, clouded though they now were by reason of prolonged suffering. Lanzky was astonished. He had come to do honour to a redoubtable prophet, and here was the most affable, the simplest, and, as it seemed to him, the most modest of German professors.

As the two men went out together, Lanzky avowed his surprise—" Master," he began....

"You are the first to call me by that name," said Nietzsche with a smile. But he let the word pass, for he knew that he was a master.

"Master," continued Lanzky, "what a mistaken idea of you one gathers from your books; tell me ..."

"No, no, not to-day. You do not know Nice. I will do the honours, and show you this sea, these mountains, these walks.... Another day we shall talk, if you will."

By the time they returned it was six o'clock in the evening, and Lanzky had discovered how tireless a walker was his prophet.

They organised their life in common. At six o'clock in the morning it was Nietzsche's custom to make himself a cup of tea, which he took alone; towards eight Lanzky would knock at his door and ask how he had passed the night—Nietzsche often slept badly—and how he intended to employ his morning. Usually Nietzsche began the day by skimming the newspapers in a public reading hall; he then went to the shore, where Lanzky either joined him or respected his desire for a solitary walk. Both of them lunched in their pension. In the afternoon they walked out together. At night, Nietzsche wrote or Lanzky read to him aloud, often from some French book, such as the *Letters* of the Abbé Galiani, Stendhal's *Le Rouge et le Noir, La Chartreuse, L'Armance.*

To live courteously, yet withhold from ordinary gaze the secret of one's life, is a whole art in itself; and this art Nietzsche had mastered. Indeed, as regards the scheme of manners that he had composed for himself, this solitary of the table d'hôte was, deliberately, hypocritical and almost cunning. More than once Lanzky was nonplussed. One Sunday a young lady asked Nietzsche had he been to church.

"To-day, no," he replied courteously.

To Lanzky, who admired his prudence, he explained that every truth was not good for everyone. "If I had troubled that girl's mind," he added, "I should be horrified."

Occasionally it amused him to announce his future greatness. He would tell his neighbours during meals that in forty years' time he would be illustrious throughout Europe.

They would say: "Well, then lend us your books."

He refused their requests most positively, and again explained to Lanzky that his writings were not for the man in the street.

"Master," asked Lanzky, "why do you print them?"

It appears that no answer was given to this reasonable question.

Nietzsche, however, dissembled even with Lanzky. The formation of a society of friends, of an idealistic phalanstery similar to that in which Emerson lived—this old dream of his he loved to repeat and elaborate for him.

He often led Lanzky to the peninsula of Saint-Jean. "Here," he would say in Biblical phrase—"Here we shall pitch our tents." He went so far as to select a group of little villas which seemed to be suitable for his purpose. But the members were not yet decided upon, and the name of Heinrich von Stein, the only friend, the only disciple whom he really wanted, was never mentioned in Lanzky's presence.

There was no news of Stein's coming, nor of his plans. To Nietzsche he gave no sign. We may assume that he had gone to Sils-Maria to conciliate, if possible, the two masters. But one of them had said that he must choose between the two: perhaps he had been disturbed for a moment. He returned, however, to his Germany, and there he saw Cosima Wagner again. Nietzsche had required that he should choose, and he remained faithful to Wagner.

Nietzsche anticipated a new desertion. He was afraid, and, yielding to a humble and mournful impulse, wrote, in the form of a poem, an appeal which he addressed to the young man:

> O midday of life! O solemn time!
> O garden of summer!
> Unquiet happiness I am there: listening, waiting!
> Night and day, living in hope of the friend;
> "Where are ye, friends? Come! It is time, it is time!"[18]

Heinrich von Stein felt it incumbent upon him to reply. He wrote: "To an appeal such as yours there is but one suitable reply. It is that I should come and give myself entirely to you, vowing, as to the noblest of tasks, all my time to the understanding of the new Gospel which you have to preach. But this is forbidden me. An idea, however, strikes me. Every month I entertain two friends and read with them some article from the Wagner-Lexicon. It is taken as text, and, on it, I speak to them. These conversations are becoming more and more lofty and free. Latterly we have found this definition of æsthetic emotion—a passage to the impersonal through very fulness of personality. I think that our meetings would please you. And how if Nietzsche should now and again send us the text? Would you communicate with us in this way? Would you not see in such a correspondence an introduction, a step towards your idea of a cloister?"

This letter was obviously the letter of an excellent pupil, and it exasperated Nietzsche. Wagner was named, doubtless intentionally, and the Wagnerian

---

[18] "Oh Lebens Mittag! Feierliche Zeit!
Oh Sommergarten!
Unruhig Glück im Stehn und Spahn und Warten!
Der Freunde harr' Ich, Tag und Nacht bereit;
Wo bleibt ihr, Freunde? Kommt! s'ist Zeit! s'ist Zeit!"

Encyclopedia, the sum of an absurd and puerile theology, was indicated as the text of Stein's meditations. Here was the old adversary again standing in the way, Wagner, the quack of thought, the seducer of young men. Förster, who was taking his sister from him, was a Wagnerian; and Heinrich von Stein, on Wagner's account, refused him his devotion. It was a cruel liberty that he had won, alone and at the cost of a struggle whose wounds he still bore. He wrote to his sister:

"What a foolish letter Stein has written me in answer to such poetry! I am painfully affected. Here I am ill again. I have recourse to the old means [chloral], and I utterly hate all men, myself included, whom I have known. I sleep well, but on waking I experience misanthropy and rancour. And yet there can be few men living who are better disposed, more benevolent than I!"

Lanzky remarked Nietzsche's trouble of mind without suspecting the cause. The crisis was very severe, but Nietzsche did not allow himself to be crushed by it and laboured energetically. More often now than heretofore he walked alone, and Lanzky would watch him trip as lightly as a dancer across the Promenade des Anglais or over the mountain paths. He would leap and gambol at times, and then suddenly interrupt his capers to write down a few words with a pencil. What was the new work on which he was busy? Lanzky had no idea.

One morning in March he entered, as was his custom, the little room which the philosopher occupied, to find him in bed notwithstanding the advanced hour. He made anxious enquiries.

"I am ill," said Nietzsche; "I have just had my confinement."

"What's that you say?" asked Lanzky, much perturbed.

"The fourth part of *Zarathustra* is written."

This fourth section does not enable us to discover at length an advance in the work, an attained precision of thought. It is merely a singular fragment, an "interlude," as Nietzsche called it. It illustrates a strange episode in the life of the hero, one which has disconcerted many a reader. We may perhaps best understand it if we consider the deception to which Nietzsche has just been subjected.

The superior men go up to Zarathustra and surprise him in his mountainous solitude: an old pope, an old historian, an old king, unhappy beings who are suffering from their abasement and wish to ask succour of a sage whose strength they feel. Was it not thus that Stein, that distinguished young man, etiolated by Bayreuth, went to Nietzsche?

Zarathustra admits these superior men to his presence, and keeping in check his savage humour, makes them sit down in his cave, is sorry for their disquietude, listens and talks to them. Was it not thus that Nietzsche had received Stein?

Zarathustra's soul is in its depths less hard than it should be, and he allows himself to be seduced by the morbid charm and delicacy of the superior men; he takes pity on them and, forgetting that their misery is irremediable, yields to the pleasures of hope. He had looked for friends, and, perhaps, with these "superior men" they have come at last. Had not Nietzsche hoped for some help from Stein?

Zarathustra leaves his friends for a moment, and ascends alone to the mountain. He returns to his cave to find the "superior men," all of them prostrate before a donkey. The aged pope is saying Mass before the new idol. In this posture Stein, interpreting a Wagnerian bible with two friends, had been surprised by Nietzsche.

Zarathustra hunts his guests away, and calls for new workmen for a new world. But will he ever find them?

"My children, my pure-blooded race, my beautiful new race; what is it that keeps my children upon their isles?

"Is it not time, full time—I murmur it in thine ear, good spirit of the tempests,—that they should return to their father? do they not know that my hair grows gray and whitens in waiting?

"Go, go, spirit of the tempests, indomitable and beneficent! Leave thy gorges and thy mountains, precipitate thyself upon the seas and bless my children before the night has come.

"Bear them the benediction of my happiness, the benediction of that crown of happy roses! Let these roses fall upon their isles, let them remain fallen there, as a sign, which asks: 'Whence can such a happiness come?'

. . . . . .

"Then they shall ask: 'Still lives he, our father Zarathustra? What, can our father Zarathustra be still alive? Does our old father, Zarathustra, still love his children?'

"The wind breathes, the wind breathes, the moon shines bright—Oh my far-off, far-off children, why are ye not here, with your father? The wind breathes no cloud passes over the sky, the world sleeps. Oh, joy! Oh, joy!"

Nietzsche omitted this page from his work. Perhaps he felt ashamed of so plain and so melancholy an avowal.

The fourth part of *Zarathustra* found no publisher. A few months earlier Schmeitzner had informed Nietzsche that "the public would not read his aphorisms." He now contented himself with stating that the public had chosen to ignore *Zarathustra;* and there the matter rested, so far as he was concerned.

Nietzsche then made certain overtures which only hurt his pride and had no result; then he took a more dignified course and had the manuscript printed at his own expense in an edition limited to forty copies. To tell the truth, his friends were not so numerous. He found seven consignees—none of whom were truly worthy. If we may guess, these were the seven: his sister—whose loss he never ceased to deplore; Overbeck -a strict friend, an intelligent reader, but cautious and reserved; Burckhardt, the Basle historian—who always replied to Nietzsche's messages, but was too polite to be easily fathomed; Peter Gast—the faithful disciple whom, no doubt, Nietzsche found too faithful and obedient; Lanzky—his good companion of the wintertide; Rohde—

who scarcely disguised the ennui that these forced readings gave him. These were the seven, we may presume, who received copies of the work, and not all of them troubled to read this fourth and last section, the interlude which ends, and yet does not complete, *Thus Spake Zarathustra.*

CHAPTER VII

THE FINAL SOLITUDE

I

Beyond Good and Evil

The lyrical work was abandoned. At moments Friedrich Nietzsche was to regret and wish to resume it; but these were brief velleities. "Henceforth," he wrote (this time the assurance is exact), "I shall speak, and not Zarathustra."

The work remained in an incomplete condition. Nietzsche knew it, and the mass of thoughts which he had not expressed saddened him like a remorse. He was about to attempt another test. It was without joy that he returned to philosophy and strove to express in abstract terms what, as poet, he had failed to utter. He opened new notebooks, he essayed titles: *The Will to Power, a new interpretation of Nature ... The Will to Power, an essay towards a new interpretation of the universe ....* These formulas, the first that he had found, were to stand. Nietzsche resumed and developed here the Schopenhauerian datum. The foundation of things, he thinks, is not a blind *will to live;* to live is to expand, it is to grow, to conquer: the foundation of things may be better defined as a blind *will to power,* and all the phenomena that arise in the human soul may be interpreted as a function of this will.

It was an immense work of prudent reflection which Nietzsche envisaged with fear. How should one discern in the soul of men what is power and what is, without doubt, weakness? Perhaps the anger of Alexander is weakness, and the mystic's exaltation power. Nietzsche had hoped that disciples, philosophers or physiologists, would have made the necessary analyses for him. Heinrich von Stein's help would have been precious. But, being alone, he had to assume every task. He grew sad. Denuded of lyricism, thought had no attraction for him. What does he love? Instinctive strength, finesse, grace, ordered and rhythmical sounds—he loves Venice and dreams of the fine weather which will allow him to fly from this Nice pension where the food and the company are so bad. On the 30th of March he writes to Peter Gast:

"DEAR FRIEND,—It seldom happens that I consider a removal with pleasure. Bat on this occasion:—when I think that I shall soon be at Venice, and near you, I grow animated, am ravished; it is like the hope of cure after a long and terrible sickness. I have made this discovery: Venice remains till to-day the only place which is always sweet and good to me.... Sils-Maria as a place of passage suits me very well; but not as a residence. Ah! if I could contrive to live there worthily as a hermit or solitary! But—Sils-Maria becomes fashionable!

"My dear friend and maestro, you and Veñlur are linked for me. Nothing gives me more pleasure than your persistent taste for this town. How much I have thought of you in these times! I was reading the memoirs of old De Brossé (1739-40) on Venice and on the maestro who was then admired there, Hasse (il detto Sassonne). Do not get angry, I haven't the least intention of making disrespectful comparisons between you.

"I have just written to Malvida: thanks to Peter Gast, our friends the low comedians, the self-styled geniuses of music, gone hence very soon, will cease to corrupt taste. 'Gone hence very soon'—is, perhaps, a gross exaggeration. In a *democratic* period few men discern beauty: *pulchrum paucorum est hominum,* I rejoice that for you I am one of these 'few.' The profound and joyous men who please me, *avec des ames mélancoliques et folles*[19] like my defunct friends Stendhal and the Abbé Galiani, could not have stayed on the earth if they had not loved some musician of joy (Galiani without Puccini, Stendhal without Cimarosa and Mozart).

"Ah, if you knew how alone I am in the world at present! and how I must play a comedy to prevent myself from spitting, now and again, in some one's face, out of satiety. Happily some of the courteous manners of my son Zarathustra exist also in his rather crazed father.

"But when I shall be with you, and in Venice, then, for a time, there will be an end of 'courtesy' and 'comedy' and 'satiety' and of all the malediction of Nice, won't there, my good friend?

"Not to be forgotten: we shall eat *baïcoli*!

"Cordially,

"F. N."

In April and May Nietzsche sojourned at Venice, and found the joy for which he had hoped. He wandered through the little sheltered and murmurous streets, he contemplated the beautiful town. He listened to the music of his friend. The galleries of St. Mark's Square shaded his walks and he compared them to those porticoes of Ephesus whither Heraclitus went to forget the agitation of the Greeks and the sombre menace of the Persian Empire. "How easily," he thinks, "one here forgets the sombre Empire—our own; let us not defame our Europe; she still offers us beautiful refuges! It is my finest workroom, this Piazza San Marco...." This shortlived happiness awoke the poetic impulse in him. He wished to chant the triumph and death of Zarathustra, now for some hours drawn from oblivion. He wrote out a sketch, but soon abandoned it; it was his last.

June brought him back to the Engadine. The chances of hotel life procured him a secretary; a certain Madame Röder, otherwise unknown, offered to help him. He dictated and tried to grasp his problem more closely. What was his end? To criticise that multitude of moral judgments, prejudices and routines which fetter modern

---

[19] In French in the text.

Europeans; to appraise their vital value, that is to say, the quantity of energy which they express, and thus to fix a hierarchy of virtues. He wished finally to realise the *Umwerthung aller Werthe* (he found this formula), "the transvaluation of all values." "All," he writes; his pride was not content with less. He then recognised, and succeeded in defining, certain modes of virtue which the professional moralists knew not how to observe: mastery over oneself, dissimulation of one's intimate sentiments, politeness, gaiety, exactitude in obedience and command, deference, exigence of respect, taste for responsibilities and for dangers. Such were the usages, the tendencies, to-day depreciated, of the old aristocratic life, the sources of a morality more virile than our own.

It is probable that he then undertook some serious enough readings. He studied the *Biological Problems* of Rolph, where he could find the analysis of that vital growth which was the basis of his metaphysic. Perhaps he then read again some book by Gobineau (he admired the man and his works); one may hazard this conjecture. But what mattered his readings? Nietzsche was forty-two years old. He had passed the age of learning, he had gathered in all his ideas. Reading helped, nourished his meditations, but never directed them.

The difficulty of his work was great and insomnia overcame him. Nevertheless he persevered, and denied himself the sad joy of a final embrace of his sister Lisbeth, who was about to follow her husband to South America. "You will live down there then," he wrote to her, "and I here, in a solitude more unattainable than all the Paraguays. My mother will have to live alone and we must all be courageous. I love you and I weep.—FRIEDRICH."

A week passed, and he had formed other projects. He was negotiating with his publisher in regard to the repurchase of his books and their republication. It was a pretext that he grasped for going to Germany. "A business matter, which makes my presence of use, comes to the aid of my desire," he wrote, and set out for Naumburg without delay.

The meeting was a grave one: brother and sister conversed tenderly on the eve of a separation which they knew to be definitive. Nietzsche made no secret of the difficulties of his life. "Alone I confront a tremendous problem," he said; "it is a forest in which I lose myself, a virgin forest— *Wald und Urwald.* I need help. I need disciples, I need a master. To obey would be sweet! If I had lost myself on a mountain, I would obey the man who knew that mountain; sick, I would obey a doctor; and if I should meet a man capable of enlightening me on moral ideas, I would listen to him, I would follow him; but I find no one, no disciples and fewer masters. "... I am alone." His sister repeated the advice which she had constantly given: that Friedrich should return to some University; young men had always listened to him, they would listen to him, they would understand him. "Young men are so stupid!" answered Nietzsche, "and professors still more stupid! Besides, all the German Universities repel me; where could I teach?" "In Zürich," his sister suggested. "There is only one town that I can tolerate, and it is Venice."

He went to Leipsic to negotiate with his publisher, who received him without much attention; his books did not sell. He returned to Naumburg, said a final farewell, and left.

Where was he to find a refuge for the winter? On the last occasion he had been irritated by the noisy swarms of Nice. He thinks of Vallombrosa. Lanzky had recommended this beautiful forest in the Tuscan Apennines, and was waiting for him at Florence. Before leaving Germany, Nietzsche, passing through Munich, visited a former friend, the Baron von Seydlitz, who introduced him to his wife and showed him his Japanese collection. The wife was young and charming, the Japanese things pleased Nietzsche; he discovered this art, he liked these stamps, these little gay objects which conformed so little to the sad modern taste, so very little to the sad taste of the Germans. Seydlitz understood beautiful things, and knew how to live; Nietzsche envied him a little. "Perhaps it is time, dear Lisbeth," he wrote to his sister, "for you to find me a wife. Let us say, still young, pretty, gay; in short, a courageous little being à la Irène von Seydlitz (we almost 'thee and thou' each other)."

He reached Tuscany. Lanzky received him, accompanied him, and brought him to the observatory of Arcetri, on the heights of San Miniato, where lived a man of a rare kind—a reader of his books. Leberecht Tempel kept on his table, near his bizarre instruments, the works of Herr Friedrich Nietzsche, many passages of which he knew by heart and willingly recited. Leberecht Tempel was a singularly noble, sincere, and disinterested nature. The two men talked for half an hour and, it seems, understood each other. When Nietzsche left he was deeply moved.

"I wish that this man had never known my books," said he to Lanzky. "He is too sensible, too good. I shall harm him."

For he knew the terrible consequences of his thoughts and feared for those who read them suffering similar to his own.

He did not stay in Tuscany: the harsh, cold air which descended from the mountains upon Florence incommoded him. He was recaptured by memories of Nice, the town with two hundred and twenty days of full sunshine—it was from Nice that he wrote to his sister, on the 15th of November, 1885:

"Do not be astonished, dear sister, if your brother, who has some of the blood of the mole and of Hamlet in his veins, writes to you not from Vallombrosa, but from Nice. It has been very precious to me to experiment almost simultaneously with the air of Leipsic, of Munich, of Florence, of Genoa, and of Nice. You would never believe how much Nice has triumphed in this group. I have put up, as last year, at the Pension de Genève, Petite Rue Saint-Etienne. I find it recarpeted, refurnished, repainted, become very comely. My neighbour at table is a bishop, a Monsignor who speaks German. I think of you a great deal. Your

"PRINCE EICHORN."

"Here I am returned to Nice," he wrote in another letter, "that is to say to reason." His pleasure is such that he observes with some indulgence the cosmopolitan city, and is amused by it. "My window looks out on the square of the Phœnicians," he wrote to Peter Gast. "What a prodigious cosmopolitanism in this alliance of words! Don't you laugh? And it's true, Phœnicians lived here. I hear sounding in the air something of the conqueror and the Super-European, a voice which gives me confidence and says to me: *Here thou art in thy place* .... How far one is from Germany here—'*Ausserdeutsch!* I cannot say it with force enough."

He returned to his habit of walking in the sun over the white roads which overlook the waves. The memories of seven years linked his thought with this sea, these strands, these mountains; his fantasy awoke, he listened to it and followed it. Not an hour passed vainly; each one was happy, and left, as the souvenir and witness of the gladness which it brought, an epigram, a poem in prose, a maxim, some *lied* or song.

He defamed the moderns; it was his pleasure, and, as he thought, his duty as a philosopher, who, speaking for coming times, must contradict his own period. In the sixteenth century a philosopher did well to praise obedience and kindliness. In the nineteenth century, in our Europe impaired by Parisian decadents and Wagnerian Germans, in this feeble Europe which is ever seeking the co-operation of the masses, the line of least effort and the least pain, a philosopher had to praise other virtues. He had to affirm: "That man is great who knows how to be the most solitary, the most hidden, the most distant; who knows how to live beyond good and evil, the master of his virtues, powerful in his will. Greatness is there. And he must urgently ask: Is greatness possible to-day?"—*Ist Veredlung möglich?* We never cease to hear this question which he first put at twenty-six.

He defamed the Germans; this was his other pleasure, a more intimate and lively one. Germanised Europe had unlearned freedom. She dissimulated her spites, her immodesties, her cunning. She needed to recover the spirit of the old world, of those Frenchmen of former times who lived in so fine a liberty, with so fine a clear-sightedness and force. "We must *mediterraneanise* music," wrote he, "and our taste, our manners also." Across these pages of Nietzsche, it is easy to hear the counsels of his "defunct friends," Stendhal and the Abbé Galiani.

"Men of profound melancholy," he wrote, "betray themselves when they are happy: they seize upon their happiness as though they would strangle it and stifle it out of jealousy.... Alas, they know too well that happiness flies before them!" December neared its end, and those festivals, the memories of which moved his faithful heart, approached; Nietzsche had seen his happiness in flight before him. The pleasure of lively thoughts, of beautiful images, did not entirely satisfy him. He was no longer amused by the crowd at Nice, the square of the Phœnicians diverted him no more. What mattered to him the *Gai Saber* and its precepts—sunlight, wind and Provençal song? He was a German, the son of a pastor, and it was with an oppressed heart that he watched Christmas and Saint Sylvester's day approach—that venerated time.

He took a disgust for the poor pension in which he lodged: its furniture was touched by too many hands, its sitting-room degraded by being common property. Then the cold weather came. Being poor, he could not get the warmth he needed; he froze, bitterly regretting the stoves of Germany. Wretched places where he cannot ever be alone! To the right, a child is clattering its scales; above, two amateurs are practising on the trumpet and violin. Friedrich Nietzsche, yielding to bitterness, wrote to his sister, who was spending a last Christmas at Naumburg:

"How stupid it is that I have no one here who might laugh with me! If I were stronger, and if I were richer, I should set up in Japan, to know a little gaiety. At Venice I am happy because there one can live in the Japanese manner without too great difficulty. All the rest of Europe is pessimist and mournful; Wagner's horrible perversion of music is a particular case of the perversion, of the universal trouble.

"Here is Christmas again, and it is sad to think that I must continue to live, as I have done for seven years, like a man proscribed, like a cynical contemner of men. No one bothers about my existence any more; the Lama has 'better to do,' and in any case enough to *do*.... Isn't it fine, my Christmas letter? Long live the Lama!

"Your F.

"Why do you not go to Japan? It is the most sensible life, and so gay."

Eight days later he wrote a better letter; perhaps he had reproached himself for his confession.

"*Chérie*, the weather is magnificent to-day, and your Fritz must afresh put on a good face for you, though in these latter times he has had nights and days that were most melancholy. By chance my Christmas was a real festival day. At noon, I receive your kind presents; very quickly I pass round my neck your watch-chain, and slide your pretty little calendar into my waistcoat pocket. As to the 'money,' if there was money in the letter (our mother wrote me that there was), it escaped my fingers. Excuse your blind animal who undid his packet in the road; something no doubt fell from it, as I opened your letters very impatiently. Let us hope that a poor old woman, passing there, found her 'little child Jesus' on the pavement. Then I go on foot to my peninsula of Saint Jean, I walk a great round along the coast, and finally install myself not far from the young soldiers who are playing at skittles. Fresh-blown roses, geraniums in the hedges, everything green, everything warm: nothing of the north! There, your Fritz drinks three glasses of a sweet wine of the country, and perhaps gets a trifle tipsy; at least he begins to talk to the waves, and, when they foam as they break too strongly against the shore, he says to them, as one does to fowl: 'Butsch! Butsch! Butsch!' Finally, I re-enter Nice and, in the evening, dine at my pension in princely style in the glitter of a great Christmas-tree. Would you believe it, I have found a baker *de luxe* who knows what 'Quackkuchen' is; he told me that the King of Würtemburg had ordered some of it, similar to the kind I like, for his birthday. I remembered this while I was writing *'in princely style.'* ... In alter liebe,

"Your F.

"N.B.—I have begun to sleep again (without narcotics)."

In January, February, and March, 1886, his melancholy appeared to be less acute. He gave a form to his work, to those notes which his fantasy had dictated to him. For four years he had ceased to publish his aphorisms, his short essays. The matter with which his notebooks supplied him was immense. He proposed to extract a volume from it; his whole task was to arrange and select.

Had he forgotten the systematic work of which he had thought the previous winter? No, for he always felt the heavy necessity and the reproach of it. He wished to make peace with his own conscience in regard to the delay: he needed a little pleasure, the amusement of a lively book, before commencing the immense work. He found a title, *Beyond Good and Evil;* a sub-title, *Prelude to a Philosophy of the Future.* Thus he announced the more important and always deferred work. He deceived himself in connecting by an artificial tie his pleasure and his duty.

Remember how joyously he used to announce the completion of the book; how communicative he was and how confident! Confidence and joy are gone. He knows that he will not be read. But his ill-fortune always exceeds his expectation, and Nietzsche, once again, has not foreseen the ordeal which he must endure: *Beyond Good and Evil* finds no publisher. He negotiates with a house in Leipsic which declines his proposals. He writes to Berlin without better success. Everywhere his book is refused. What is he to do with it? He thinks of cutting it up into pamphlets which will perhaps reach the public more easily. He writes an experimental preface.

"These pamphlets," he is to say, "form a sequel to the 'Thoughts out of Season' which I published some ten years ago in the hope of drawing to me 'my fellows.' I was then young enough to go fishing for associates with an impatient hope. To-day—after a hundred years: I measure the time by my measure—I am not yet old enough to have lost all hope and confidence."

But he soon abandoned this idea too. "There is nothing else for me to do," he wrote to his sister, "but to tie up my manuscript with a string and put it in a drawer."

In the spring he stayed at Venice, as his custom was, but did not meet his friend, who was visiting the German towns in the vain hope of "placing" his music. Peter Gast had composed an opera, *The Lion of Venice,* which was being rejected by one theatre after another. Nietzsche wrote to comfort and encourage him. Like Nietzsche, Gast was a German by birth, a Mediterranean in taste. The one lived at Nice, the other at Venice; they had the same ambition, the same unhappy destiny.

"Come back," he wrote to him, "come back to the solitude in which we both know how to live, in which we alone know how to live! It is Wagnerism which bars your road, and it's also that German grossness and thickness which, since the 'Empire,' goes growing, growing. We must be circumspect and march under arms, you and I, to prevent ourselves from being forced to die of silence...."

Friedrich Nietzsche felt his solitude alleviated by this comradeship in a difficult lot. Peter Gast's distress was similar to his own; he spoke to him as to a brother. Peter

Gast was poor: "Let us share my purse," said Nietzsche; "let us share the little that I have." Peter Gast grew discouraged and lost confidence in himself. Nietzsche knew this agony; he knew the great necessity of confidence to the man who worked, and how quickly the contempt of the public must overwhelm him. "Courage," he wrote; "do not let yourself be cast down; be sure that I, at least, believe in you; I need your music; without it I could not live." We need not doubt that Nietzsche was sincere when he thus expressed himself. All his power of love and admiration, which was immense, he brought to bear upon this last companion who remained to him, and his friendship transfigured the music of Peter Gast.

He was unhappy, even at Venice; the light hurt the delicate nerves of his eyes. As at Basle in former times, he was obliged to shut himself up behind closed shutters, and deny himself the pleasure of the fine Italian days. What refuge could he find? He recalled the vast German forests, so shady and beneficent to his eyes, and he took to regretting his country. Though she angered him, though he revolted against her, he loved Germany; how could he help loving her? Without her divine music, which had governed the impulses of his first desires, his soul would have been other; without her tongue, that splendid and difficult instrument, his thought would have been other. Schopenhauer and Wagner, two Germans, were his real masters, and remained so (he secretly avowed it); his true disciples, if ever they were to exist, would be born in Germany, that cruel Fatherland which he could not abjure.

Thence he received a piece of news which moved him: Rohde was appointed professor in the University of Leipsic. Nietzsche was happy for his friend, and congratulated him in exquisite terms. Nevertheless, he could not prevent himself from sadly drawing a personal moral. "At present," he wrote to Peter Gast, "the Faculty of Philosophy is half composed of my 'good friends' (Zarncke, Heinze, Leskien, Windisch, Rohde, &c.)." Suddenly he wished to depart; he wanted to see his mother, whom her two children had left; he wished to attend his old comrade's course; lastly, he wished to confront those famous publishers who printed twenty thousand volumes a year, and refused his own. He left Venice and went straight to Leipsic.

He stepped up to Rohde's rooms; the time was badly chosen. He found a busy and preoccupied man, who received this unexpected visitor, this too singular personage who had failed in life, with vexation and constraint. "I saw Nietzsche," Rohde wrote later in a few lines in which he explained his cold welcome. "All his person was marked with an indescribable strangeness, and it disquieted me. There was about him something that I had never known, and of the Nietzsche whom I had known many features were effaced. He seemed to have come from an uninhabited land." Nietzsche said: "I would like to hear you speak." Rohde brought him, and put him to sit among young men who were ignorant of his work and of his very name. Nietzsche listened, then went away. "I have heard Rohde at the University," he wrote to his sister briefly. "I can no longer communicate with any one. Leipsic is, it is clear, no place of refuge or of repose for me."

He would have fled from Leipsic, as he had fled from Venice and Nice; but the difficulty of his negotiations obliged him to remain there. He applied to various publishers, and applied in vain. Finally, his dignity revolted. He wished his book to appear, and, however heavy the cost, he resolved to pay out of his own pocket the cost of the printing.

His mother was waiting for him at Naumburg, where since Lisbeth's departure she lived alone. Nietzsche felt a very lively pity for her; he knew her to be desolated by the loss of her family, and in despair over the impieties which he published in his books. "Don't read them, ignore them," he told her ceaselessly: "it is not for you that I write." Nevertheless, she could not repress her curiosity, and her discontent was never appeased. Nietzsche did not wish to leave without giving her a little happiness. He went to spend a week at home; but he had not the strength to keep the secret of his vexations to himself; he bewailed himself, he grew exalted; he saddened the poor woman, whom finally he left in a more unhappy condition than ever.

Passing through Munich, he called on the Baron and Baroness von Seydlitz. He wished to snatch a brief repose under the roof of his amiable host; but Seydlitz was away from home, and his house was shut up.

Nietzsche, having left this Germany which he was never again to see, continued on his road towards the Upper Engadine, from which he always expected some benefit. Here in July he found himself among icy fogs, and felt the first symptoms of a long crisis of neuralgia and melancholy.

II

The Will to Power

Shall we say that he met friends? Is the word suitable to those vague figures, to those Russian, English, Jewish, and Swiss women who, seeing this charming man return each season, did not refuse him their quick sympathy? We set down their names: Mesdames Röder and Marasoff; Miss Zimmern and Fräulein von Salis Marschlins (this last a friend of Fräulein von Meysenbug); others, whose names remain unknown, may be guessed.

How did they judge him? Carefully he avoided any speech that might have pained or surprised them. He kept his dangerous thoughts to himself. So far as they were concerned, he wished to be, and knew how to be, an amiable companion ... learned, refined, and reserved. Still, whatever secret he made of his work, his friends did not fail to get an inkling into the mystery of his reserve. One of them, an Englishwoman in delicate health, whom he often went to visit and distract, broached the subject.

"I know, Herr Nietzsche, why you won't let us see your books. If one were to believe what you say in them, a poor, suffering creature like myself would have no right to live."

Nietzsche was apologetic, and warded off the accusation as best he could.

Another, having said to him one day: "I have been told about your books. You've written in one of them, '*If thou goest among women, do not forget thy whip.*'"

"Dear lady, dear friend," answered Nietzsche, in a pained voice, taking the hands of her who reproached him in his own; "do not misunderstand me; it is not thus that I am to be understood."

Did they admire him? To dare to admire an unrecognised author a very sure judgment is needed; and no doubt they lacked in necessary daring. They esteemed, they liked their hotel companion, and recognised his singular genius in conversation; at the *table d'hôte* they looked to have the place near his: little enough it seems if one consider his present fame; then it was a great deal to him. He recovered in the Engadine, thanks to them, a little of the confidence which was necessary to his soul and which he had been losing in Germany. During the summer of 1886, some good musicians passed through Sils. In Nietzsche they discovered a very rare listener, and they liked to be heard by him. This courtesy touched him: "I notice," he wrote to Peter Gast, "that our artists only sing and play for me. I should be greatly spoilt if this continued."

A certain Oriental story narrates the adventures of a masked sovereign who travels in his provinces; he is not recognised but divined; an instinct of respect awakes at his approach. In this mountain hotel, does not Nietzsche appear as a masked, a half-divined sovereign?

Nevertheless it was but a poor comfort. Could these women lighten a distress which they could not measure? Nietzsche was traversing that grave moment of life in which a man, however unwilling to be taught, must learn at last what his fate with inexorable constancy gives and refuses him; he had to tear his last hopes from his heart. "I have been unspeakably sad in these latter days," he wrote to Peter Gast, "and cares have deprived me of sleep." The information is brief. To his sister he avows more; he addresses to her pages upon pages that are terrible in their power and monotony.

"Where are they, those old friends, with whom I formerly felt so closely bound? We inhabit different worlds, we no longer speak the same tongue! As a stranger, a proscribed man, I wander among them; never a word, never a look now reaches me. I hold my peace—for none understands my speech—ah, I can say it, they have never understood me! ... It is terrible to be condemned to silence, when one has so many things to say. Am I created for solitude, never to find any one with whom I may make myself understood? Incommunicability is in truth the most awful of solitudes, to be *different*, to wear a mask of brass harder than any mask of brass—perfect friendship is only possible *inter pares. Inter pares!* a phrase which intoxicates me: what confidence, what hope, what perfume, what beatitude it promises the man who necessarily and constantly lives alone; to a man who is *different*—who has never met any one of his race. And nevertheless he is a good seeker; he has sought much. Ah, the swift folly of those hours in which the solitary thinks he has found a friend, embraces him and holds him in his arms; it is a present from heaven, an inestimable gift. An hour later he rejects him with disgust, he rejects himself with disgust, as though soiled, diminished, sick from his own society. A *profound* man needs friends, unless indeed he has a God. And I have neither God nor friend! Ah, my sister, those whom you call by this name, once they were friends—but now?

"Excuse this burst of passion; my last journey is the cause....

"My health is neither good nor bad; it is only the poor soul which is wounded and thirsting. Give me a little circle of men who will listen to me and understand—and I am in good health.

"Here everything takes its course; the two English-women and the old Russian lady, the musician, have come back; the latter very ill...."

Nietzsche now went on with his labours on the *Wille zur Macht*. His unfortunate passage through Germany had modified his arrangements. He thought: "What use is it my writing warlike books? Without allies, without readers, I cannot prevent the abasement of Europe; let it be brought about then. One day it will find its goal—a day which I shall not see. Then my books will be discovered, then I shall have my readers. For them I should write, for them I should determine my fundamental ideas. To-day, I cannot fight, for I have not enemies even...." At the beginning of July, when leaving the Germany which had tried him so hardly, he drew up a detailed plan. In September he wrote:

"I announce, for the next four years, the completion of my work in four volumes. The title alone is alarming: *The Will to Power, an essay towards a Transvaluation of all Values.* For this all is necessary to me—health, solitude, good humour—perhaps a wife *(eine Frau)* also."

In what retirement should he compose this new work? Genoa had inspired the two books which he wrote as a convalescent, *The Dawn of Day* and *The Gay Science;* Rapallo, Nice, had inspired *Zarathustra.* He now thought of Corsica. For long he had been curious about this savage island, and, in the island itself, of a town, Corte—

"There Napoleon was not born but—what is perhaps more important—conceived, and is it not the clearly indicated spot in which I should undertake the transvaluation of all values? ... For me, too, it is a *conception* that is in question."

Alas! this Napoleonic work, the title of which alone should strike terror, thus struck its author. Nietzsche was not unaware whither that *"via mala des consequences"* which he had been long following led him. Since a covetous, conquering force is at the heart of nature, every act which does not correspond precisely with this force is inexact and feeble. He said this, he wrote it, and such indeed was his thought: man is never so great as when he combines an alertness and refinement of mind with a certain native brutality and cruelty of instinct. Thus the Greeks understood *virtu,* and the Italians *virtù.* The French politicians, and, after them, Frederick II., Napoleon and Bismarck, acted in accordance with these maxims. Troubled by his doubts, lost in his problem, Nietzsche firmly grasped this fragmentary but certain truth: *one must have the courage of psychological nudity,* he was to write. He trained himself to it, but remained dissatisfied. His mind was too clear, his soul too pensive, and this definition of the strongest men was too curt and icy for his dreams. Formerly he had chosen Schiller and Mazzini for masters. Did he admire them no longer? No soul was ever as constant as his. Only he feared that, in following them, he would gratify a certain feebleness, and the masters whom he now wished to prefer were called Napoleon and Cæsar Borgia.

On this occasion, too, he turned away from his task, shunning harsh affirmations. The publisher Fritsch consented, on the condition that he received pecuniary aid, to publish a second edition of the *Origin of Tragedy, The Dawn of Day,* and *The Gay Science.* This had long been one of Nietzsche's desires: he wished to add prefaces to these old works, to touch them up, and perhaps to add to them. He undertook this new work and became absorbed in it.

Instead of going to Corsica he returned to the Genoese coast, to Ruta, not far from Rapallo, above Portofino, which thrusts its wooded crest out into the sea. Again he found the walks and familiar places in which Zarathustra had spoken to him. How sad he had then been! He had just lost his two last friends, Lou Salomé and Paul Rée. Nevertheless he had continued his task and, indeed, created, at the moment of his profoundest sorrow, his bravest book. Friedrich Nietzsche let himself be stirred by these memories of the past.

He now received a letter which was the first sign of his coming fame. In August, 1886, in despair of being listened to by his compatriots, he had sent his book, *Beyond Good and Evil,* to two foreign readers, to the Dane Georges Brandes, and to the Frenchman Hippolyte Taine. Georges Brandes did not reply. Hippolyte Taine wrote (October 17, 1886) a letter which gave Nietzsche some joy.

"On my return from a voyage, I found the book which you were good enough to send me; as you say, it is full of 'thoughts from behind' (*'pensées de derrière'*); the form, which is so lively, so literary, the impassioned style, the often paradoxical turn, will open the eyes of the reader who wants to understand; I will in particular recommend to philosophers your first piece on philosophers and philosophy (pp. 14, 17, 20, 25); but the historians and critics will also have their share in the booty of new ideas (for example 41, 75, 76, 149, 150, &c). What you say of national genius and character in your eighth essay is infinitely suggestive, and I shall re-read this piece, although I find there a far too flattering word relative to myself. You do me a great honour in your letter by putting me by the side of M. Burckhardt of Basle, whom I greatly admire; I think that I was the first man in France to announce in the press his great work upon the *Culture of the Renaissance in Italy....* With best thanks, I am,

"Yours sincerely,

"H. TAINE."

Paul Lanzky rejoined Friedrich Nietzsche at Ruta. Not having seen him for eighteen months, he was struck by the change which he observed in him. The body was weighed down, the features altered. But the man remained the same; however bitter his life had become, he was still affectionate and naïve, quick to laughter like a child. He brought Lanzky up the mountain which gives at every instant such magnificent views over the snowy Alps and the sea. The two rested in the most beautiful spots; then they gathered up bits of old timber and twigs from the autumn vines and lit fires, Nietzsche saluting the flames and the rising smoke with cries of joy.

It was then, it was in this inn at Ruta, that Nietzsche drew up the prefaces to *The Dawn of Day* and *The Gay Science,* in which he recounted with so strange a vivacity his spiritual *Odyssey:* Triebschen and Wagner's friendship; Metz and the discovery of war; Bayreuth, hope and mishap; the rupture with Richard Wagner; the bruising of his love; the cruel years which he spent deprived of poetry and of art; finally Italy, which gave him back both; Venice and Genoa, the two towns which saved him, and the Ligurian coast, Zarathustra's cradle.

While Nietzsche wrote thus and struggled against depression, may it not be that he was taking drugs to excite himself to work? There is some evidence to suggest it. But we shall never have exact information on this point. We know that he was absorbing chloral and an extract of Indian hemp which, in small doses, produced an inward calm; in large doses, excitement. Perhaps he handled a more complicated pharmacopoeia in secret; it is the habit of nervous persons.

Friedrich Nietzsche liked this coast. "Imagine," he wrote to Peter Gast, "a little island in the Greek archipelago, pushed down here by the winds. It is a coast of pirates, swift, deceitful, dangerous...." He proposed to pass the winter there. But soon he modified his plans, and wished to return to Nice. Lanzky sought in vain to keep him back.

"You complain of being abandoned," he said to him. "Whose fault is it? You have disciples and you discourage them. You call me here, you call Peter Gast; and you leave."

"I need the light, the air of Nice," answered Nietzsche; "I need the Bay of the Angels."

He went alone. During this winter, he completed his prefaces, he re-read and touched-up his books. He lived, it seems, in a singular condition of relaxation, indecision and melancholy. He sent his manuscripts to Peter Gast, as he always did, but his requests for advice have an unusual accent of unrest and humility. "Bead me," he wrote in February, 1887, "with more distrust than you generally do; say simply: this will do, this won't do I like this, why not alter that, &c, &c."

He read, and his readings seemed guided by a queer curiosity and less under the rigorous sway of his prejudices.

He familiarised himself with the works of the French decadents. He appreciated Baudelaire's writings on Richard Wagner, Paul Bourget's *Essais de Psychologie Contemporaine.* He read the *Contes* of Maupassant and admired this "great Latin."

He ran through some volumes by Zola and did not allow himself to be seduced by a merely popular style of thought, by a merely decorative art. He bought, and commented in pencil on the margin, the *Esquisse d'une Morale sans obligation ni sanction*. Guyau, like Nietzsche and at the same moment, had had the idea of founding a system of morals on the expansive modalities of life. But he understood them in another sense and interpreted as a force of love what Nietzsche understood as a conquering force. Nevertheless the initial agreement was certain. Nietzsche valued highly the purity and intelligence of idea which he found in the work of the French philosopher. The vogue of the Russian novelists was then beginning. Nietzsche took an interest in these poets of a young, violent, and sensitive race, whose charm he always felt. "Do you know Dostoievsky?" he wrote to Peter Gast. "No one, with the exception of Stendhal, has so satisfied and ravished me. There is a psychologist with whom I am in agreement!" He indicated the new author to all his correspondents. The religious fervour of the Slavs interested him and found him indulgent. It was not a symptom of weakness, he thought; it was the return of an energy which could not accept the cold constraints of modern society and whose insubordination took the form of a revolutionary Christianity. These barbarians, thwarted in their instincts, were disconcerted and self-accusatory; they had precipitated a crisis which was still undecided, and Nietzsche wrote: "This bad conscience is a malady, but a malady of the nature of pregnancy." For, hoping always, he obstinately defended his thoughts against his disgusts. He wished his thoughts to remain free, kindly and confident, and when there rose within him and towards them a hatred of Europe and of its debased peoples; when he feared that he might yield to his bitter humour, he corrected himself at once: "No," he kept on saying, "Europe is at present richer than ever in men, in ideas, in aspirations, better prepared for great tasks, and we must, contrary to all semblance, hope everything from these multitudes, though their ugly disposition seems to forbid hope."

During these early months of 1887, Friedrich Nietzsche became intimate with a certain Madame V. P. They went together to San Remo and Monte Carlo. We do not know this woman's name; we have no letter, either written by her or addressed to her. We may infer some mystery, perhaps a mystery of love.

Madame V. P. was no doubt Nietzsche's companion[20] when he heard the prelude to *Parsifal* at the concerts in the Casino at Monte Carlo. He listened without any bitterness, with the sudden indulgence of a worn-out adversary. "I loved Wagner," he wrote in September to Peter Gast; "I still love him." Assuredly he still loved him, when he could speak as he did of this symphony which he had just heard.

"I do not seek to know whether this art can or should serve some end," he wrote to Peter Gast, "I ask myself: Has Wagner ever done better? And I find this: the most

---

[20] Morals are free in the pensions on the Mediterranean, and no doubt we are unaware of all the episodes of Friedrich Nietzsche's life. But this reservation must be made. According to evidence which we have been able to gather, his manner of life, in the Engadine, never gave occasion for the least gossip. On the contrary he seems, we are told, to have avoided young women.

exact conscience and psychological precision in the manner of relating, expressing, and communicating emotion; the shortest and most direct form; every nuance of sentiment defined with an almost epigrammatical brevity: such descriptive clearness that in listening to this music one thinks of some buckler of marvellous workmanship; lastly, a sentiment, a musical experience of a soul which is extraordinary and sublime; a "haughtiness," in the formidable meaning of the word; ... a sympathy, a penetration, which enters like a knife into the soul—and a pity for what he has discovered and judged at the bottom of that soul. Such beauties one finds in Dante and nowhere else. What painter has ever painted so melancholy a look of love as Wagner in the last accents of his prelude?"

How easy it would have been for him to be a great critic, equal in his delicacy, superior in the largeness of his views, to that Sainte-Beuve whom he esteemed so highly! He knew it, and found it hard to resist the seductions of that "dilettantism of analysis"—the expression is his own. His best readers of ten remarked this. "What a historian you are!" Burckhardt used to say, and Hippolyte Taine repeated it. It did not satisfy Nietzsche. He despised the calling of historian or of critic. He was informed by a young German whom he met at Nice that the professors of Tübingen took him as a merely dissolvent mind, radical and nihilistic; it saddened him. He had not torn himself from the romanticism of pity and love to sink at last in the inverse romanticism of violence and energy. He admired Stendhal, but did not intend to be a Stendhalian. The Christian belief had nourished his infancy, the disciplines of Pforta had ripened it, Pythagoras, Plato, Wagner had increased, elevated his desires. He wished to be a poet and a moralist, an inventor of virtues, venerations, and serenities: none of his readers, none of his friends, had understood this intention. In correcting the proofs of *The Dawn of Day,* he re-read this old page, the truth of which still held good.

"We are still on our knees before power—according to the old custom of slaves—and yet, when the degree of *venerability* shall have to be fixed, only the degree of *rationality in power* will be decisive; we have to investigate to what extent power has indeed been overcome by something higher of which it is now the tool and instrument. But as yet there is an absolute lack of eyes for such investigations; nay, in most cases the appraisement of genius is even considered a crime. And thus perhaps the most beautiful of all spectacles still takes place in the dark and, after bursting into bloom, soon fades into perpetual night—I mean the spectacle of that power which a man of genius employs, not in his works, but in the development of himself, regarded as a work, that is, in the task of self-mastery, in the purification of his imagination, in his deliberate choice and ordering of the course of his tasks and inspirations. And yet the great man is still invisible in the greatest thing which claims worship, invisible like a distant star; his triumph over power continues to be without eyes, hence also without song and poets. As yet the order of greatness has not been settled for the sum total of human history...."

Alas, for victory over force, one must possess some exterior force, reason or faith. Nietzsche, denying to the one or to the other all their rights, has disarmed himself for the combat.

At the beginning of March a violent earthquake terrified the cosmopolitan *flaneurs* of Nice. Friedrich Nietzsche admired these movements of nature which reminded man of his nothingness. Two years earlier the catastrophe of Krakatoa, which destroyed two thousand human beings in Java, had filled him with enthusiasm. "It's grand," he said to Lanzky, whom he had asked to read the telegrams to him; "two thousand human beings annihilated at a stroke! It's magnificent. This is how humanity should come to its end—how one day it will end." And he hoped that a tidal wave would at least do away with Nice and its peoples. "But," observed Lanzky, "we should be done away with ourselves." "What matter!" answered Nietzsche. His almost realised desire amused him. He did not advance his departure by a single day.

"Hitherto," he wrote on March 7th, "among these thousands of people in a condition of folly, I have lived with a sentiment of irony and cold curiosity. But one cannot answer for oneself; perhaps to-morrow I shall be as unreasonable as any one. Here there is an *imprévu* which has its charm."

By the middle of March he would have ended his work on the prefaces; and, as he says in one of them: "What do Herr Nietzsche, his illnesses and recoveries, matter to us? Let us speak frankly, let us go straight to the problem." Yes, surely, let us go straight to the problem; determine, among the many ends which men propose to themselves, those which truly elevate and ennoble them; succeed at last in gaining our *triumph over power.* On March 17th he sketched out a plan:

First Book: *European Nihilism.*
Second Book: *Criticism of Superior Values.*
Third Book: *Principle of a New Evaluation.*
Fourth Book: *Discipline and Selection.*

He had sketched a very similar programme in July, 1886: two books of analysis and criticism; two books of doctrine and affirmation; in all four books—four volumes.

Every springtime brought him back to a condition of uncertainty and uneasiness; between Nice and the Engadine; he did not know where to find an air which should be bright enough and not too warm; a fine light that would not hurt his eyes. In this year, 1887, he let himself be tempted by the Italian lakes, and, leaving Nice, set out for Lake Maggiore. This midget Mediterranean, enclosed in the mountains, pleased him infinitely at first. "This place strikes me as more beautiful than any part of the Mediterranean," he wrote, "and more moving—how is it that I took so many years to discover it? The sea, like all huge things, has something stupid and indecent which will not be found here." He corrected the proofs of the *Gaya Scienza;* he re-read *Human, Too Human,* and again paused to contemplate with pity his unrecognised work.

But he recovered possession of himself. The coming work alone mattered. He forced himself to recommence his meditations, and at once became enervated and exhausted. He had planned a visit to Venice; suddenly he gave it up. "My health is against it," he wrote to Peter Gast. "I am unworthy of seeing such beautiful things."

From aggravation of ennui, an epistolary quarrel arose between Erwin Rohde and himself. He had occasion to write a word to the most intimate friend of past days, and could not resist the pleasure of adding a malicious touch. "I suit old people only," he wrote; "Taine, Burckhardt, and even you are not old enough for me...." Erwin Rohde did not like this touch. A professor, whereas Nietzsche was nothing; a scholar with a reputation among European scholars, whereas Nietzsche was still unknown despite his eccentric books, he would not permit irreverence, and defended his dignity. His letter must have been strongly worded, for he had it restored to him later, and destroyed it.

This misadventure tried Nietzsche. His health was in every respect impaired; he resolved to follow a régime of waters, massage and baths, in a special establishment in Switzerland, at Coire. He went there, and surrendered himself to the doctors.

He kept on working, however, and made an energetic effort to discover and define the moral values which he wished to propound. But in vain; do what he would, the problem of his third book—*Principle of a New Evaluation*—remained unsolved. "We may here transcribe the more precise definition with which we are furnished by another draft.

"*Third Book:* the problem of the legislator. To bind anew the unregulated energies in such a manner that they are not mutually annihilated by running foul of one another; to mark the *real augmentation* of force."

What does this mean? What real augmentation, what real direction of things is indicated us by these words? Is it an augmentation of intensity? Then every shade of energy, provided it be intense, will be good. But we must not take it in this sense. Nietzsche selected, preferred, excluded. This augmentation is then the sign of an order, of a natural hierarchy. But in every hierarchy there must be a criterion by which the ranks are distributed; what should this criterion be? Nietzsche would formerly have said: It will be my logical affirmation, the beliefs which I shall have given. Does he still think it? Doubtless; his thoughts hardly vary. But his audacity was lessened by his sorrows, his critical mind had been rendered more exacting by long indecisions. He desired, he sought, he seemed to ask science, the "doctor-philosopher," for a real basis which all his habits of thought refused him.

Mournful news completed the ruin of his courage. Heinrich von Stein died, before his thirtieth year, of a heart failure.

"This has put me out of my senses," wrote Nietzsche to Peter Gast; "I truly loved him. I always thought that he was reserved for me some day. He belonged to that little number of men whose *existence* rejoiced me; and he too had great confidence in me....

In this very place how we laughed! ... He paid a two days' visit to Sils, he had not a glance for Nature or Switzerland—he came straight from Bayreuth; he went back straight to Halle, to his father;—one of the rarest and most delicate homages I have ever received. It made an impression. He had said at the hotel: 'If I come, it is not for the Engadine.'"

Three weeks passed. He complained of bitter inclinations, of susceptibility which lowered his soul. Nevertheless, he announced a new work. What was it?

It is not *The Will to Power*. His impatience, which is added to by fatigue, does not easily bend to the delays of meditation. Of his old gifts, his genius for improvising, his polemical genius alone survive. Herr Widmann, a Swiss critic, had just written a study on *Beyond Good and Evil* and saw in this work but a manual of anarchism: "This is dynamite," he said. Friedrich Nietzsche wished to reply, and at once drew up at a spurt in fifteen days one, two, three short essays which he entitled as a whole, *A Genealogy of Morals*. "This work," he wrote on the title-page, "is destined to complete and elucidate my last book, *Beyond Good and Evil*."

"I have said," he wrote in substance, "that I place myself beyond Good and Evil— *Gut und Böse*. Does this mean that I wish to liberate myself from every moral category? No. I challenge the exaltation of meekness which is called good; the defamation of energy which is called bad; but the history of the human conscience— do the moralists know that such a history exists?—displays to us a multitude of other moral values, other ways of being good, other ways of being bad, numerous shades of honour and of dishonour. Even here the reality is moving, initiative is free; one must seek, one must create."

But Nietzsche developed his thought further: "I have wished," he wrote some months later à propos of this little book, "I have wished to fire a cannon-shot with more sonorous powder." He exposed the distinction between the two moralities, the one dictated by the masters, the other by the slaves; and he thought to recognise in the verbal roots of the words "good" and "evil," their old meaning. *Bonus, buonus,* said he, comes from *duonus,* which signifies warrior; *malus* comes from μέλας, black: the blonde Aryans, the ancestors of the Greek, indicated by this word the type of conduct habitual to their slaves and subjects, the Mediterraneans crossed with Negro and Semitic blood. These primitive notions of what is noble and what is vile, Friedrich Nietzsche does not challenge.

On the 18th of July, writing from Sils-Maria, he announced the new work to Peter Gast.

"I have energetically employed these last days, which were better," he wrote. "I have drawn up a little piece of work which, as I think, puts the problem of my last book in a clear light. Every one has complained of not having understood me; and the hundred copies sold do not permit me to doubt that in effect I am not understood. You know that for three years I have spent about 500 thalers to defray the cost of my books; no honorarium, it goes without saying, and I am 43 years old, and I have written fifteen books! Further: experience, and many applications, more painful to me than I care to say, force me to certify, as a fact, that no German editor wants to have anything to do with me (even if I abandon my author's rights). Perhaps this little book which I am completing to-day will help to sell some copies of my last book (it always pains me to think of the poor Fritzsch on whom all the weight of my work rests). Perhaps my publishers will some day benefit from me. As for myself, I know only too well that when people begin to understand me, *I shall not benefit from it.*"

On the 20th of July, he despatched the manuscript to the publisher. On the 24th July, he called it back by telegram in order to add a few features, a few pages. All his summer was spent in discomfort, melancholy, and the correction of his book, which he never ceased to touch up, to draw out, to render more violent and more alive. Towards the end of August, perceiving an empty space on the last page of the first section, Nietzsche added this curious note, in which he indicated the unstudied problems which he was to have neither strength nor time to attack.

"*Remark.*—I take the opportunity presented by this essay to express publicly and formally a wish which, so far, I have only mentioned occasionally to certain scholars, in chance conversations. Some Faculty of Philosophy ought, by a series of academical prize-dissertations, to further studies in the *history of morality;* perhaps this book will serve to give a vigorous impetus in this direction. I would propose the following question:

" *What hints are furnished by philology, more especially by etymological research, with reference to the history of the development of moral concepts?*

"On the other hand it will be as necessary to interest physiologists and doctors in these problems. In fact and above all, all tables of values, every 'thou shalt' known to history and ethnological research, need to be explained and elucidated in the first place from their *physiological* side, before any attempt is made to interpret them through psychology.... The question: What is this or that table of values and morality *worth?* must be considered from the most varied perspectives. Especially 'the worth for what?' must be considered with extraordinary discernment and delicacy. A thing, for instance, which has evident value with reference to the greatest durability of a race might possess quite another value, if it were a question of creating a higher type. The good of the greatest number and the good of the smallest number are antithetical points of view in valuation; we shall let the simplicity of English biologists suppose that the former is *by itself* of higher value. All sciences must prepare the way for the philosopher of the future, whose task will consist in solving the *problem of values* and determining *their hierarchy.*"

September came. The proofs were corrected, the Engadine became cold. The wandering philosopher had to find new quarters and new work.

"To tell the truth," he wrote to Peter Gast, "I hesitate between Venice and Leipsic; I should go there to work, I still have a lot to learn, many questions to ask and much to read for the great thought of my life of which I must now acquit myself. It would not be a matter of an autumn, but of a *whole winter* spent in Germany. And, weighing everything together, my health dissuades me very strongly from essaying a like experience this year. It will be then Venice or Nice; and from a quite personal point of view, that is better perhaps. Moreover, I need solitude and contemplation rather than study and inquiry into five thousand problems."

Peter Gast was at Venice, and Venice, as one might have foreseen, carried the day. Nietzsche lived for some weeks, a *flaneur* and all but happy, in the town with a "hundred profound solitudes." He scarcely wrote: his days, according to Peter Gast, were idle or seemed to be so. It was not to shut himself up in a room in Venice that he gave up the libraries of Leipsic. He walked, frequented the poor "trattoria," where at midday the humblest, the most courteous of lower classes sit down to eat; when the light was too strong he went to rest his eyes in the shade of the basilica; when day began to decline he recommenced his perpetual walks. Then he could look at St. Mark, with its flocks of familiar pigeons, without suffering, at the lagoon with its islands and temples. He kept on thinking of his work. He imagined it logical and free, simple in its plan, numerous in its details, luminous with a little mystery, a little shade on every line; he wished in short that it should resemble that city which he loved, that Venice whose sovereign will allied itself to the play of all fantasy and grace.

Let us read this page of notes, written in November, 1887; L'*Ombra di Venezia,* is it not obvious there?

"*A perfect* book to consider:

"(1) Form. Style. *An ideal monologue,* all that has a learned appearance, absorbed in the depths. All the accents of profound passion, of unrest and also of weakness. Alleviations, sun tasks—short happiness, sublime serenity. To go beyond demonstration; to be absolutely personal, without employing the first person. Memoirs as it were; to say the most abstract things in the most concrete, in the most cutting manner. The whole history as if it had been *lived* and *personally suffered.* Visible things, precise things, examples, as many as possible. No description; all the problems transposed into sentiment as far as passion.

"(2) Expressive terms. Advantage of military terms. To find expressions to replace philosophical terms."

On the 22nd of October he was at Nice.

Two events (the word is assuredly not too strong) occupied the first two weeks of his stay. He lost his oldest friend; he acquired a reader.

The lost friend was Erwin Rohde. The quarrel begun in the previous spring was then consummated. Nietzsche wrote to Rohde, and his first intention was not to wound. "Do not withdraw from me too lightly," he wrote in announcing the despatch of his last book, *The Genealogy of Morals;* "at my age and in my solitude I can hardly bear to lose the few men in whom I formerly confided." But he could not limit himself to these words. He had received a second note, a very amiable one, from Hippolyte Taine,[21] whom Erwin Rohde had criticised disrespectfully in his letter of May. Nietzsche wished to defend his French correspondent, and continued:

"N.B.—I beg that you judge M. Taine more sensibly. The scurrilities that you express and think about him irritate me. I pardon them to the prince Napoleon, not to friend Rohde. It is difficult to me to think that any one who misunderstands this great-hearted and severe-minded race can understand anything of my task. Besides, you have never written me a word which shows that you have the least suspicion of the destiny which weighs me down. I have forty-three years behind me and am as alone as if I were a child."

All relations were broken off.

The new reader acquired was Georges Brandes, who acknowledged the despatch of the *Genealogy* in an extraordinarily intelligent and vivid letter.

"I get the breath of a new mind from your books," he wrote: "I do not always entirely understand what I read, I do not always see whither you are bound, but many features are in accord with my thoughts and sympathies; like you I hold the ascetic ideal in poor esteem; democratic mediocrity inspires in me, as in you, a profound repugnance; I appreciate your aristocratic radicalism. I am not quite clear with regard to your contempt for the ethic of pity ...

"Of you I know nothing. I see with astonishment that you are a professor. In any case I offer you my best compliments on being, intellectually, so little of a professor.... You are of the small number of men with whom I would like to talk."

It would seem as if Nietzsche ought to have felt very strongly the comfort of having found two witnesses to his work, and of so rare a quality: Brandes and Taine. Did he not learn, about this time, that Brahms was reading *Beyond, Good and Evil* with much relish? But the iron had entered into his soul, and the faculty of receiving happy impressions was, as it were, extinguished in him. He had lost that interior joy, that resistant serenity of which he was formerly so proud, and his letters displayed only melancholy.

With this disaster there survived the activity of his mind alone, which worked with singular energy. We can with difficulty enumerate the objects which occupied his attention. Peter Gast transcribed his *Hymn to Life* for the orchestra; Nietzsche superintended, sometimes corrected, always naïvely admired, this new form of his work.

The journal of the Goncourts appeared; he read this "very interesting novelty," and sat down to table at Magny's with Flaubert, Sainte-Beuve, Gautier, Taine, Gavarri and Renan. All these distractions did not prevent him from embarking resolutely on his new work, the decisive work in which his wisdom and not his rage would speak;

---

[21] "I am very happy," wrote Taine, "that my articles on Napoleon have struck you as true, and nothing can more exactly sum up my impression than the two German words which you use: *Unmensch* und *Uebermensch*."—Letter of July 12, 1887.

the calm work in which polemics would be without rights. He defined in six lines the design which he had formed.

"To have run through every chamber of the modern soul, to have eaten in each of its corners: my pride, my torture, and my joy. To transcend pessimism effectively, and, in short, a Goethean regard full of love and good-will."

Friedrich Nietzsche in this note designated the inspirer of his last work; it was to be Goethe. No nature differed so much from his own, and this very difference determined his choice. Goethe had humiliated no mode of human activity, he had excluded no idea from his intellectual world; he had received and administered as a benevolent lord the immense heritage of human culture. Such was Friedrich Nietzsche's last ideal, his last dream. He wished, in this extremity of life (he knew his destiny), to spread, like the sinking sun, his softest lights; to penetrate everywhere, to justify and illumine everything, so that not one shadow should exist upon the surface of things, not one sorrow in the privacy of souls.

He easily determined the directing ideas of his first two volumes: *European Nihilism, The Criticism of Higher Values.* For four years he had not written a line which was not a part of this analysis or criticism. He wrote rapidly, angrily. "A little fresh air," he cried; "this absurd state of Europe cannot last much longer." It was only a cry, and very quickly suppressed. Nietzsche put patience behind him, like a weakness; with a song of love that he would answer the attacks of life. He wished to return, and did, in fact, return, to calmer thoughts. He put this question: "Is it true that the condition of Europe is absurd? Perhaps a reason for the facts exists, and escapes us. Perhaps in this debility of the will, in this democratic abasement, one should rightly recognise a certain utility, a certain value of conservation. They seem irrepressible; perhaps they are necessary, perhaps in the long run salutary, though to-day, and, so far as we are concerned, they must be deplored.

"*Reflexion:* It is madness to suppose that all this victory of values can be anti-biological; one must seek to explain it by a *vital* interest for the maintenance of the type *man,* even though it must be attained by the preponderance of the feeble and the disinherited. Perhaps if things went differently, man would cease to exist?—Problem.

"The elevation of the type is dangerous to the conservation of the species. Why?

"The strong races are the prodigal races.... Here we are confronted by a problem of economy...."

He repressed all disgust, refused to allow himself the use of abusive speech, tried to consider, and did consider, serenely, those tendencies which he condemned. He asked: Must we deny to the masses the right to seek their truths, their vital beliefs? The masses are the basis of all humanity, the foundation of all cultures. Without them, what would become of the masters? They require that the masses be happy. We must be patient; we must suffer our insurgent slaves (for the moment our masters) to invent the illusions which are favourable to them. Let them believe in the dignity of work! If they thus become more docile in work, their belief is salutary.

"The problem," he writes, "is to render man as utilisable as possible, and make him approximate, as far as may be done, as closely as possible to the machine which never makes a mistake; for this, he must be armed with the virtues of the machine, he must be taught to endure ennui, to lend to ennui a superior charm ...; the *agreeable* sentiments must be put back to a lower rank.... The mechanical form of existence, considered as the noblest, the highest, should adore itself.

"A high culture can only be raised on a vast site, over a firm and well-consolidated mediocrity....

"The sole end must, for a long while yet, be the *lessening* of man: for there must first be created a large foundation on which the race of strong men may be raised....

"The *lessening* of the European man is the great process which may not be impeded; it should be accelerated again. It is the active force which allows one to hope for the arrival of a stronger race, of a race which should possess to excess those very qualities which the impoverished species lack (will, responsibility, certitude, the faculty of fixing an end for oneself)."

Thus at the end of 1887, Nietzsche had succeeded in drawing up a first sketch of the work of synthesis which he had proposed to himself. He concedes a certain right, a certain dignity, to those motives which he formerly reviled. The final rough drafts of *Zarathustra* had already given us similar indications. "The disciples of Zarathustra," wrote Nietzsche, "give to the humblest, not to themselves, the expectation of happiness. ... They distribute religions and systems, according to a hierarchy." Nietzsche now writes, and the intention is similar: "The humanitarian tendencies are not anti-vital, they suit the masses who live slowly, and thus suit humanity which needs the satisfaction of the masses. The Christian tendencies are also benevolent, and nothing is so desirable," writes Nietzsche, "as their permanence; for they suit all those who suffer, all the feeble, and it is necessary for the health of human societies that suffering, that inevitable weaknesses, be accepted without revolt, with submission, and, if possible, with love." "Whatever I may happen to say of Christianity," wrote Nietzsche in 1881 to Peter Gast, "I cannot forget that I owe to it the best experiences of my spiritual life; and I hope never to be ungrateful to it at the bottom of my heart." This thought, this hope, has never left him; and he rejoices to have found a word of justice for the religion of his childhood, the only one which still offers itself to souls.

On December 14, 1887, he addressed a letter to an old correspondent of the Basle days, Carl Fuchs. The accent is a proud one.

"Almost all that I have written should be erased. During these latter years the vehemence of my internal agitations has been terrible. To-day, at the moment when I should be rising higher, my first task is to modify myself, to *depersonalise* myself towards higher forms.

"Am I old? I do not know, and moreover I do not know what kind of youth is necessary to me.

"In Germany, people complain strongly of my 'eccentricities.' But as they do not know where my centre is, they can hardly discern when or how I happen to be eccentric."

From the dates of his notes, it seems that Nietzsche approached a different problem in the month of January, 1888. Those humble multitudes whose rights he admits and measures would not deserve to live, if their activity were not, in the last instance, governed by an élite, utilised for glorious ends. What would be the virtues of this élite, what ends would it serve? Nietzsche was thus brought back to the problem which was his torment. Would he define at length this unknown, and perhaps unattainable grandeur, towards which his soul had for so long aspired? He was again a prey to sadness. He complained of his sensibility, of his irritability, which had become such that each day, on the arrival of the post, he hesitated and shivered before opening his letters.

"Never has life appeared so difficult to me," he wrote to Peter Gast on January 15th. "I can no longer keep on terms with any sort of reality: when I do not succeed in forgetting them, they break me.... There are nights when I am overwhelmed with distress. And so much remains to be done—all, so to say!—Therefore I must hold out. To this wisdom I apply myself, at least in the mornings. Music, these days, gives me sensations which I had never known. It frees me, it lets me recover from the intoxication of myself; I seem to consider myself from a great height, to *feel* myself from a great height; thus it renders me stronger, and regularly, after an evening's music (I have heard *Carmen* four times), I have a morning full of energetic perceptions and lucky discoveries. It is quite admirable. It is as though I had bathed myself in a *more natural* element. Without music life is merely a mistake, a weariness, an exile."

Let us try to follow the course of his work. He subjected himself to an historical research and attempted to discover the social class, the nation, the race or the party which authorised the hope of a more noble humanity. Here was the modern European:

"How could a race of strong men disengage itself from it? a race with the classical taste? The classical taste, that is, the will to simplification, to accentuation ... the courage of psychological nudity.... To raise oneself from this chaos to this organisation, one must be constrained by a *necessity*. One must be without choice; disappear or impose oneself. A dominant race can only have terrible and violent origins. Problem: where are the *barbarians* of the twentieth century? Evidently they will only be able to appear and impose themselves after huge socialistic crises—these will be the elements most capable of the most persistent hardness in respect of themselves, and who will be able to become the guarantees of *the most persistent will*."

Is it possible to discern in modern Europe these elements predestined to victory? Nietzsche busied himself with this problem, and wrote down the results of his researches in his notebook.

"The most favourable impediments and remedies against modernity.

"And first:

"1. *Obligatory military service,* with genuine wars which put an end to all lightness of mind.

"2. *National narrowness* which simplifies and concentrates."

Other indications corroborate the above.

"The maintenance of the *military state,* which is the only means left to us, whether for the maintenance of the great traditions, or for the institution of the superior type of man. And all circumstances which perpetuate unfriendliness, distance between states, find themselves thus justified."

What an unforeseen conclusion to Nietzschean polemics! He had dishonoured nationalism; and for the support which he sought in this grave hour he fell back on nationalism. A yet more unexpected discovery was to come. Nietzsche, proceeding with his researches, foresaw, defined, and approved of a party which can be but a form or a reform of Positivist democracy. He discerned the lineaments of the two vigorous and sane groupings which suffice to discipline man.

"*A party of peace,* not sentimental, which denies war to itself and its members, which also denies them recourse to the courts of law; which provokes against itself, struggle, contradiction, persecution: a party of the oppressed, at least for a time; soon the great party opposed to sentiments of rancour and vengeance.

"A *party of war,* which with the same logic and severity against itself, proceeds in an opposite sense."

Should we recognise in these two parties the organised forces which will produce that *tragical era of Europe* which Nietzsche announces? Perhaps; but let us be careful not to exaggerate the value of these notes. They are rapidly written; as they surged and passed in Nietzsche's mind, they should surge and pass before us. His view pierces in every direction: it never settles upon one object. No working-class Puritanism can satisfy him, for he knows that the brilliancy of human culture stands or falls with the freedom of the aristocracies. No nationalism can satisfy him, for he loves Europe and her innumerable traditions.

What resource is left to him? He has bound himself to seek in his own time the points of support for a higher culture. For a moment he thinks he has found them; he has deceived himself, and turns away, for these supports impose a narrowness of direction which his mind cannot tolerate. "There is this that is extraordinary in the life of a thinker," he wrote in 1875—the age of the text proves the permanence of the conflict—" that two contrary inclinations oblige him to follow, at the same moment, two different directions and hold him under their yokes; on the one hand he wishes to know and, abandoning without weariness the firm ground which sustains the life of men, he adventures into unknown regions; on the other hand he wishes to live, and, without ever wearying, he seeks a place in which to five...." Nietzsche had abandoned Wagner, wandered in uncertain regions. He seeks a final security; what does he find? The narrow refuge of nationalism. He withdraws from it: it may be a vulgar recourse, a useful artifice for maintaining some solidity in the crowds, a certain principle of taste and of severity; it may not be, it must not be, the doctrine of the European élite, a scattered and, no doubt, non-existent élite to whom his thoughts are addressed.

Nietzsche put the idea of nationalism out of his mind; it was the expedient of a weak century. He ceased to devote himself to his search. What mattered to him the beliefs which should be beneficent to the humble? He thought of Napoleon and of Goethe, both of whom rose superior to their times, and to the prejudices of their countries. Napoleon was contemptuous of the Revolution, but artfully turned its energy to advantage; he despised France, but ruled her. Goethe held Germany in poor esteem and took little interest in her struggles: he wished to possess and reanimate all the ideas, all the dreams of men, to conserve and enrich the vast heritage of moral riches which Europe had created. Napoleon knew the grandeur of Goethe, and Goethe joyfully observed the life of the conqueror, *ens realissimum*. The soldier, the poet, the one who kept men in submission and silence, held them to effort, the other who watched, meditated, and glorified, such is the ideal couple that reappear at every decisive instant in Friedrich Nietzsche's life. He had admired the Greece of Theognis and Pindar, the Germany of Bismarck and Wagner; a long winding course led him back towards his dream, towards that unrealised Europe of strength and beauty of which Goethe and Napoleon were, upon the morrow of the Revolution, the solitary representatives.

We can tell, from a letter addressed to Peter Gast (February 13, 1887), that Nietzsche was at this date by no means satisfied with his work. "I am still in the tentative, the introductory, the expectant stage ..." he wrote, and he added: "The first rough draft of my *Essay towards a Transvaluation* is ready; it has been, on the whole, a torture, and I have no longer the courage to think of it. In ten years I shall do better." What was the cause of this dissatisfaction? Was he weary of that tolerance, that condescension to the needs of the feeble and of the crowd which he had imposed on himself for three months? Was he impatient to express his anger?

The letters which he then addressed to his mother and sister let us approach him in a more intimate manner. (They have not all been published.) He wrote to these two women from whom he was separated with a tenderness which rendered difficult dissimulation and even courage itself. He let himself go, as though it pleased him to find himself at their knees a child again. He was gentle, obedient with his mother; he signed himself humbly: *ta vieille créature.* With his sister he talked like a comrade; he seemed to have forgotten all the grievances he had had against her in other times; he knew that she would never return from far-off Paraguay: he regretted her, he loved her because she was lost. She is energetic, is Lisbeth, and valiantly risks her life. Nietzsche admired in her the virtues which he esteemed above all virtues, and which are, he thinks, the virtues of his race, the noble race of the Counts Nietzki. "How strongly I feel," he wrote her, "in all you do and say, that the same blood runs in our veins." He hearkened to her, but she did not cease to offer him overwise advice. As he complains of being alone, why does he not get made a professor, why does he not marry? Nietzsche answered too easily: "Where would I find a wife? and if by chance I did find one, would I have the right to ask her to share my life?" He knew nevertheless, and said so, that a wife would be sweet to him.

"NICE, *January* 25, 1888. "I must relate a little adventure to you: yesterday, as I was taking my usual walk, I heard, not far off, a warm and frank laugh (I thought that I heard your laugh); and when this laughing person came near me—I saw a very charming girl, with brown eyes, delicate as a deer. The sight warmed my heart, my old solitary philosopher's heart—I thought of your matrimonial advice, and for the rest of my walk, I could not rid myself of the image of this young and gracious girl. Assuredly it would do me good to have so gracious a thing by me—but would it do her good? Would not I, with my ideas, make this girl unhappy? And would not my heart break (we assume that I love her) if I saw so amiable a creature suffering? No, no marriage!"

Was it not now that a singular and unwholesome idea fixed itself in his thought? At every moment he was picturing to himself the joys of which he was deprived: fame, love, and friendship; he thought rancourously of those who possessed them, and above all of Richard Wagner, whose genius had been always so sumptuously rewarded. How beautiful she had been, when he knew her at Triebschen, this incomparable woman Cosima Lizst, come, while yet married, to the scandal of the world, to live with Wagner and help in his work! Attentive and clear-minded, active and helpful, she assured him the security which he had hitherto lacked. Without her, what would have become of him? Could he have mastered his impatient, restless, excitable temperament? would he have been capable of realising those great works which he was for ever announcing? Cosima appeased him, directed him; thanks to her, he achieved the Tetralogy, he reared Bayreuth, he wrote *Parsifal*.... Nietzsche recalled those fine days at Triebschen. Cosima welcomed him, listened to his ideas and projects, read his manuscripts, was benevolent, talked brightly to him. Suffering and irritation deformed his memories; he became infatuated with the thought that he had loved Cosima Wagner and that she, perhaps, had loved him. Nietzsche wished to believe this, and came to believe it. Yes, there had been love between them, and Cosima would have saved him, as she saved Wagner, if, by lucky chance, she had only known him a few years earlier. But every circumstance had been unfavourable to Nietzsche. Here again Wagner had robbed him. He had taken all, fame, love, friendship.

We can divine this strange romance in the last works of Friedrich Nietzsche. A Greek myth helps him to express and veil his thoughts; it is the myth of Ariadne, Theseus, and Bacchus. Theseus was lost; Ariadne has met him and led him to the exit from the labyrinth; but Theseus is treacherous: he abandons upon the rock the woman who has saved him; Ariadne would die alone and in despair if Bacchus did not intervene, Bacchus-Dionysios who loves her. The enigma of these three names may be solved: Ariadne is Cosima; Theseus, Wagner; Bacchus-Dionysios, Nietzsche.

On the 31st of March he wrote again, and his language was that of a lost soul.

"Night and day, I am in a state of unbearable tension and oppression, by reason of the duty imposed upon me and also on account of my conditions of life, which are absolutely opposed to the accomplishment of this duty; here no doubt the cause of my distress must be sought.

"... My health, thanks to an extraordinarily fine winter, to good nourishment, to long walks, has remained sufficiently good. Nothing is sick, but the poor soul. Besides, I will not conceal the fact that my winter has been very rich in spiritual acquisitions for my great work: so the mind is not sick; nothing is sick, but the poor soul."

Nietzsche left Nice next day. He wished, before going up to the Engadine, to make the experiment of a stay in Turin. Its dry air and spacious streets had been praised in his hearing. He travelled with difficulty; he lost his luggage and his temper, quarrelled with the porters, and remained for two days ill at Sampiedarena, near Genoa; in Genoa itself, he spent three days of rest, fully occupied with the happy memories which he found again. "I thank my luck," he wrote to Peter Gast, "that it led me back to this town, where the will rises, where one cannot be cowardly. I have never felt more gratitude than during this pilgrimage to Genoa...." On Saturday, April 6th, he arrived at Turin, broken with fatigue. "I am no longer capable of travelling alone," he said to Peter Gast in the same letter. "It agitates me too much, everything affects me stupidly."

III

Towards the Darkness

Here we should discontinue our story to forewarn the reader. Hitherto, we have been following the history of Nietzsche's thought. Nietzsche's thought has now no longer a history, for an influence, come not from the mind, but from the body, has affected it. People sometimes say that Nietzsche was mad long before this. It may be that they are right; it is impossible to reach an assured diagnosis. At least he had retained his power of reflection, his will. He could still hold himself and his judgments in check. In the spring of 1888 he lost this faculty. His intelligence is not yet darkened; there is not a word he writes but is penetrating and trenchant. His lucidity is extreme, but disastrous, since it exercises itself only to destroy. As one studies the last months of this life, one feels as though one were watching the work of some engine of war which is no longer governed by the hand of man.

Friedrich Nietzsche abandoned those moral researches which had strengthened his work till now, enriched and elevated it. Let us recall a letter addressed to Peter Gast in February, 1888: "I am in a state of chronic irritability which allows me, in my better moments, a sort of revenge, not the finest sort—it takes the form of an excess of hardness." These words shed light on the three coming books: *The Case of Wagner, The Twilight of the Idols, The Antichrist.*

We shall hurry on with the story of those months in which Nietzsche is no longer quite himself.

About the 7th of April he received an unexpected letter at Turin. Georges Brandes wrote informing him of a projected series of conferences which were to be devoted to his philosophy. "It annoys me," wrote Brandes, "to think that no one knows you here, and I wish to make you known all of a sudden." Nietzsche replied: "Truly, dear sir, this is a surprise. Where did you get such courage that you can speak in public of a *vir obscurissimus?*... Perhaps you imagine that I am known in my own country. They treat me as something singular and absurd, which it is not at all necessary *to take seriously"* He ended by remarking, "The long resistance has exasperated my pride a little. Am I a philosopher? What does it matter?"

The letter should have been an occasion of great joy; and, perhaps, had it been possible to save him, the occasion of his salvation. Assuredly he felt some happiness, but we scarcely discern it. The hour was late, and Nietzsche now followed the tracks whither his destiny had drawn him.

During these days of weariness and tension, he procured a translation of the *Laws of Manu,* for he wished to become familiar with the model of those hierarchic societies for whose renovation he hoped. He read, and his expectations were not deceived; this, the last study of his life, turned out to be one of the most important he had ever undertaken. It delighted him to ecstasy—here was a code on which were established the customs and the order of four castes, a language that was beautiful, simple, human in its very severity, a constant nobleness of thought. And the impression of security, of sweetness which detached itself from the book as a whole! Here are some commandments from its earlier pages:

"Before the cutting of the navel string, a ceremony is prescribed at the birth of a male; he must be made, while sacred texts are pronounced, to taste a little honey and clarified butter from a golden dish.

"Let the father fulfil the ceremony of the giving of a name, on the tenth or twelfth day after birth, on a propitious lunary day, at a favourable moment, under a star of happy influence.

"Let the first name in the compound name of a Brahman express the propitious favour; that of a Kshatriya, power; that of a Vaisya, riches: that of a Sudra, abjection.

"Let the name of a girl be soft, clear, agreeable, propitious and easily spoken, terminating in long vowels, and resembling words of benediction."

Friedrich Nietzsche read and admired. He copied out many a passage, recognising in the old Hindu text that *Goethean gaze, full of love and of good will,* hearing in its pages that *canto d'amore,* which he had himself wished to sing.

But if he admired, he also judged. That Hindu order had as basis a mythology of which the priests who interpreted it were not the dupes. "These sages," wrote

Nietzsche, "do not believe in all this—or they would not have found it...." The laws of Manu were clever and beautiful lies. Necessarily so, since Nature is a chaos, a derision of all thought and of all order, and whoever aspires to the foundation of an order, must turn away from her and conceive an illusory world. Those master builders, the Hindoo lawgivers, are masters also in the art of lying. If Nietzsche were not careful, their genius would drag him into the path of falsehoods.

Here was the instant of a crisis of which we know nothing but the origin and the term. Nietzsche was alone at Turin, no one was by him as he worked, he had no confidant. What was he thinking? Doubtless he was studying, meditating continually over the old Aryan book which gave him the model of his dreams, that book which was the finest monument of æsthetic and social perfection, and, at the same time, of intellectual knavery. How he must have loved and yet hated it! He mused, was amazed, and suspended his work. Four years earlier a similar difficulty had prevented him from completing his *Zarathustra*. It was no longer a question of the *Superman,* of an *Eternal Return.* These naïve formulæ were abandoned, but the tendencies which they cloaked—the one, lyrical, avid of construction and of order, even though illusory; the other, avid of destruction and of lucidity—these unvarying tendencies again exercised their influence at this point. Nietzsche hesitated: should he finally listen to these Brahmins, these priests, these crafty leaders of men. No; loyalty is the virtue upon which he can never compound. Later perhaps, much later, when a few centuries are gone by, humanity, more learned in the meaning of its life, in the origins and values of its instincts, in the mechanism of heredities, may essay new lawgivings. To-day it cannot: it would only add falsehoods and hypocrisies to the old lies, the old hypocrisies, which already fetter it. Nietzsche turned away from the thoughts which he had followed with such energy for six months, and suddenly found himself exactly as he had been in his thirtieth year, indifferent to all that was not in the service of truth.

"All that is suspect and false must be brought into the light!" he had then written. "We do not wish to build prematurely, we do not know that we can build, and that it may not be better to build nothing. There are pessimists who are cowardly and resigned—of those we do not wish to be."

When he had thus expressed himself, Nietzsche still possessed strength enough to consider calmly a labour made the easier by hope. But in ten years he has lost his old force, his old calm, and all hope has left him. His sick soul can no longer offer any resistance—irritability overcomes it. He gives up the composition of his great work, relinquishes it to write a pamphlet. By this circumstance our conjectures are solved and, indeed, terminated.

The days of serenity have gone by. Wounded to the death, Nietzsche wishes to return blow for blow. Richard Wagner is his mark, the false apostle of *Parsifal,* the illusionist who has seduced his period. If he formerly served Wagner, now he will disserve him, out of passion as out of a sense of duty. He thinks: "It is I who made Wagnerism; it is I who must unmake it." He wishes to liberate, by means of a violent attack, those of his contemporaries who, weaker than himself, still submit to the prestige of this art. He wants to humiliate this man whom he has loved, whom he still loves; he wishes to defame this master who was the benefactor of his youth; in short, if we do not mistake, he wishes to take vengeance on a lost happiness. So he insults Wagner; calls him a decadent, a low comedian, a modern Cagliostro. This indelicacy— an unheard-of thing in Nietzsche's life—suffices to prove the presence of the evil.

No scruple haunted him. A happy excitement favoured and hastened on his work. Alienists are familiar with those singular conditions which precede the last crises of general paralysis, and Friedrich Nietzsche seemed to abandon himself to an afflux of joy. He attributed the benefit to the climate of Turin, which he was now trying.

"Turin, dear friend," wrote he to Peter Gast, "is a capital discovery. I tell you with the idea at the back of my mind that you may perhaps also profit from it. My humour is good, I work from morning to night—a little pamphlet on music occupies my fingers—I digest like a demi-god, I sleep in spite of the nocturnal noises of carriages: so many symptoms of the eminent suitability of Turin to Nietzsche."

In July, in the Engadine, some damp and cold weeks did him a great deal of harm. He lost his sleep. His happy excitement disappeared, or transformed itself into bitter and febrile humours. It was then that Fräulein von Salis-Marschlins, who has recounted her recollections in an interesting brochure, saw him, after a separation of ten months. She remarked the change in his condition; how he walked alone, his hurried carriage, his sharp salute—he would stop scarcely or not at all, in such a hurry was he to get back to his inn and put down the thoughts which his walk had inspired in him. On the visits he paid her he did not conceal his preoccupations. He was in dread of pecuniary embarrassments: the capital which had constituted his little fortune was almost gone; and could he, with the three thousand francs which the University of Basle allowed him as a pension, provide for his everyday needs and for the publication, always onerous, of his books? It was in vain that he regulated his journeys and restricted himself to the simplest lodgings and food. He was reaching the limits of his resources.

The Case of Wagner was completed; to the text, a preliminary discourse, a postscript, a second postscript, and an epilogue were added. He could not cease extending his work, and making it more bitter. Nevertheless he was not satisfied, and felt, after having written it, some remorse.

"I hope that this very *risqué* pamphlet has pleased you," he wrote to Peter Gast on the 11th of August, 1888. "That would be for me a comfort by no means negligible. There are certain hours, above all, certain evenings, when I do not feel enough courage in myself for so many follies, for so much hardheartedness; I am in doubt over some passages. Perhaps I went too far (not in the matter, but in my manner of expressing the matter). Perhaps the note in which I speak of Wagner's family origins could be suppressed."

A letter addressed about this time to Fräulein von Meysenbug gives food for thought.

"I have given to men the most profound book," he writes; "one pays dearly for that. The price of being immortal is sometimes life! ... And always on my road that cretinism of Bayreuth! The old seducer Wagner, dead though he be, continues to draw away from me just those few men whom my influence might touch. But in Denmark—how absurd to think!—I have been celebrated this winter. Dr. Georges Brandes, whose mind is so full of vitality, has dared to talk about me before the University of Copenhagen. And with brilliant success! Always more than three hundred listeners! And a final ovation!—And something similar is being arranged in New York. I am the most *independent* mind in Europe and the *only* German writer— which is something!"

He added in a postscript: "Only a great soul can endure my writings. Thus I have had the good luck to provoke against myself all that is feeble and virtuous." No doubt the indulgent Fräulein von Meysenbug saw in these lines a point directed against herself. She answered, as usual, in her kindly manner: "You say that everything feeble and virtuous is against you? Do not be so paradoxical. Virtue is not weakness but strength, words say it plainly enough. And are you not yourself the living contradiction of what you say? For you are virtuous, and the example of your life, if men could only know it, would, as I am assured, be more persuasive than your books." Nietzsche replied: "I have read your charming letter, dear lady and dear friend, with real emotion; no doubt you are right—so am I."

How headlong a thing is his life! Days spent in walking, in getting the rhythm of phrases, in sharpening thoughts. Often he works through the dawn and is writing still when the innkeeper rises and goes noiselessly out to follow the traces of the chamois among the mountains. "Am I not myself a hunter of chamois?" thinks Nietzsche, and goes on with his work.

The *Case of Wagner* being completed, Nietzsche began a new pamphlet, directed not against a man, but against ideas—against all ideas that men have found whereby to guide their acts. There is no metaphysical world, and the rationalists are dreamers; there is no moral world, and the moralists are dreamers. What then remains? "The world of appearances, perhaps? But no; for with the world of truth we have abolished the world of appearances!" Nothing exists but energy, renewed at every instant. "Incipiet Zarathustra." Friedrich Nietzsche looked for a title for his new pamphlet: *Leisure Hours of a Psychologist* was his first idea; then, *The Twilight of the Idols, or The Philosophy of the Hammer.* On September 7th he sent his manuscript to the publisher. This little book—he wrote—must strike, scandalise, and strain people's minds, and prepare them for the reception of his great work.

Of it he is always thinking, and his second pamphlet is scarcely finished when he starts on this labour. But we no longer recognise the calm and Goethean work which it had been his desire to write. He tries new titles: *We other Immoralists, We other Hyperboreans:* then returns to his old title and keeps to it—*The Will to Power: An Essay towards the Transvaluation of all Values.* Between September 3rd and September 30th he draws up a first section: *The Antichrist;* and it is a third pamphlet. This time he speaks outright, he indicates his Yea and his Nay, his straight line and his goal: he exalts the most brutal energy. All moral imperatives, whether dictated by Moses or by Manu, by the people or by the aristocracy, are lies. "Europe was near to greatness," he writes, "when, during the first years of the sixteenth century, it was possible to hope that Cæsar Borgia would seize the Papacy." Are we bound to accept these thoughts as definitive, because they are the last that Nietzsche expressed?

While he was drawing up *The Antichrist,* he returned again to his *Dionysian Songs,* outlined in 1884, and completed them. Here we find the sure expression of the presentiments that then agitated him.

"The sun sets,
Soon thy thirst shall be quenched,
Burning heart!
A freshness is in the air,
I breathe the breath of unknown mouths,
The great cold comes....

The sun is in its place, and burns upon my head at noon.
I salute ye, ye who come,
O swift winds,
O fresh spirits of the afternoon

The air stirs, peaceable and pure.
Has it not darted towards me a sidelong glance,
A seductive glance,
To-night?

Be strong, brave heart!
Ask not: why?
Eve of my life!
The sun sets."

On the 21st September we find him at Turin. On the 22nd *The Case of Wagner* was published. Here at last was a book of which the newspapers spoke a little. But Nietzsche was exasperated by their comments. With the exception of a Swiss author, Carl Spiteler, no one had understood him. Every word gave him the measure of the public ignorance as regards his work. For ten years he had been seeking and following ideas found by him alone: of this the German critics knew nothing; they knew only that a certain Herr Nietzsche, a disciple of Wagner's, had been an author; they read

The Case of Wagner and surmised that Herr Nietzsche was just fallen out with his master. Besides, he felt that he had incurred the blame of some of his later friends. Jacob Burckhardt, always so precise, did not acknowledge the receipt of the pamphlet; the good Meysenbug wrote an indignant and severe letter.

"These are subjects," Nietzsche answered him, "with regard to which I cannot permit any contradiction. Upon the question of *decadence* I am the highest authority (instance) in the world: the men of to-day, with their querulous and degenerate instinct, should consider themselves fortunate that they have by them some one who offers them a generous wine in their most sombre moments. That Wagner succeeded in making himself believed in, assuredly proves genius; but the genius of falsehood. I have the honour to be his opposite—a genius of truth."

In spite of the agitation thus displayed, his letters expressed an unheard-of happiness. There is nothing which he does not admire. The autumn is splendid; the roads, the galleries, the palaces, the cafés of Turin, are magnificent; repasts are succulent and prices modest. He digests well, sleeps marvellously. He hears French operettas: there is nothing as perfect as their buoyant manner, "the paradise of all the refinements." He listens to a concert: each piece, whether Beethoven, Schubert, Bossaro, Goldmarck, Vibac, or Bizet be its author, seems to him equally sublime. "I was in tears," he wrote to Peter Gast. "I think that Turin, from the point of view of the musical sense, as from every other point of view, is the *most solid* town that I know."

One might hope that this intoxication of spirit kept Nietzsche from knowledge of his destiny. But a rare word sufficiently indicates his clairvoyance. He has a sense of the approaching disaster. His reason escapes from him and he measures its flight. On the 13th of November, 1888, he expressed to Peter Gast a desire to have him near, his regret that he could not come; this was his constant plaint, the very constancy of which indeed diminished its significance. Nietzsche, who knew this, warned his friend: "What I tell you, take tragically," he wrote. On the 18th of November he sent a letter which seemed quite happy. He spoke of operettas which he had just heard, of Judic, and of Milly Meyer. "For our bodies and for our souls, dear friend," he wrote, "a light Parisian intoxication, 'tis salvation." He concluded: "This letter also, I pray you to take tragically."

Thus the condition of physical jubilation to which imminent madness brought him let him escape neither presentiment nor anguish. He wished to reassemble for the last time the memories and impressions which life had left to him, and to compose a work which should be bizarre, triumphant, and desperate. Look at the titles of the chapters: "Why I am so prudent.—Why I am so wise.—Why I have written such good books.—Why I am a fatality.—Glory and eternity...." He calls his last work: *Ecce Homo.* What does he mean? Is he Antichrist or another Christ? He is both together. Like Christ, he has sacrificed himself. Christ is man and God: He has conquered the temptations to which He made Himself accessible. Nietzsche is man and Superman: he has known every feeble desire, every cowardly thought, and has cast them from him. None before him was so tender or so hard; no reality has alarmed him. He has taken upon himself not the sins of men, but all their passions in their greatest force. "Jesus on the Cross," he writes, "is an anathema upon life; Dionysos broken in bits is a *promise* of life, of life indestructible and ever-renewed." The solitary Christian had his God: Nietzsche lives alone and without God. The sage of old had his friends: Nietzsche lives alone and without friends. He lives nevertheless, and can sing, in his cruel extremity, the Dionysian hymn. "I am not a saint," he writes, "but a satyr." And again, "I have written so many books, and such beautiful ones: how should I not be grateful to life?"

No; Nietzsche was a saint, not a satyr, and a wounded saint who aspired to die. He said that he felt grateful to life; it was false, for his soul was quite embittered. He lied, but sometimes man has no other way to victory. When Arria, dying from the blow she had given herself, said to her husband as she passed him her weapon: *"Pœte, non dolet..."* she lied, and it was to her glory that she lied. And here, may we not pass on Nietzsche himself the judgment that he had passed upon her? "Her holy falsehood," he wrote in 1879, "obscures all the truths that have ever been said by the dying." Nietzsche had not triumphed. *Ecce Homo:* he was broken but would not avow it. A poet, he wished that his cry of agony should be a song; a last lyrical transport uplifted his soul and gave him the force to lie.

Thou sinkst to eve!
Thine eye already
Gleams half-bruised;
Drops from thy dew,
Like tears outstrewn,
Stream; the purple of thy love
Goes silent over the milky sea,
Thy ultimate, tardy blessedness....

All around, only the waves and their mirth.
What once was hard
Has foundered in a blue oblivion—
My boat lies idle now.
Tempest and travel—how unlearnt
Hope and desire are drowned,
The soul and the sea he sleek.

Seventh solitude
Never felt I
Closer to me the sweet serenity,

Warmer the rays of the sun.
—Shines not even the ice of my summit?

A rapid, silvery fish,
My bark glides away, afar."

Nevertheless he was conscious that the fame, so long desired, approached. Georges Brandes, who was going to repeat and publish his lectures, found him a new reader, the Swede Auguste Strindberg. Very pleased, Nietzsche announced it to Peter Gast. "Strindberg has written to me," he said, "and for the first time I receive a letter in which I find a world-historic *(Welthistorik)* accent." In St. Petersburg they were getting ready to translate his *Case of Wagner.* In Paris, Hippolyte Taine sought and found him a correspondent: Jean Bordeau, contributor to the *Débats* and the *Revue des Deux Mondes.* "At last," wrote Nietzsche, "the grand Panama Canal towards France has been opened." His old comrade Deussen handed him two thousand francs, the offering of an unknown who wished to subscribe to an edition of his works. Madame de Salis Marschlins offered him a thousand. Friedrich Nietzsche should have been happy, but it was too late.

How were his last days spent? We do not know. He lived in a furnished apartment, the guest of a humble family, which lodged him and, if he wished, fed him. He corrected the proofs of *Ecce Homo,* adding a postscript to the early text, then a dithyrambic poem; meanwhile he prepared a new pamphlet for publication, *Nietzsche contra Wagner.* "Before launching the first edition of my great work," he wrote to his publisher, "we must prepare the public, we must create a genuine tension—or it will be *Zarathustra* over again." On the 8th of December he wrote to Peter Gast: "I have re-read *Ecce Homo,* I have weighed every word in scales of gold: literally it cuts the history of humanity into two sections—the highest superlative of dynamite." On the 29th of December he wrote to his publisher: "I am of your opinion, as to *Ecce Homo;* let us not exceed 1,000 copies; a thousand copies for Germany of a book, written in the grand style, is indeed rather more than reasonable. But in France, I say it quite seriously, I count on an issue of 80,000—or 40,000 copies." On the 2nd of January another letter (in a rough and deformed hand): "Return me the poem—on with *Ecce!"*

There exists a tradition, difficult to verify, that, during these latter days, Nietzsche often played fragments of Wagner to his hosts. He would say to them: "I knew him," and talk of Triebschen. The thing does not seem improbable, for now his memories of his greatest happiness may well have visited him, and he may have found delight in recounting them to simple people ignorant of his life. Had he not just written in *Ecce Homo:*

"Since I am here recalling the consolations of my life, I ought to express in a word my gratitude for what was by far my most profound and best-loved joy—my intimacy with Richard Wagner. I wish to be just with regard to the rest of my human relationships; but I absolutely cannot efface from my life the days at Triebschen, days of confidence, of gaiety; of sublime flashes—days of *profound* happiness. I do not know what Wagner was for others: our sky was never darkened by a cloud."

On the 9th of January, 1889, Franz Overbeck was sitting, with his wife, at the window of his quiet house in Basle, when he saw old Burckhardt stop and ring at his door. He was surprised: Burckhardt was not an intimate, and some intuition warned him that Nietzsche, their common friend, was the cause of this visit. For some weeks he had had disquieting notes from Turin. Burckhardt brought him a long letter which all too clearly confirmed his presentiments. Nietzsche was mad. "I am Ferdinand de Lesseps," he wrote, "I am Prado, I am Chambige [the two assassins with whom the Paris newspapers were then occupied]; I have been buried twice this autumn."

A few moments later Overbeck received a similar letter, and all Nietzsche's friends were likewise advised. He had written to each of them.

"Friend Georges," he wrote to Brandes, "since you have discovered me, it is not wonderful to find me: what is now difficult is to lose me.

"THE CRUCIFIED."

Peter Gast received a message the tragic significance of which he did not understand:

"*A mon maestro Pietro.*

"Sing me a new song. The world is clear and all the skies rejoice."

"Ariadne, I love you," he wrote to Cosima Wagner.

Overbeck started immediately. He found Nietzsche, watched over by his hosts, ploughing the piano with his elbow, singing and crying his Dionysian glory. He was able to bring him back to Basle, and introduce him, without too painful a scene, into a hospital, where his mother came to seek him.

He lived another ten years. The first of them were cruel, the later more kindly; sometimes even there seemed to be hope. He would recall his work.

"Have I not written fine books?" he would say.

He was shown portraits of Wagner.

"Him," he would say, "I loved much."

These returns of consciousness might have been frightful; it seems that they were not. One day his sister, as she sat by his side, could not restrain her tears.

"Lisbeth," he said, "why do you cry? Are we not happy?"

The ruined intellect could not be saved, but the uncorrupted soul kept sweet and charming, open to pure impressions.

One day a young man who was occupied with the publication of his work was out with him on his short walk. Nietzsche perceived a little girl at the side of the road, and was charmed. He went up to her, stopped, and with a hand drew back the hair which lay low on her forehead; then, contemplating the frank face with a smile, he said:

"Is it not the picture of innocence?"

Friedrich Nietzsche died at Weimar on the 25th of August, 1900.